This pragmatic and sympathetic study of Henry James's fiction is an attempt to reclaim James from the Jamesians and from the anti-Jamesians—from those modern critics who have transformed his novels into formal and abstract exercises, and from those others who have dismissed him as a writer isolated from reality. By examining closely the dramatic textures and rhythms of seven works that span James's career—*Madame de Mauves*, *Daisy Miller*, *Roderick Hudson*, *The Aspern Papers*, *The Tragic Muse*, *The Spoils of Poynton*, and *The Wings of the Dove*—the author shows how James's characteristic theme of the search for personal expansion and fulfilment awakens the novelist's full sense of life and evokes in the reader an intimate sense of recognition and discovery.

Kenneth Graham, Senior Lecturer in English in the University of Southampton, is the author of *English Criticism of the Novel 1865–1900*.

HENRY JAMES
THE DRAMA OF FULFILMENT

HENRY JAMES
The Drama of Fulfilment

An Approach to the Novels

by

KENNETH GRAHAM

CLARENDON PRESS · OXFORD
1975

Oxford University Press, Ely House, London W.1

GLASGOW NEW YORK TORONTO MELBOURNE WELLINGTON
CAPE TOWN IBADAN NAIROBI DAR ES SALAAM LUSAKA ADDIS ABABA
DELHI BOMBAY CALCUTTA MADRAS KARACHI LAHORE DACCA
KUALA LUMPUR SINGAPORE HONG KONG TOKYO

ISBN 0 19 812058 3

*Printed in Great Britain by
Billing & Sons Limited, Guildford and London*

for SHEILA
whose own Henry James I hope it comes near
and for ANGUS *and* EUAN
who love the written word

Acknowledgements

I AM grateful to my colleagues and students who have heard or read various versions of this material over the past few years, and who have helped me by their interest, their comments, and their forbearance; to Viola Winner, whose friendly response gave me encouragement at an important juncture; to F. T. Prince, whose knowledge of James and whose own sense of style were a constant criterion; and to Jacques Berthoud, who read the entire manuscript for me with a generous assiduity and a sympathetic understanding that made him the most creative of critics.

Contents

Introduction

THIS is an approach to Henry James's fiction, and only an approach. It is not a large-scale study of his development and achievement, but a limited attempt towards reappropriating the novels to our sympathetic imagination and to our full sense of life—faculties from which they are in some danger of being estranged. One reason why this book has been written is that I find myself more and more failing to recognize the James I think I know in the criticism I read—almost in proportion to its increasing sophistication. The air around the novels is being pumped a little dry and thin. One of the hazards of James criticism—it is the hazard of all modern criticism, more or less—is that of becoming bemused by the idea of its own completeness and intellectual dignity as 'discourse', and therefore of fitting literary works to its own uses and to its own more abstract modes. Criticism is not a primary activity but thoroughly auxiliary and disposable, and I would wish this present example of it—this exercise in submitting my own mind and language to the dramatic life of James's fiction—to be judged purely by whether it affords to others some freshness of access to the fiction itself: some slightly increased sense of personal encounter and possession.

To favour this directness of response I have tried to avoid making too many generalities about James, or drawing together too many of his works in the kind of web of cross-references and thematic connections that can make everything he wrote sound the same. I prefer to suggest any larger patterns only from within the analyses of individual works, partly from personal predilection, but also in the hope that the reader might in this way find phrases or perceptions that he can adapt to his own needs, and apply usefully in his continued reading of James. Criticism has to leave some space: when it is too comprehensive it tends to dry up the individual applications and modifications that it ought to stimulate. James's own inclination as a writer should discourage any attempt at providing a conspectus of his practice or a 'key' to his thinking. It is difficult to discuss with confidence topics like his over-all view of manners, or of renunciation, or of innocence, for example, because his ideas and even his vocabulary always take on the colour of the particular book he is writing. And I have tried to approach James's ideas through each book, rather than directly, and in the terms which each book provides. My method, therefore, may have something of the impressionistic about it, since it is the actual impression and effect of reading a James novel that I wish my own criticism to be guided by. And my preference for cumulative commentary that runs roughly parallel to the progress of each book's action will always result in some recapitulation, and even in some (I hope) brief statements of the mildly obvious, since such a method, if it purports to be full, cannot aim only at the recherché but at absorbing the new into the familiar, and vice versa. I have also tried to make only limited reference to the great variety of critical interpretations and critical controversies which most of these works have elicited, the reason not being that I have failed to find things to admire and envy in other critics—Dorothea Krook and the earlier Richard Poirier, for example—but that in order to be fairly representative of other views one would have to be numbingly comprehensive. It is all very well to demonstrate all those other readings from which one has diverged, but there may be better things to try to do: among them to preserve a readability, a narrative flow, and, if possible, a dramatic rhythm in one's own writing. Full lists of appropriate articles, therefore, should be looked for in other books about James (the lists are very long).[1] And I hope it can be assumed after this (as the application of a general law of James studies) that virtually any single comment I make in these pages could be provided with a footnoted reference to someone who has said exactly the opposite. I want to confront James's works as closely and as personally as possible, free from much of the smoke of battle.

There are seven works to be discussed in this study, and they have been chosen and arranged just as much for their variety of type, of appeal, and of length as for their representativeness. From the early period there are two novellas, *Madame de Mauves* and *Daisy Miller*, followed by a full-length novel, *Roderick Hudson*. Then from the middle period one novella, *The Aspern Papers*, and one long work, *The Tragic Muse*. And finally, a short novel from the later period, *The Spoils of Poynton*, leading up to a very lengthy discussion of *The Wings of the Dove*. These titles combine the familiar and the rather less familiar. They cover James's career more or less chronologically. And they all illustrate that consistent feature of his imaginative vision which I have chosen, not primarily as a discovered 'theme' in its own right, but as a sensitive point of entry into the characteristic life and unity of a James novel—his image of life as a search for personal wholeness and expansiveness, and for a place of equilibrium in the midst of contrariety and contention.

James was a post-Romantic, a Victorian, an early modern, and an American; and on at least four counts, therefore, it is not surprising

[1] The best starting-place would be the selective checklist by Maurice Beebe and William Stafford in *Modern Fiction Studies*, xii, 1966-7, 117-77.

that his books should be concerned with the fulfilment and frustration of the individual—a matter as interesting to each of these four categories of writer as the concept of kingship was to the Elizabethans (and at times with some of the same meaning). At one level the idea is so patent and so universal that we must see it as part of the air James breathed—part, even, of the novel-form itself from its inception as a genre—and what counts, of course, is his individual expression of it: how it becomes, through his sensibility, a source of insight, feeling, and dramatc energy. There is no writer in English more committed than James to the ironies of the contrast between thought and action, between the perceived possibilities of life and the realities of compromise and inadequacy—and these ironies are presented dramatically and not abstractly or dogmatically. Out of the irony, for example, that some people are morally scrupulous, unaesthetic, and self-restricting while others are self-glorifying, glamorously dishonest, and wilful comes much of the comedy of his 'International Theme'. And out of similar essential contrasts—the elements modified and exchanged with perpetual subtlety—comes his greatest social tragedies. The prime interest is not that some types or races come nearer to fulfilling themselves than others, but that in the to-and-fro between them we see the desire or the need of all individuals for a fuller quality of being. At its highest, even, the desire is for that ultimate integration within the self, and between the self and the world, that is one of the latent aspirations of human consciousness—including the consciousness of the reader who has been trapped by sympathy into experiencing the particular book. That trap is sprung by the quality and urgency of emotion in these works, along with their other qualities and their technical skills. There is a great fount of lyric, heroic, and elegiac feeling at the very centre of James's creativity, and a strong imaginative urge towards heightened images, scenes, and situations where the face of a tantalizing power and reality reveals itself momentarily to his various questers and moral travellers. Certain characters who complement one another seek to move together; lovers try to join their talents; single figures seek involvement with others and with a social reality; divided men desperately look for an inner and an outer fusion—all of them trying to resist life's tendency to fragment and to decline. More often than not, humorously or catastrophically, their goal of unity is thwarted. But at any rate they all—except for the few who are quite sterile, the Gilbert Osmonds, the Selah Tarrants, the Urbain de Bellegardes—take up their individual lives as a specific challenge thrown down by some larger 'life'. And this greater reality is not left as some merely nebulous grand harmony, but is a force and a desire that is expressed through particular things: a woman, an artist, a landscape, a beautiful house, a pile of letters, a social situation, and above all, and again and again, a personal relationship.

The search was Henry James's, too—that of the contemplative, open-minded *déraciné* keenly responsive to the appeal of practical action and total self-expenditure; that of the shy observer and 'restless analyst' who literally dreamed of triumphing gloriously over personal dread down the glittering halls of the Louvre, and babbled of Napoleon on his death-bed. Here was a painfully insecure and repressed man whose writing could itself be seen as an imaginative pursuit of 'the real thing', a compensation for inexpressiveness and personal incompleteness. But here is an area I very much wish to avoid. The connection between James's life and his art is one that readers will always, and very properly, wish to explore at various times. But the result of such conjecture is so often unhappy, since it tends to reduce the complexity of the fiction to a sham covering up the 'real' truth—which often proves to be itself something of a sub-literary metaphor and Freudian cliché, such as James's voyeurism, or his 'wound', or his sibling rivalry with William, or his father's wooden leg, or above all his own guilty fear of exposure to 'real' experience. Speculative critico-biography, of the kind that runs through Leon Edel's five-volume biography of James, favours a clear pattern at the expense of the artist's multifariousness, and discounts that capacity to create illusion—illusion of event and character—which makes the novels viable as art. And when such criticism thinks it is being favourable to James it seems to be playing straight into the hands of those who deride his work as the expression of a purely private neurosis. Leon Edel, in all his good faith, casts the shadow of a Maxwell Geismar, whose *Henry James and his Cult* is the ultimate in diatribes. It is perfectly plain that James's personality had serious inadequacies, but his best books simply do not read like works of neurosis or perversity—no matter what neurosis or perversity may conceivably have touched on their most profound and unseeable origins. Like any artist, James was able to objectify and give an independent dramatic life to his personal predicaments and incapacities—the beasts in his own jungle. They become part of the recognizable human scene his books explore, transformed through fiction into the predicaments and incapacities of all of us. And what I have chosen to examine is that fictional scene, its imaginative correspondences with our life, and the dramatic methods by which it is created.

The partly biographical interpretation always appeals to us by seeming to offer a healthy alternative to purely formalist criticism. But ironically, through its use of argument by analogy, it sometimes feeds back into the most hermetic of all formalist approaches to James. This is the one which suggests that the novels are really *about* the methods of their own creation, and that, for example, Chad is to be seen as Strether's *Ambassadors*, and Milly Theale is 'betrayed' more by the aesthetic form and language of *The Wings of the Dove* than by two characters called Kate and Densher.[2] The act of writing becomes the protagonist of the fiction it creates; mirror is held up to mirror; and the novel's self-sustaining structure—dazzlingly analysed—becomes the shape of the author's mind contemplating itself. This is unfair to James, for it makes him out to be almost as dazzling—and as mandarin—as his critics. It is false, I suggest, to the actual experience of reading the novels: in particular their representational, moral, and emotional qualities. And it comes near to turning James into some writer-god of the Modern Movement, contemplating his navel while his intricate works disappear, like bathwater, down their own vortices.

Nevertheless, though James is far from this parody-version of Joyce or Wallace Stevens or Jorge Borges, there are certain strains in his writing that might seem to encourage the mandarin approach. As even the admirer of James would admit, there are places where one fears for the direction taken by his sensibility: places marked by a slightly flaccid religiosity and morbidity, an unclear and self-indulgent emotionality (for example, in *The Great Good Place* or *The Bench of Desolation*). Above all, there are more than a few places where James's life-hunger turns aside into a form of exaggerated mental mastication, where his virtuosity in dissection is not supported by a consistent grasp of ordinary human behaviour and values, and where there are gaps and unnatural assumptions in characterization. And then there are the ever-dangerous Prefaces, in all their exotic, exasperating brilliance, and in their unconscious self-parody, which always remind us of just how far James can go on the path of the self-regarding consciousness. But the point that has to be emphasized is that James when at his best precisely goes to this brink of over-cerebration and no further; and that this exposure to danger can become a source of strength, of unique strength, and not weakness. When so active and so luminous an intelligence is accompanied by engaged feeling and a humane sensitivity it turns the brink into a vantage-point, and is able to bring back from it a series of complex and poetic insights, an introduction to whole new ranges of feeling and expression, all within some of the most firmly based fictions in the language. James's performance considered as a whole, I think, is an unsettled and hazardous one, but therefore the more heroic. And one could take almost as a motto to it the memorable cry of warning and exhortation he committed to his Notebooks, as he

---

[2] The most influential example of this criticism has been Laurence Holland's much-admired *The Expense of Vision* (Princeton, N.J., 1964). See also Leo Bersani, 'The Jamesian Lie', *Partisan Review*, xxxvi, 1969, 53–79.

pulled himself up half-way through the writing of that not-quite-convincing story, *The Altar of the Dead*:

But the thing is a 'conceit', after all, a little fancy which doesn't hold a great deal. Such things betray one—that I more and more (if possible) feel. *Plus je vais*, the more intensely it comes home to me that solidity of subject, importance, emotional capacity of subject, is the only thing on which, henceforth, it is of the slightest use for me to expend myself. Everything else breaks down, collapses, turns thin, turns poor, turns wretched—betrays one miserably. Only the fine, the large, the human, the natural, the fundamental, the passionate things.[3]

I wish in this study to be fair to the James of 'the natural, the fundamental, the passionate things', and to suggest that high style and spiritual vision can be made to take their place among these things. All criticism of Henry James veers back to this at some point (perhaps a little wearily): the eternal question of whether he is on the side of the natural or of the stylized and the spiritualized; 'life' or 'art'; 'real' experience or the Emersonian (or Swedenborgian—or Proustian!) imagining and reshaping of experience. Does he primarily celebrate the autonomous powers of consciousness and aesthetic form? Does he fear and despise life, and so transmute it into beautiful safe shapes? Does he ruefully accept and reveal the given conditions of life; or is he an unrelenting moral idealist who believed, in G. H. Bantock's words, that 'It is not in passion that life consists, but in pursuing an ideal of conduct which *transcends* the forms of current society'? Is he absolutist or relativist, Platonist or realist, post-Christian visionary or stoic humanist, a Mallarmé or a Balzac?—and so on, an unceasing battle of the books.[4] These questions, I think, need not always be confronted directly or polemically—and never for very long in terms of such stark alternatives. When is imagination (and art) not a part of 'experience' in our lives, we might ask, and when is 'experience' not realized through the imagination? Every man is an 'observer', a shaper, and an imaginer; and every novel, too, is an act of observation and filtering. Also, to deal with such

[3] *The Notebooks of Henry James*, ed. F. O. Matthiessen and K. B. Murdock, New York, 1947, pp. 165–6.

[4] Bantock's view of the idealist James is given in his essay, 'Morals and Civilization in Henry James', *Cambridge Journal*, vii, 1953, 158–81. The Emersonian (or post-Emersonian) emphasis is exemplified in Tony Tanner, *The Reign of Wonder*, 1965, pp. 261–335; the Swedenborgian in Quentin Anderson, *The American Henry James*, London, 1958; the Proustian in Leon Edel, *Henry James: the Conquest of London*, London, 1962, p. 169. And the familiar argument about James's retreat from the real is spelled out afresh in one of the more recent books on him, Philip Weinstein's *Henry James and the Requirements of the Imagination*, Cambridge, Mass., 1971. But really, the battle of the books is by now virtually beyond the bibliographer's reach.

issues always brings us up against James's many-sidedness—the way his emphases vary subtly, and even diametrically, from book to book—and the fact that one aspect of his achievement as an essentially dramatic and exploratory writer was precisely to reveal the *naïveté* of those very distinctions and oppositions. If, in the controversy with H. G. Wells, he offered the famous (or notorious) statement, 'It is art that *makes* life', he accompanied it with the statement that his personal 'poetic' was one of 'fulness of life and of the projection of it'.[5] No doubt it is a matter of personal choice and emphasis. James's work will support many approaches: the approach that emphasizes his language and narrative technique more than mine will do; the approach metaphysical, the approach social, the approach polemical. My own approach is a limited one, and for the most part it leaves the general 'case' of Henry James as only an implicit element in its method of concentrating on the actual experience of reading certain of his writings. But the element is there, and I hope by the end of this book to have done a little towards defending James from certain adversaries, and equally from certain friends. It would be difficult to decide which is the more invidious: the view that James is an alienated observer, obsessed by renunciation, detachment, and the creation of pure form, and drifting therefore towards his aesthete's limbo, like Ezra Pound's Mauberley;[6] or such praise as Richard Poirier's in *A World Elsewhere*, which hails him as the architect of a private, shifting world, the first and bravest American Narcissus, forerunner of the anti-static art of dandyism and ecstasy.[7] I hope to demonstrate that James's novels can involve us in many of the rhythms and contradictions of our common experience, and that his dominating vision of the struggle for fullness and reality is not one that leads only to the ivory tower and to the 'religion of consciousness'—though that tower and that religion loom up as possible goals in not a few of his books. James was too much a modern to be all affirmation. His touch is not at all the common touch; and his analytical and syntactical extravagance (along with his high valuation of consciousness) is always capable of breeding monsters. But because his artistic vision is in the end more dramatic than idealist or judicial it is to the extent an implicating vision, not an alienating one, and it expresses his feelings for people as powerfully as it does his intelligence and his mimetic capacity. Art and Mind are of course, for James, ways of trying to master the world; but they are also ways of

[5] *Henry James and H. G. Wells*, ed. L. Edel and G. N. Ray, London, 1958, pp. 267, 262.

[6] See, for example, Maurice Beebe, *Ivory Towers and Sacred Founts*, New York, 1964, pp. 197–231. Beebe compares James to Pater—and to Axel Heyst!

[7] *A World Elsewhere*, London, 1967, pp. 124–43.

submitting to it more profoundly—especially since they have their own flaws to keep them earth-bound and humble. His characters' imaginations and their fallible sensibilities are part of their very individual and very human nature, and subject to their particular situations and conditions—they are not absolute, not self-validating. And in this fact lie the roots of tragedy, rather than of a 'religion of consciousness'. James's characters do care greatly for the abstract 'quality' of an experience, but in most cases not obsessively, for they pursue passion and power and practical rewards and knowledge and selfhood with no less intentness—the conflict of these values being the guarantee for us of their humanity as well as the basis of their tragedy. The 'life' which some of them fear, and which some of them are driven to renounce, in fact impinges on them in a thousand unavoidable ways, making their fear a kind of tribute, and making apparent renunciation a torment, or else a realistic recognition of certain constricting facts, or else a clearly portrayed mistake and perversity.

If 'truth' lay anywhere for James, it lay within interplay and flow: among other things, interplay between the individual mind, circumstance, and society—hence the protean shiftings of sympathy, the techniques of ambiguity, irony, obliquity, and patient accretion by which he pursued that fugitive truth. Hence also the elemental human drama of pursuit and experiment—the search for consummation, personal being, personal truth—in which his characters are shown to be engaged. And the aim of this book is simply to catch and to re-create just a little of this drama, which is the Jamesian vision, in its practical working. For all its uncommonness of style and perception, the vision is fundamental enough to attach us to him, and him to the existence we know—and it is fundamental to art, too, since the search he describes is the same as the creative urge itself. Within James's actual rendering of it—within the drama of fulfilment—we might hope to come closer to the pulse of each novel's life: the life that goes on flowing, back and forth, between art and the world, and between the reader and the book.

Views from a Terrace: *Madame de Mauves* and *Daisy Miller*

I

AN approach to Henry James should open at once on a balcony or a terrace.

The view from the terrace at Saint-Germain-en-Laye is immense and famous. Paris lies spread before you in dusky vastness, domed and fortified, glittering here and there through her light vapors, and girdled with her silver Seine. Behind you is a park of stately symmetry, and behind that a forest, where you may lounge through turfy avenues and light-checkered glades, and quite forget that you are within half an hour of the boulevards. One afternoon, however, in mid-spring, some five years ago, a young man seated on the terrace had chosen not to forget this. His eyes were fixed in idle wistfulness on the mighty human hive before him. He was fond of rural things, and he had come to Saint-Germain a week before to meet the spring half-way; but though he could boast of a six months' acquaintance with the great city, he never looked at it from his present standpoint without a feeling of painfully unsatisfied curiosity. There were moments when it seemed to him that not to be there just then was to miss some thrilling chapter of experience. And yet his winter's experience had been rather fruitless, and he had closed the book almost with a yawn. Though not in the least a cynic, he was what one may call a disappointed observer; and he never chose the right-hand road without beginning to suspect after an hour's way-faring that the left would have been the interesting one.

This is not only the opening of James's finest early novella, *Madame de Mauves*;[1] it is also in its way an emblem for the unfolding of James's imagination. Here, within his first published volume—at the outset of his career, as at the end—James confronts full face the greatest promise of life and the greatest

---

[1] *The Complete Tales of Henry James*, ed. Leon Edel, vol. 3, London, 1962, p. 123. Future page-references are to this edition, which reprints the first book-form of the story, from *A Passionate Pilgrim*, 1875.

uncertainties of life. The two together form a vista that excites
his own feelings and challenges his sense of craft. And above all it
draws him as an author out of himself into objective narration and
the interplay of characters. There is a view of experience—a
theme, a latent idea—behind James's frequent metaphors of
balcony and window and theatre. But what gives such typical
dramatic life to each of the two early stories I wish to discuss is
the way the grand terrace-view of Parisian and other possibilities
becomes at once the view taken by a particular man of a particular
enigmatic young woman. In both stories it is really the movement and quality of feeling that counts, and the way in which
feeling and determining idea are totally expressed through scene
and dialogue, the sense of character, and the shape of a plot. It is
this dramatization, when successfully achieved by James and
successfully submitted to by a reader, that prevents us dismissing
figures like Longmore and Winterbourne—the hesitant young men
in each case—as merely caricatures, or as projections of the
author's own weaknesses. We are made to discover too much of
ourselves in these men for the biography of their creator to loom
very large[2]—too much of the power of generality-through-
particularity that marks the distinguished writer even in such
comparatively undeveloped works as these. *Madame de Mauves*,
in the end, is moving in the way that *Daisy Miller* and so many
of the novels are moving: that is, in the words James in this same
year applied to Turgenev, 'moving, not in the sense that it makes
us shed easy tears, but as reminding us vividly of the solidarity,
as we may say, of all human weakness'.[3] Any man, not just an
ingenuous American of thirty, has stared at the enigma of life
stretching before him, and has been forced to measure the distance

[2] The curious, however, can be referred to Leon Edel, *Henry James: the
Conquest of London*, London, 1962, pp. 119–23, for a characteristic 'psychobio-
graphical' reading of *Madame de Mauves*. According to Edel the story is a
conversion of James's own embarrassed relationship with Mrs. Sarah Wister
(whose name suggests 'lilac wistaria' and hence the colour *mauve*!), and
represents his renunciation of personal passion for art. Edel's method may have
its point for his particular purposes, but it has proved unhappy in its influence
on other, more specifically literary, critics—witness S. Gorley Putt's summing-
up of *Madame de Mauves*, that 'it does rub in the moral, now second nature to
the bachelor author, that, one way or another, marriage kills' (*A Reader's Guide
to Henry James*, 1966, p. 73).

[3] 'Ivan Turgénieff' (1874), *French Poets and Novelists*, New York, rptd. 1964,
p. 218.

between his private terrace and that 'thrilling chapter of experience'. And if this story is to make us respond fully to its central situation of a man and a woman seeking for their true selves at the point where roads diverge and possibilities begin to multiply, it can only do so by compelling us into a plot that must itself bristle with the tantalizing and the tentative. This it achieves from its first words (quite literally) its last. Here is a young, or a youngish man who is dissatisfied and bored, but uncynical, fond of the country and fascinated by the city, and now sitting uneasily at a point between the boulevards, a formal park, and a natural forest. The woman he meets on the terrace, almost immediately, is similarly composed of contradictions. Madame de Mauves is 'naturally pale' but now 'flushed . . . with recent excitement'. She is 'not obviously' a beauty or an American, but 'essentially both, on a closer scrutiny'. She is 'at once alert and indifferent, contemplative and restless'. And when Longmore quickly discovers that she is unhappy in her marriage to the faithless Baron, we feel as readers, almost as warmly as Longmore does as protagonist, a 'sense of unwonted opportunity' and suspense.

James's handling of tone is as important and successful as his handling of plot: there is an air of suave authorial banter, especially in the more panoramic opening chapters, an amused and sympathetic detachment that will nevertheless allow a sharp commitment of feeling at exactly the right juncture of the action. This double effect is very familiar in reading James. Even in his maturer works we are dramatically convinced by scenes and characters and yet simultaneously very much aware of the medium that expresses them: an authoritative narrating voice that savours its own language and its own wit. We know we are in the theatre of James's mind, watching people on the stage who are nevertheless independent and diverse. As in a book like *The Europeans*, so in this story there is a distinctly choreographic manner to its balanced encounters and crises, on terrace and in drawing-room and forest walk, with its well-turned debates between Longmore and Euphemia, and the voice of James's regulating wit as it elucidates and shapes his characters into life:

[M. de Mauves] was a placid sceptic, and it was a singular fate for a man who believed in nothing to be so tenderly believed in. What his original faith had been he could hardly have told you; for as he came back to his childhood's home to mend his fortunes by pretending to fall in love, he was a thoroughly perverted creature, and overlaid with more corruptions than a summer day's questioning of his conscience would have released him from. Ten years' pursuit of pleasure, which a bureau full of unpaid bills was all he had to show for, had pretty well stifled the natural lad, whose violent will and generous temper might have been shaped by other circumstances to a result which a romantic imagination might fairly accept as a late-blooming flower of hereditary honor. The Baron's violence had been subdued, and he had learned to be irreproachably polite; but he had lost the edge of his generosity, and his politeness, which in the long run society paid for, was hardly more than a form of luxurious egotism, like his fondness for cambric handkerchiefs, lavender gloves, and other fopperies by which shop-keepers remained out of pocket. In after years he was terribly polite to his wife. He had formed himself, as the phrase was, and the form prescribed to him by the society into which his birth and his tastes introduced him was marked by some peculiar features. That which mainly concerns us is its classification of the fairer half of humanity as objects not essentially different—say from the light gloves one soils in an evening and throws away. To do M. de Mauves justice, he had in the course of time encountered such plentiful evidence of this pliant, glove-like quality in the feminine character, that idealism naturally seemed to him a losing game. (p. 137)

If there is detachment in this style there is also the opposite. There is energy underneath its elegance, and a delight in its own self-control, that make it seem very classical. And the wit, which is active not just verbally and locally but also in larger structural effects, makes us enter more closely into the process of the story by implicating us in the very play and dance of James's creative mind at work.

As the little drama of Longmore and Madame de Mauves begins to take its shape, through such a style, and as their mutual scruples begin to proliferate and intensify, the fundamental problem in the story's interpretation comes to declare itself. What attitude does James take to such spiritual rigour as Euphemia de Mauves's, the wronged wife who refuses her unfaithful husband's injunction to console herself in kind; and to such self-questioning, half-passionate hesitations as those of her admiring compatriot? He of course takes no attitude simple enough to be detached from a detailed reading of the whole tale in its varying movements. For one thing, it belongs to its basic conception that Euphemia should remain partly enigmatic to the end. We see into her mind directly, though briefly, on more than one occasion; but for the most part our view of her is through Longmore. And for him she is fully as tantalizing as his initial view of Paris, and of life, from the terrace. What he is obsessed by, from the first, is the 'hovering mystery' of her 'authentic self' which she herself describes: 'in my mind, it's a nameless country of my own'. Where does that authentic self exist, behind the mask of beauty and calmness that reminds him of 'the serious cast of certain blank-browed Greek statues'? Can one person ever know another person 'authentically', any more than he can ever find complete issue for himself in a fulfilling 'chapter of experience'? Full knowledge, and the full expressive act—it is the latent Jamesian dream (if not yet the full Jamesian vision) that begins to reveal itself behind all the questioning about Euphemia de Mauves.

Of course she is not a total mystery. There are things we know about her that link her closely to Longmore, in a perfectly recognizable human predicament: for example, her early excess of imaginative idealism, fostered by a convent education upon a native American propensity, which James demonstrates with fine clarity in the second chapter, that early *locus classicus* in the development of his International Theme. Euphemia's youthful idealism (naïve, but nevertheless, like Daisy Miller's *naïveté*, the root of something notable) traps her into marrying the Baron. And it is Longmore's similar 'radical purity' and 'active imagination' which draw him with passionate sympathy towards Euphemia, and which in the end condemn him (as they have condemned her) to frustration. Although the disillusioned Euphemia has by now developed in a different direction from Longmore, it is the similarity of the moral bases and origins of their lives that gives their relationship its anguish and its destructiveness. There is something too transcendent about the mind of each of them—though this excess may have some merit when the alternative is the worldly corruption, the Old Worldly corruption, of the de Mauves clan. Such idealism, James makes very clear, has more than a touch of sterility about it. It is genuinely self-transcending, but it also leads back to the self, by some ironic by-ways. Reality can rarely match the imaginative ideal for long, and a retreat into isolation or coldness or hardness is often suggested by James as the tragic part of the moral imagination's working. The most important sign of Euphemia's tragedy—and surely there are the makings of tragedy in all this?—is the threatened atrophy of feeling, indicated by her very denial of the tragic:

'I hate tragedy', she once said to [Longmore]; 'I have a really pusillanimous dread of moral suffering. I believe that—without base concessions—there is always some way of escaping from it. I had almost rather never smile all my life than have a single violent explosion of grief.' (p. 153)

One begins to feel, early on in the story, that the Baron may have a point (though not more than a point) when he complains cynically that his wife needs to 'bend a trifle' and also to travel: 'It would enlarge her horizon.'

Longmore, being the character in the book closest to us, is in a much more dramatically realized dilemma than Euphemia, and is much further from atrophy. His feelings still exist—savingly, as well as bewilderingly:

This sentimental tumult was more than he had bargained for, and, as he looked in the shop windows, he wondered whether it was a 'passion'. He had never been fond of the word, and had grown up with a kind of horror of what it represented. He had hoped that when he fell in love, he should do it with an excellent conscience, with no greater agitation than a mild general glow of satisfaction. But here was a sentiment compounded of pity and anger, as well as admiration, and bristling with scruples and doubts. (p. 163)

His confusions and humiliations are not simply to be laughed at, though the reader does laugh. His contradictions are too human— as when, despite his total moral abhorrence of him, he nevertheless envies the Baron his 'superb positiveness', his 'luxurious serenity', and his 'vigorous and unscrupulous temperament'. This is not enough to make Longmore a fool or a hypocrite, but only a victim, like anyone else, to the fact that the desirable things in life, such as virtue and luxury, moral value and material interest, remain obstinately apart—Longmore's whole story being shaped by the irony and pathos of this separation.

Longmore's troubles reach a turning-point in the fifth chapter —or, at least, a point of significant intensification, since his essential dilemma can hardly change or be resolved. By now, he is on the very brink of his terrace, as it were. And one of his alternatives is that of retreat from worldly temptation (the temptation of forcing a liaison on Euphemia) by escaping to his friend Web-

ster in Belgium (not one of Henry James's favourite countries!).
It is not the Belgium of Rubens but, more ascetically, of the
'fair-tressed saints of Van Eyck and Memling'. Yet it is Rubens,
figuratively, who wins (or even Renoir!), in the very pictorial
episode at the café in the Bois de Boulogne. From his table in the
garden among the June roses, Longmore gazes through the
window at a bold, wine-stained, strawberry-crunching woman of
the world whose naked neck receives a kiss from—a flushed Baron
de Mauves. James's mild sensuality plays over the incident in a
very characteristic way: ironic, but far from uninvolved. It
touches the reader, and helps him to realize, sympathetically, that
the tumult which ensues in Longmore's mind is as much his
rekindled awareness of the flesh's demands as his more conscious
sense of redoubled moral outrage on Madame de Mauves's behalf.
Each impulse in Longmore, the fleshly and the spiritual, seems to
use the vocabulary of the other: a subtle and entirely natural
confusion. He rushes back to Saint-Germain with 'rapture' and
'ardour'. 'Doubts and scruples' have gone, leaving room for 'pity
and anger' to 'throb' and 'rage'. He will abandon the tranquillity
of the past for direct action, for a new zestful consciousness of
'tending with all his being to a single aim'. And all this self-
expressiveness in the name of moral outrage and ideal honesty.

In such a mood, Longmore is brought together with Euphemia
in the forest—and finds her in an unaccustomed state of 'grief and
agitation'. There has been a climactic quarrel with the Baron,
which at last seems to have forced her towards that tragic disturbance she has so avoided, and towards the maturing insight that
'deep experience is never peaceful.' The feelings of the two are
now in as close and as heated a proximity as they are ever to be.
Their language is suddenly at its most eloquent. Each is open to
the other—'He felt his heart beating hard; he seemed now to
know her secrets'—and each makes a profession of belief. And it
is only at this delayed point that the story—as is so often the case
with James—comes to its full seriousness and inwardness, a note
that it will sustain to the end. The narrator has begun to brood
down over the sight of his absurd half-lovers with something added
to his amusement: a deep and admonitory pity.

Longmore and Euphemia's meeting in the forest is certainly an
affair to move pity—partly because, with two such Americans, it
inevitably becomes a debate, and a debate through which they

blunder, as though in a maze. Euphemia's outburst of tears, which
had removed Longmore's instinctive fear of her 'deeper faith' and
'stronger will', soon changes into an 'impatient resignation'. And
in that oxymoron lies a hint that Euphemia's part in their debate
is no more single-minded than Longmore's. He makes a heart-felt
appeal to the idealism in her which is so like his own: 'You are
truth itself, and there is no truth about you. You believe in purity
and duty and dignity, and you live in a world in which they are
daily belied.' Yet the practical end of his appeal to a nobler
discontent could only in this context be fleshly and adulterous.
And the idealist Euphemia, in her disillusionment, seems to
argue on the side of realistic compromise: 'Life is hard prose,
which one must learn to read contentedly'; and then, 'You are very
kind to go to the expense of visions for me. Visions are vain things;
we must make the best of the reality.' Yet the basis of her prag-
matism is in fact impregnably idealist, and even religious. Her old
romantic faith, she tells Longmore, 'has faded, but it has not
vanished. Some feelings, I am sure, die only with ourselves; some
illusions are as much the conditions of our life as our heart-beats.
They say that life itself is an illusion,—that this world is a shadow
of which the reality is yet to come' (p. 169). The spokesman for
this ultimate reality is her conscience. And Euphemia, under the
mounting stress of the scene, the stress of seeing tears in Longmore's eyes, is then granted a moment's insight into the doubleness
of the conscience, and the fact that it can constrict, rather than
exalt: 'I have nothing on earth but a conscience, . . . nothing but a
dogged, clinging, inexpugnable conscience. Does that prove me to
be indeed of your faith and race, and have you one for which you
can say as much? I don't say it in vanity, for I believe that if my
conscience will prevent me from doing anything very base, it will
effectually prevent me from doing anything very fine' (p. 171).
And yet she at once proceeds to re-endow that conscience with
full religious value when Longmore desperately disparages it:
' "Don't laugh at your conscience", she answered gravely; "that's
the only blasphemy I know".' And is it to add too much to the
ironies of so brief a scene to point out that the ultimate faith from
which Euphemia draws her dogged conscience and her strength to
renounce what Longmore offers her is possibly, at a great distance,
the same romantic vision by which Longmore hopes to win her:
the vision of a life without compromises, in which goodness can be

reconciled with present worldly happiness and serenity with love?

The vision of harmony is given its fullest embodiment in the climax of Chapter 7—a real vision, set in the French countryside, and one in which the reader's feelings, awakened by the wranglings of these self-destructive people, can at last flow out into one representative and firmly constituted scene. All the interplay of frustration and hesitant desire that has given the story its psychological and moral life is now at once externalized in a dramatic image which remains in the mind after the tale is done, and which seems to comprise its kernel.

Despite the moral disgust reawakened in Longmore by an encounter with the insidious Mme Clairin, his worldly self has also been excited by learning from her that her brother the Baron has now deliberately placed his wife and Longmore in a form of total intimacy *malgré eux*. Each has been told that the other knows an *affaire* is possible, and indeed, from the family's point of view, desirable, as a way of humbling Euphemia and making her tractable. And now Longmore, heated and anguished, full of joy and pain—that is, full of the 'deep experience' to which he is being initiated—strides off into the French landscape, where the fulfilment he yearns for takes on the clear forms of a picture, a view, a meal, and a pair of lovers. The landscape is itself a perfect blend of stillness and vigour, of the human and the non-human, the natural and the aesthetic—'the grass looked as if it might stain your trousers, and the foliage your hands.' The colours, man-made and otherwise, blend in harmonious tones. Even the hostess of the little inn is a 'true artist' at an omelette. And as the expression of it all, Longmore has a reverie, a painterly reverie, of 'an unhappy woman strolling by the slow-moving stream before him, and pulling down the blossoming boughs in the orchard'. The burden of his reveries is *carpe diem*— a rejection of the 'spiritual zeal' that seems at odds with so much natural harmony:

. . . he now felt all the vehemence of rebellion. To renounce—to renounce again—to renounce forever—was this all that youth and longing and resolve were meant for? Was experience to be muffled and mutilated, like an indecent picture? Was a man to sit and deliberately condemn his future to be the blank memory of a regret, rather than the long reverberation of a joy? Sacrifice? The word was a trap for minds muddled by fear, an ignoble refuge of weakness. To insist now seemed not to dare, but simply to be, to live on possible terms. (p. 185)

This positiveness comes like a clarion in the book, bringing a sense of stir and release—especially when, as if in response to its summons and to Longmore's needs, a young painter and his mistress emerge from the inn and move into the centre of the scene. The girl seems both heavenly and of the earth, with her pink muslin dress, her white hat, and her 'clear brown skin and a bright dark eye, and a step which seemed to keep time to some slow music, heard only by herself'. Before she appears, Longmore is misled, by envy of the young painter's talent, into wondering whether 'it was better to cultivate an art than to cultivate a passion', and into asking himself, 'Was a strong talent the best thing in the world?' (questions and themes we shall meet again, especially in *Roderick Hudson* and *The Tragic Muse*). But he is posing false alternatives, since it soon appears that here before him is a man who can combine art *and* passion, self-expression with another's commitment to him—and have ahead of him, on top of everything, the prospect of the landlady's artistic lamb chops and spinach and *tarte à la crème* at the end of the day. For Longmore, it all constitutes a 'vision of bliss', mocking him by its distance yet urging him to emulation.

But James (and these are the minute touches of discrimination that will mark the fullest maturity of his art) can see through the vision itself, and can see through his own ineradicable commitment to its appeal. For the little idyll is strongly qualified by a shadow of realism, though not destroyed by it. Claudine, the girl, is only one of many for the painter, and she will not always be the one on the river-bank with him. 'Those artists', clucks the landlady, as she reveals this fact, '*ça n'a pas de principes!*' It is revealing of the distance Longmore still has to cover in his life (it is the distance that an idealistic Lambert Strether still had to cover at the age of fifty, when faced by a similar revelation on a French river-bank) that his stimulated passion soars even now, *à l'américaine*, above the landlady's knowledge of infidelity, as he cries 'No!' to the possibility of love's impermanence. But the landlady's sardonic insight rises up again in Longmore's subconscious, and bulks larger into the story itself, in the shape of the disturbed dream that ends his expedition. The idyll evokes its attendant nightmare, and together they cover more truth than either alone. On each side of a deep stream (goes his dream) stand the separated lovers, he and Euphemia. To cross the gap, to be joined together,

requires the help of the fatal boatman with the visage of the Baron.
That is, to achieve union and happiness, which has been the
original dream of each, they must utilize those worldly principles
that infringe so much of their moral identity as persons. In his
dream, Longmore accepts the boatman and crosses. But like
Eurydice, Euphemia has gone, betrayed by his decision, betrayed
by something in her nature and in his—and by the incompleteness
that, for James, is endemic to all human nature and human effort.

The last major encounter between Longmore and Euphemia
takes place on a terrace in the darkness—and in confusion. She is
in vestal white like a 'marble statue', and urges on him honour,
sacrifice, parting. He is in his old chaos, torn between the desire
to worship and the desire to take the goddess in his arms. Just as in
the earlier scene where Longmore stormed back to Saint-Germain
from the café in the Bois de Boulogne with an 'ardour' that was
spiritual in one aspect and sexual in another, so now, at the end,
each of them uses the language and gestures of idealism in so
ambiguous and sophistical a way as almost to amount to parody.
Their postures on the terrace are elaborate and extreme, suffused
with the violence of the conflicting demands within each of them:

'*Don't disappoint me* [Euphemia urges on him]. If you don't understand me now, you will to-morrow, or very soon. . . . You have made
too good an impression on me not to make the very best. If you wish to
please me forever, there's a way'. She was standing close to him, with
her dress touching him, her eyes fixed on his. As she went on her manner
grew strangely intense, and she had the singular appearance of a
woman preaching reason with a kind of passion. Longmore was confused, dazzled, almost bewildered. The intention of her words was all
remonstrance, refusal, dismissal; but her presence there, so close, so
urgent, so personal, seemed a distracting contradiction of it . . . she
drew a long breath; Longmore felt it on his cheek, and it stirred in his
whole being a sudden, rapturous conjecture. (pp. 194–5)

Longmore's last assertive movement along the terrace to grasp her,
as a woman and not as a statue, is inspired by a feeling that has
passed in the space of one sentence from exaltation at her 'ideal of
conduct' to excitement at 'something he might immediately enjoy'.
Negation turns into passion, and passion into negation—in oscillations so intense that it takes all of James's wit and stagecraft,
here, near his conclusion, to hold everything together.

As Euphemia recedes from us, drawing the Baron with her,

James's emphasis changes, slightly but importantly. We have always been kept aware of the element of hardness in her, among the other elements—and we have seen her own awareness of it. But now James chooses to bring out more clearly his perception that personal integrity, on which so much depends, has often some accompanying abrasiveness, even destructiveness—like that rocky soil of New England selfhood that Gertrude Wentworth uncovers, just as she escapes into a kind of fulfilment, in *The Europeans*. James is no more the apostle of self-reliance than he is of renunciation—though there are those who have always claimed him to be one or the other. Certainly, he makes it plain that if you give up your integrity, if Euphemia were to be untrue to her conscience and the continuity of her faith, then the loss would be great, even though the gain to passionate feeling might be considerable. But if Euphemia remains true to herself, and to the more insistent of her inner voices, as she does, then others must suffer as victims of that 'truth'. The main casualty, of course, is the Baron. 'Be yourself' is what old Madame de Mauves, the Baron's mother, had urged on Euphemia with terrible unconscious irony years before; 'Be persistently and patiently yourself, and a De Mauves will do you justice!' (pp. 140–41). But justice is a chilling principle to apply within a marriage, and the Baron, faced with a woman who is persistently herself, and who never bends, or sins, or forgives, is to blow his brains out in humiliation and despair —justice, no doubt, thereby being satisfied. It is part of the change of emphasis—and typical of how James can discover new things up to the last—that the Baron himself, before his end, becomes an anguished and pitiable walker on terraces. When he bumps into a now indifferent and weary Longmore in a boulevard café, the Baron reacts to him as to a second Euphemia, 'exasperatingly impenetrable' and full of cold 'self-possession' (it was precisely Euphemia's 'self-control' that Longmore recognized as the root of the Baron's disgust at his wife, in Chapter 3). The New World seems to him united in its revenge. The Baron is taken off into the social underworld (by a consumptive-looking dandy smelling of heliotrope) only after some unusual inner reluctance, and Longmore is dismayed to suspect that jealousy is stirring within the Baron. And jealousy, that 'passion with a double face', might even signify a newly kindled love in the Baron for his wife (the man who told his wife to take a lover becomes sexually jealous only when she refuses to do so!). But of course it is too late for the Baron. Euphemia, recoiling from both men, has passed into that slightly arid 'nameless country' of her own. She parts with Longmore on the big terrace where it all began, with words of cold comfort and exclusion. 'It's better to have done nothing in bitterness,—nothing in passion', she says; and in the distance a corrupt Paris twinkles and flashes in derision at her words (p. 204). And the Baron, at home for once after rejecting his mistress, now wanders through his garden in the darkness, exasperated and alone, while his wife sits wordless and pure (and pathetic, too) on the terrace. It makes an eloquent and painful tableau.

The account of the Baron's suicide two years later, on which the novella ends, is heavily qualified. It apparently makes him out to be a pure victim, and Euphemia to be a moralistic avenger (a 'female Chillingworth', Marius Bewley calls her):[4] 'He was the proudest man in France, but he had begged her on his knees to be readmitted to favor. All in vain! She was stone, she was ice, she was outraged virtue. People noticed a great change in him: he gave up society, ceased to care for anything, looked shockingly. One fine day they learned that he had blown out his brains' (pp. 208–9). But James, characteristically, is taking up one interpretation which his own narrative has already suggested to us only in order to query its completeness. It is important to notice that the account reaches Longmore only after it has filtered through no fewer than three narrators, each of them essentially hostile to Euphemia and her way of life. It is told him by his friend Mrs. Draper, who, though American, is far from unwordlly, and has previously criticized Euphemia for her rigidity. 'Just a little folly is very graceful', she has told Longmore (who himself prefers to attach a more ethereal meaning to the word 'grace'). Mrs. Draper has had the story from 'a clever young Frenchman' at Vichy, a society spa (one can almost presume he smelled of heliotrope). And the young Frenchman had the story from, of all unbiased authorities, Mme Clairin. The question is, why did James carefully allow us to hear a version hostile to Euphemia and at the same time draw some of its sting by using it to reflect unfavourably on those who tell it? And why—it is essentially the same question, and the one that seems to have annoyed many readers—why does the tale end so quizzically on Longmore's reluctance to return to France to claim

[4] *The Eccentric Design*, London, 1959, p. 230.

the newly widowed Euphemia, and on his 'singular feeling' that
has grown up in the midst of remembered tenderness, 'a feeling
for which awe would be hardly too strong a name'?[5]

Fear of Euphemia, fear of the lengths to which her idealism can
take her, has been an acknowledged and a justified element in
Longmore's response to her from the very beginning. His failure
to go back to her now comes as a shock in the narrative—a twist
in the very last line—but it is not incongruous or contrived, and
the shock is one that brings about a fuller understanding and a
slightly different assimilation of all that has gone before. It is, in
fact, a genuine *coup de roman*. Can it be mere indecisiveness or an
intellectual tease on James's part to suggest that admiration and
desire can coexist with an incipient repulsion, and that the
repulsion might grow during a period of absence? Or that this
repulsion and fear may partly arise out of Longmore's doubts of
himself and of his own similarity to the woman who arouses such
tenderness and awe? Or that a great force for goodness, such as
Euphemia's idealism, may have for its obverse a face of vindictive-
ness and self-petrification? Or that renunciation is one of the
noblest of human acts, yet pride can lie inextricably coiled within
it—as bewilderingly as the Baron's first impulse of love may lie
within his futile jealousy? The ending of *Madame de Mauves* helps
to express all this, and more, by its very ambiguity. This is not
the kind of open-endedness that defeats significance. There is a
coherent shape that is drawn around the dubiety, enclosing it,
making it graspable, as in all the best instances of James's ambiguity. And this is the shape, simply, of the total action, which has
represented certain recognizable conflicts within individuals and
their relationships, and has not tried to adjudicate finally among
them. A lifelike and shapely image of an ambiguity in human
behaviour and values is not the same as artistic meaninglessness.
To represent life truly, but more intensely and compactly and
pleasingly than life itself allows; not to offer definitive judgement
or intellectual or ethical system, but a clearer view of the human
scene within which judgement itself moves, and is judged; and to
clarify the emotional and imaginative responses in which idea and

---

[5] Gorley Putt, for example, finds James's final touch 'factitious', 'contemp-
tuous', and 'out of character' (*A Reader's Guide to Henry James*, p. 73); and
Krishna Vaid calls it 'trite' and puzzling (*Technique in the Tales of Henry James*,
Cambridge, Mass., 1964, p. 144).

value must be rooted—these are among the most essential elements of James's aesthetic, and elements to which a sympathetic reading of any of his best works will always lead us.

Madame de Mauves seems a simple tale, but it is rich in texture and dovetailed in structure.[6] Its lines of careful contrast or similarity give it an evident formal unity, but equally they serve to extend greatly the range of its meaning. Longmore clearly dominates the foreground, but only as a part of the whole. Beyond him stands Euphemia, the fainter but more suggestive outlines of her character gaining from the greater immediacy and detail of his. And beyond both of them extend all the other figures, in a vista full of ironic comparison, down to the shade of Mme Clairin's husband, who had blown his brains out after failing to reconcile his bourgeois background and the aristocratic wife who could not understand him—the Baron, the *grand seigneur* who married an American *bourgeoise* and finds that he cannot understand her, doing exactly the same. These are characters caught in the same trap. They look out through the bars, in ways we recognize, at a receding vision of total happiness and utterance, where the mind and heart can be fulfilled in natural action. And for them all (except, no doubt, Mme Clairin), for Euphemia and her husband, even for the Baron's mother who had longed wearily to join her worldly experience to the young Euphemia's innocence, even for the painter and his temporary Claudine, it has been and will be what it proves for Longmore, an encounter with a fact and a suffering more universal than their individual loss: 'Something of infinite value was floating past him, and he had taken an oath not to raise a finger to stop it. It was borne by the strong current of the world's great life and not of his own small one' (p. 205).

II

There is a terrace with a view in *Daisy Miller*—two terraces, rather: one confronting Lake Geneva and the Alps, and the other the Roman sunset over the Pincian Garden. And more directly than in *Madame de Mauves*, the interest of the work centres on the puzzle of the young woman who stands there taking the view and belonging to the view. This time there is a rather less complicated relationship between her and her observer, Winterbourne,

[6] The structure is exhaustively analysed in J. A. Ward, *The Search for Form: Studies in the Structure of James's Fiction*, Chapel Hill, N.C., 1967, pp. 77–94.

the unspontaneous and Europeanized young American. He does not fill the picture as much as did Longmore, in his more vivid wrestlings, and we find ourselves more closely engaged with Daisy than with Euphemia, and with the 'case' presented by her situation. Is her innocence compromised for all worldly purposes, social and marital, by her vulgarity? Does this kind of innocence throw as much of a blight on day-to-day living as Euphemia de Mauves's idealism? And has Daisy's innocence ceased to be true innocence anyway? Belonging to the 'European' world of conventions and conventional judgements as Winterbourne mostly does (and as the reader mostly does), what is the source of the deep appeal for him in such a girl's nature, the unconscious nature that seems to reveal and disturb so much of the life around her? It is a quality that exists not only inside her but outside, hinted at in details of landscape and Roman ruin. It seems to exist, in an etiolated form, within Winterbourne himself, though he fights it down successfully by a conventional judgement. And it seems to exist somewhere in us, the readers, as we respond to all the little touches and hints by which James builds up her character. The story is subtitled 'A Sketch', and it seems to work as fine sketches do, and with the advantages a sketch has over a finished picture, that the tentativeness and quickness of its lines can best convey the living mystery of a personality like Daisy's. James, for all the detail of his later works, is always something of a sketcher, too. After all the analysis is done, he still leaves his characters room to move, and believes in the fleeting impression, the subtle areas of untouched paper.

In some ways, this book is a tragicomedy of judgement and knowledge—of the ways the mind endeavours to grasp the real. For there are two ways of judging Daisy, and each is allowed its validity: the 'external' way of a traditional and stereotyped social ethic, and the 'internal' way of intuitive personal response. It is tempting to exaggerate James's adherence to the latter in this story—just as it is tempting, and mistaken, to imagine in Chapter 19 of *Portrait of a Lady* that James discounts Madame Merle's belief that the self is as much external, expressed in objects and circumstances, as it is private and inexpressible (as Isabel Archer argues, too simply). James is always very careful to keep before us the rebarbative nature of Daisy's crudity and her lack of real imagination, deficiencies that would seem partly to justify the 'external' criticisms made of her by Mrs. Costello and Mrs. Walker, and half-accepted by Winterbourne. And though in the actual ending the intuitive response on James's part is clearly dominant over the rational, social judgement, the story as a whole is characteristically devoted to the interaction of the two.

Winterbourne is caught between the two worlds. And as always, James uses the America–Europe dichotomy not as a subject in itself but as an extended metaphor for more general dichotomies. After all, 'America' is never clearly represented here. If it has its innocent freshness, as in the young woman from Schenectady, it has its Mrs. Costellos and Walkers, who are always at pains to point out how un-American Daisy is. And New York society, it seems, has a 'minutely hierarchical constitution' that can appear more restrictively 'European' than Europe. Winterbourne is let down by both worlds of judgement when he is confronted by the ambivalent 'prospect' of a Daisy Miller at Vevey: '[he] had lost his instinct in this matter, and his reason could not help him.'[7] Through the rest of the story he tries alternately to recover each, and in the end is satisfied (or almost satisfied) by a rational 'formula'. Even at Vevey he finds momentary relief from un-certainty in a formula, a cliché of judgement that he repeats to himself, 'she was only a pretty American flirt'—though at once his composure is destroyed by the chance of an expedition with Daisy to the Château de Chillon (the first of two obliquely ironic references in the story to Byron and the Byronic life, the life hostile to limiting formulae!). Later on, in Rome, when Daisy seems perfectly content that he should accompany her in her assignation with the disreputable Giovanelli, Winterbourne is vexed that she thereby does not quite fit his next phrase for her: 'It would . . . simplify matters greatly to be able to treat her as the object of one of those sentiments which are called by romancers "lawless passions" ' (p. 182). And his final formula in the Colosseum at the end—'She was a young lady whom a gentleman need no longer be at pains to respect' (p. 202)—is one that damns him far more than it damns its subject, in the context of our increasing pity for Daisy. It is also one that links Winterbourne closely to the figure of Robert Acton in *The Europeans*, another torn man who

---

[7] *The Complete Tales of Henry James*, ed. Leon Edel, vol. 4, p. 151. Future page-references are to this edition, which reprints the first English book-form of the story, published in 1879.

seeks to protect himself against a temptress (Eugenia) by an
absurdly reductive judgement on her, 'She is not honest, she is not
honest.'

The inadequacy of such clinical judgement is revealed even by
the language it is delivered in, and confirms Winterbourne's
kinship with the other Roman-Americans. For example, when he
is with Mrs. Costello in St. Peter's and they catch sight of Daisy
and Giovanelli, this exchange occurs:

'And what is it', he asked, 'that you accuse me of thinking of?'
'Of that young lady's—Miss Baker's, Miss Chandler's—what's her name?
—Miss Miller's intrigue with that little barber's block.' (p. 194)

Mrs. Costello expresses her derisive judgement of Daisy by the
stereotyped proletarian associations of certain names. And it is
interesting (though untypical of James) that in this tale the use of
French phrases—'a young lady *qui se passe ses fantaisies*'; '*elle
s'affiche*'; or, 'actual or potential *inconduite*, as they said at Geneva'
—seems to be related to those fixed linguistic tags by which a
deadening judgement, and even the moral deadness of the judger,
are conveyed. They are at one not only with Winterbourne's
formulae but also with such a mechanistic attitude as Mrs. Walker's,
who in her parties made a point of 'studying European society',
and had 'collected several specimens of her diversely born fellow-
mortals to serve, as it were, as text-books'. And even Winterbourne
is at times moved to regret the ossified and schematic response of
the whole American colony to Daisy, 'because it was painful to
hear so much that was pretty and undefended and natural assigned
to a vulgar place among the categories of disorder'. 'Assigned' to a
'category'—James can express so much about moralism by the
choice of two words.

And yet one has to add at once what James knows equally well:
that the 'categories' are often helpful and necessary in a life of
manners. Winterbourne's language and his concepts may imprison
him. He may seem a victim to his own priggery when he uses the
word 'gentleman' as a shibboleth with which to destroy Giovanelli, who patently is not what that word suggests. But does
James laugh unreservedly at Winterbourne's use of 'gentleman',
and at his annoyance that Daisy cannot tell the difference between
a real and a spurious specimen? Surely not, when he goes to
lengths to emphasize that Giovanelli, for all his one major insight

denied to the others—into the full quality of Daisy's innocence—nevertheless *is* spurious, a sponger and a vulgarian (the later revisions of the story degrade poor Giovanelli even further: 'that man' becomes 'that thing', 'he' becomes 'it', and is even 'glossy' and 'greasy').[8] That is, the word and the idea 'gentleman' are not without validity, and a Giovanelli is properly devalued when judged against them. But the mistake is to believe that such validity is ever static, and that evaluation and knowledge are ever secure. Only within change and flow is any truth to be found—though in change and flow are also to be found error and suffering (and death, too). The society judgement that Giovanelli is a fortune-hunter (and Eugenio the courier his commissioned pander) has a measure of truth in it, and it is essential and even good that the Roman-American society is able to see this. After all, Mrs. Walker does have tears in her eyes as she watches Daisy make a spectacle of herself on the Pincio. But they see it at the expense of other things, and at the cost to themselves that they inevitably partake of that self-seeking lack of charity which they are the first to scent out. James, the most sophisticated of novelists, fully understands the perilous virtues of sophistication.

What this society misses (what a sophisticated America has come to miss of its own birthright), and what Winterbourne half-perceives, is something that lies behind Daisy on her terrace. This is the source of the 'poetry' in the tale that James later confessed to, in his Preface, as being 'inordinate' and 'extravagant'.[9] Without the existence of this other level, the story might appear to go no deeper than James's own description of hotel life at Vevey: 'a flitting hither and thither of "stylish" young girls, a rustling of muslin flounces, a rattle of dance-music in the morning hours, a sound of high-pitched voices at all times' (p. 141). But in front of this hotel there is also 'a remarkably blue lake' (that 'remarkably' is so Jamesian a hallmark: the coaxing, raised eyebrows of an ironic depreciation that is really an invitation to approach and to submit). And from the parapet of the hotel garden the view extends beyond the lake shore to the Château de Chillon and the crest of the Dents du Midi. The very first sight of Daisy is when she has paused in front of Winterbourne's bench and is silhouetted

---

[8] See Viola Dunbar, 'The Revision of *Daisy Miller*', *Modern Language Notes*, lxv, 1950, 311–17.
[9] *The Art of the Novel*, ed. R. P. Blackmur, New York, 1934, p. 269.

against the edge of the parapet and its view. When he addresses her, she turns from time to time to gaze, a little vacantly, at the prospect 'over the parapet, at the lake and the opposite mountains', while in the foreground is played out the comic 'flitting' and 'rustling' and 'rattle' of their contemporary young voices (with the ghastly shrill accompaniment of little Randolph), engaged in a contemporary young encounter—trivial, bathetic, embarrassed, gradually purposive and involved. The view is always there: James never lets us forget it, though it is as yet only a minor under-tone to the comedy of the scene. The second meeting with Daisy, on the same parapet, is in darkness, and James (it is a minute touch—but these are all minute touches that add up to something large) insists on the spectacular fan, that familiar image of feminine grace and feminine challenge, that Daisy carries (it is mentioned five times in the short scene): 'He found her that evening in the garden, wandering about in the warm starlight, like an indolent sylph, and swinging to and fro the largest fan he had ever beheld'. When Winterbourne is obliged to reveal to her that his aunt declines to meet her, and Daisy has to take bravely the first of many snubs, we suddenly have a glimpse into the prospect behind Daisy's fan, her 'unknown country'. James repeats his phrasing and his allusions to make his emphasis clear:

Winterbourne was embarrassed. 'She would be most happy', he said; 'but I am afraid those headaches will interfere'.

The young girl looked at him through the dusk. 'But I suppose she doesn't have a headache every day', she said, sympathetically.

Winterbourne was silent a moment. 'She tells me she does', he answered at last—not knowing what to say.

Miss Daisy Miller stopped and stood looking at him. Her prettiness was still visible in the darkness; she was opening and closing her enormous fan. 'She doesn't want to know me!' she said, suddenly. 'Why don't you say so? You needn't be afraid. I'm not afraid!' And she gave a little laugh.

Winterbourne fancied there was a tremor in her voice; he was touched, shocked, mortified by it. 'My dear young lady', he protested, 'she knows no one. It's her wretched health'.

The young girl walked on a few steps, laughing still. 'You needn't be afraid', she repeated. 'Why should she want to know me?' Then she paused again; she was close to the parapet of the garden, and in front of her was the starlit lake. There was a vague sheen upon its surface, and in the distance were dimly-seen mountain forms. Daisy Miller looked

out upon the mysterious prospect, and then she gave another little
laugh. 'Gracious! she *is* exclusive!' she said. (pp. 159–60)

The implications in such a passage are enriched by the little
reference to the fan—little, but singled out by its having been
stressed so much immediately before, and not least by the semi-
colon after the word 'darkness' that sets off the fan in a sentence
of its own. Similarly, the repetition of Winterbourne being looked
at by Daisy through the darkness (an image used again, with
devastating effect, in the last scene in the Colosseum) and of
Daisy's nervous 'You needn't be afraid' combine with the evocation
of the landscape to suggest the presence of the girl's inner life.
Beneath the external triviality there is a wayward and strangely
attractive personality, unreachable yet sensitive to pain.

Again, consider the conclusion to the later scene in Rome where
Daisy asserts her freedom (and her giddiness) by ignoring Mrs.
Walker's exhortation not to compromise herself by walking in
public with Giovanelli. Winterbourne, having allied himself with
Mrs. Walker by getting into her carriage—literally and figuratively
—now sees Daisy and Giovanelli on the parapet of the Pincian
Garden overlooking the Villa Borghese. He gets out and approaches
them, but in vain:

Winterbourne stood there; he had turned his eyes towards Daisy and
her cavalier. They evidently saw no one; they were too deeply occupied
with each other. When they reached the low garden-wall they stood a
moment looking off at the great flat-topped pine-clusters of the Villa
Borghese; then Giovanelli seated himself familiarly upon the broad
ledge of the wall. The western sun in the opposite sky sent out a brilliant
shaft through a couple of cloud-bars; whereupon Daisy's companion
took her parasol out of her hands and opened it. She came a little nearer
and he held the parasol over her; then, still holding it, he let it rest
upon her shoulder, so that both of their heads were hidden from
Winterbourne. This young man lingered a moment, then he began to
walk. But he walked—not towards the couple with the parasol; towards
the residence of his aunt, Mrs. Costello. (p. 187)

The parasol excludes Winterbourne from Daisy, and also from
what Daisy in confronting, the whole garden and the dramatic
appearance of the setting sun—the whole prospect of colour,
nature, expansiveness, potentiality. Daisy is always a little distant
from us; but we know her well by the objects and the places James

so consciously associates her with. And their ramifications are at
least as wide as the vista of Paris and of the French countryside
that tantalized Longmore in *Madame de Mauves*.

The tragedy for Daisy is that she, even more cruelly than
Winterbourne, is in the end cut off from such a prospect. She has
an idea of freedom—though very much less intelligently developed
than the young Isabel Archer's, say. And even more, she comes to
have an idea of loving Winterbourne, and being loved by him. The
idea of freedom is latent in the quizzicality of many of her attitudes.
Because Daisy, for all her apparent small-mindedness, for all her
desperate lack of maturity and support, acts as a mocker of
Winterbourne's conventional world. Not only are her nature and
her behaviour in themselves a challenge to that world; there is
something in her that seems to know she can challenge it. For
example, her request to Winterbourne to take her out unaccompanied in a rowing-boat on Lake Geneva at night is evidently
provoked by the 'stiffness' in him which she accurately diagnoses.
She really does not intend to go. When he jumps to accede to her
request, she stands still and only laughs, 'I was bound I would
make you say something' (p. 165). (One of the many interesting
revisions which James made in *Daisy Miller* for the New York
edition—interesting, though in other respects very arch and
mannered—was to add at this point, 'She only remained an
elegant image of free light irony.') Her words to the courier—'Oh,
Eugenio,—I am going out in a boat'—are similarly designed to
bring out and then to ironize his conventional disapproval. And
when he withdraws his disapproval, she laughingly abandons her
suggestion with the words: 'That's all I want—a litte fuss.' If this
behaviour seems irresponsible, it is less irresponsible than that of
Winterbourne—a man who genuinely considers the action im-
proper but is excited enough by the impropriety to pursue it. And
this is the point behind so much of Daisy's behaviour at Vevey
and Rome. Her crudity and petulance also contain a naïve irony,
sometimes instinctive, sometimes conscious and nervous. This is
something which the disapprovers, apart from Winterbourne at
times, can never appreciate: that their own hypocrisies, cruelties,
and familiarity with chicanery are being shown up by having
Daisy as a home-bred irritant and a raw little judge in their midst.[10]

[10] Against this interpretation of Daisy as a judge must be set the authority
of James himself, who wrote in a letter to Eliza Lynn Linton in 1880: '[Daisy]

And to add to this complication, the 'little fuss' Daisy wants is not only a sign of simple callowness and, in equal part, a sign of her intuitively testing this society; it is also a testimony to her interest in Winterbourne as a man, to her wish to move him, make him jealous, throw him off balance. Daisy could easily have loved Winterbourne, and Winterbourne, freed from his inhibitions, could have loved Daisy—we must never forget this simple and moving possibility, on which the whole tale deeply depends for its success, and which makes it so much more lyrical and less sardonic than the story of Longmore and Euphemia.

Daisy is the figure who changes most through this story. Winterbourne, after his gyrations, stands still, even ossifies. She comes to have a tenderness for him; and she also moves towards a greater self-awareness that brings, if not maturity, at least a pained recognition of her own failure. She loses innocence without gaining wisdom, or even a reciprocated love. United to Winterbourne, one is meant to feel, she might well have developed out of her intellectual flimsiness. And he for his part would at least have escaped from the ethic of Geneva and the atmosphere of middle-aged ladies. As it is, what we feel about Daisy in the latter part of the story is her unprotected loneliness—she is virtually motherless —and even despair, in the face of ostracism. Her notorious behaviour becomes more assertive and more self-protective. Her 'spontaneity' turns into an impudent mask because the Rome of American exiles sneers at the 'Golden Age' in which she is seen to move, and because it cannot accept the most American of qualities in its pristine state. Hence the slightly frenetic note of her late appearance at Mrs. Walker's party with the unwelcome Giovanelli—a final act of defiance against the Mrs. Walker set, and a next-to-final attempt to exasperate Winterbourne out of his stiffness.

---

never took the measure really of the scandal she produced, and had no means of doing so: she was too ignorant, too irreflective, too little versed in the proportions of things . . . to my perception she never really tried to take her revenge upon public opinion—to outrage it and irritate it. In this sense I fear I must declare that she was not *defiant*, in the sense you mean. . . . She only wished to be left alone—being herself quite unaggressive' (*Selected Letters of Henry James*, ed. Leon Edel, London, 1956, pp. 171–2). James, however, as the Preface makes clear, was very uneasy as to the degree of romantic sympathy he had shown for Daisy in the story, and perhaps his remarks in the letter can be seen partly as a reaction to this. At any rate, one can only hold to the way Daisy actually appears to exist in the reading of the story.

All she moves him to is a comment on the possibility of her being
in love with Giovanelli, which, to his bewilderment, offends a
suddenly blushing Daisy by its indelicacy (Winterbourne tested
against her natural sensibility once again, and found wanting).
And when Daisy leaves the party in distress after being snubbed by
the turned back of her hostess, Winterbourne's feelings of pity are
the more damnable in that they are safely indulged from the
distance, as a mere observer of the scene.

The last movement of the destruction of Daisy Miller, and
James's last survey of all that is lost in that destruction, are given
consummate expression by his use of the Roman landscape: a
last progression, from the Palace of the Caesars, to the Colosseum,
to the Protestant Cemetery (no novelist has ever used his impressions
as a tourist to more functional, less merely picturesque effect than
James).

A few days after his brief interview with her mother, he encountered
her in that beautiful abode of flowering desolation known as the
Palace of the Caesars. The early Roman spring had filled the air with
bloom and perfume, and the rugged surface of the Palatine was muffled
with tender verdure. Daisy was strolling along the top of one of those
great mounds of ruin that are embanked with mossy marble and paved
with monumental inscriptions. It seemed to him that Rome had never
been so lovely as just then. He stood looking off at the enchanting
harmony of line and colour that remotely encircles the city, inhaling
the softly humid odours and feeling the freshness of the year and the
antiquity of the place reaffirm themselves in mysterious interfusion.
(p. 198)

That 'mysterious interfusion' is lightly touched on—it just passes
Winterbourne, and the reader, with a brush of its wings. But a
great deal lies within it. What is interfused, so mysteriously, is
history and the present moment, 'antiquity' and 'freshness'; the
weightiness of a dead imperial society, 'paved with monumental
inscriptions', along with youth's spontaneity and spring; rugged-
ness with verdure; desolation with flowers; and all within 'the
enchanting harmony of line and colour' that encircles Rome and
the whole scene, with the figure of Daisy, strolling above the ruins,
as the centre of the circle. For only a second, all the opposing
forces of the story are held in balance; and for that second we know
the difference between equilibrium and the usual state of things.

Then Winterbourne and Daisy, drawn back to that usual state, taunt one another—he, experimentally; she, coquettishly—and go their separate ways.

If James rises above the tourist in his appreciation of place, poor Winterbourne does not, at the end. He adds a little aestheticism to the rest of his detachment, and as 'a lover of the picturesque' enters the Colosseum by moonlight to read aloud the famous description of it in Byron's *Manfred*.[11] The scene is one of chiaroscuro, visually and figuratively: 'One-half of the gigantic circus was in deep shade; the other was sleeping in the luminous dusk' (p. 201). Daisy and Giovanelli are seated at the foot of the great cross in the centre of the arena, within the shadow. Their critical observer stands in the light. And having found to his satisfaction the final formula that sums up so unrespectable a young lady, he imagines that his light is also a judicial one: 'It was as if a sudden illumination had been flashed upon the ambiguity of Daisy's behaviour and the riddle had become easy to read.' James only just stops short of making explicit all the suggestiveness of the setting: '[Winterbourne] stood there looking at her—looking at her companion, and not reflecting that though he saw them vaguely, he himself must have been more brightly visible.' He prides himself on the clarity of his view, but the real 'illumination' is that which shines on him and through him from outside, exposing to Daisy, and more clearly to us, his final collapse. He has cast Daisy into the shadows, as his society has already done—the shadow which will at once become that of the malarial *perniciosa*. [12] He has never really penetrated the obscurity in which the girl's personality and her whole 'case' lie wrapped for him. And he chooses, finally, a simple black-and-white morality that simplifies and gives him the self-righteous relief of his formula. All these metaphorical suggestions flow naturally out of a scene that is intense but quite unlaboured. There is no heavy symbolism: only a clear setting

[11] Act III, Scene iv. I wonder if the passage was in James's mind when he wrote the description of the Palace of the Caesars a few pages before, with its 'flowering desolation' and 'rugged surface'. Byron writes of the 'rolling moon' 'Which softened down the hoar austerity/Of rugged desolation, and fill'd up,/ As 'twere anew, the gaps of centuries'. And the whole passage from *Manfred* evokes a not dissimilar moment of 'mysterious interfusion'.

[12] The revision adds another variation to the chiaroscuro motif: 'She was a young lady about the *shades* of whose perversity a foolish puzzled gentleman need no longer trouble his head or his heart. That once questionable quantity *had* no shades—it was a mere black little blot.'

that blends quite indistinguishably at every point with the taken
meanings of the action.

The final exchange between Winterbourne and Daisy takes
place through this same darkness. His last thrust is a heartless and
contemptuous phrase, 'I believe that it makes very little difference
whether you are engaged or not!' As she takes the thrust, 'He felt
the young girl's pretty eyes fixed upon him through the thick
gloom of the archway'—a light failing in darkness, a perception
blinded, a communication and a love left unuttered.[13] And
Daisy's last words as she leaves the Colosseum closely echo in
their syntax Winterbourne's callous phrase, as if to emphasize his
being implicated in what is to follow: '"I don't care", said Daisy,
in a little strange tone, "whether I have Roman fever or not!"'
And as a final element in the scene, what of the fact that Daisy is
seated at the foot of the cross, and facetiously compares herself to
a Christian martyr and the approaching Winterbourne to a lion?[14]
It is certainly not enough to make us see the whole incident in
Christian terms. But despite the strongly ironic tone it is another
pointer to James's involvement here on the side of his heroine,
whose innocent sufferings move him, as suffering in his novels so
often moved him, towards at least the vocabulary of Christianity.

Daisy's last simple message of defeated affection is heart-
breaking, coming as it does through the bathetic medium of her
mother's words to Winterbourne when he visits their hotel: 'Any
way, she says she's not engaged. I don't know why she wanted you
to know; but she said to me three times—"Mind you tell Mr.
Winterbourne". And then she told me to ask if you remembered
the time you went to that castle, in Switzerland. But I said I
wouldn't give any such messages as that' (p. 205). Her death is as
succinct and final as the wry little phrase by which James records it:
'A week after this the poor girl died; it had been a terrible case of
the fever' (the raised eyebrows again, the ironic circumflex, as in
that 'remarkably' of the book's second sentence: this time to
express a compassionate pungency). And Daisy's grave, in an
equally flawless phrase, is only a 'raw protuberance among the

---

[13] Revision: 'He felt her lighted eyes fairly penetrate the thick gloom of the
vaulted passage—as if to seek some access to him she hadn't yet encompassed.'

[14] The revision even adds the doves of Christianity: 'These words [of Daisy's]
were winged with their accent, so that they fluttered and settled about him in
the darkness like vague white doves.'

April daisies' (those ugly gaping vowels in 'raw protuberance';
and the way 'protuberance' catches, in its sound, the ungainly
bulge of the earth, and also, in its generality, the startling abstraction of a death). This is what the 'mysterious interfusion', the
moment at the Palace of the Caesars, has come down to. Then,
Daisy had walked in harmony above the Empire's mounds of ruin
and above the categorical inscriptions and stony formulae of that
old law-making city, in the same way that the freshness of spring
had relieved the desolation of the Caesars. Now, her grave is dug
far down, 'in an angle of the wall of imperial Rome, beneath the
cypresses and the thick spring-flowers'. And everything else has
broken apart, gone its familiar way: Giovanelli into his urbane
obscurity; the expatriates to their salons; and Winterbourne,
perturbed and a little haunted, back to observation and 'study',
and back to some 'very clever foreign lady'—who must therefore,
in at least three ways, be the antithesis and final negation of a
Daisy Miller.

One brief word remains to be said about both these stories. Each
of them ends in failure and in a death, and contains much that is
grievous—there is a note of sorrow that is clearly James's own,
particularly at the end of *Daisy Miller*. But they are also comic—a
fact which it is easy to take for granted and to leave out of our
total estimate of them. If we remember the self-lacerating confusions of Longmore's nature, and how they implicate us all, we
also remember, in a different way, the Baron's testy description
of his wife initiating him into the 'terrible brown fog' of Anglo-
Saxon culture by making him read 'a certain Wordsworth'—an
experience like having one's noble head held forcibly 'over a basin
of *soupe aux choux*' (p. 159). And against our image of the raw
earth on Daisy Miller's grave we must also place, for example, the
laughable banality of her frizzle-headed mother:

'we have seen places', [Mrs. Miller] resumed, 'that I should put a long
way before Rome'. And in reply to Winterbourne's interrogation,
'There's Zurich', she observed; 'I think Zurich is lovely; and we
hadn't heard half so much about it'.
    'The best place we've seen is the City of Richmond!' said Randolph.
    'He means the ship', his mother explained. 'We crossed in that ship.
Randolph had a good time on the City of Richmond'.

'It's the best place I've seen', the child repeated. 'Only it was turned the wrong way'.

'Well, we've got to turn the right way some time', said Mrs. Miller, with a little laugh. (p. 175)

At any climax, no matter how serious, James's sombreness is able to take on a very particular comic or ironic edge. And this is a further mark of that sustained and unique narrative tone which we noted earlier, and which determines the way we apprehend any of James's works. It is as characteristic and as exacting as the manner of a Chekhov play, and is as functional an item of James's technique as his manipulation of dramatic scene or symbol or point of view, or any other of the devices of fiction on which he has placed his name. It is the most important single factor in the unity of any James novel, since it allows him to blend the various and opposed strains of his creative response: the intelligent, self-delighting *boulevardier* and the confirmed elegist; the satirist, the moral analyst, the romantic; the man of the theatre, the humourist, and the man of feeling. It is a formidable, subtle medium—one that often demands an effort from the reader to recognize and assimilate—and *Madame de Mauves* and *Daisy Miller* would be, even in this respect alone, invaluable as a starting-point. The mixed mode they represent establishes itself as the only appropriate vehicle for James's mingled vision: the tragicomic vision (which in a way was Chekhov's, too) of a desired but always elusive fulfilment to all human living, individual and collective; of mind and temperament striving for ultimate shape; of baffled lovers on their terraces, staring at a city or a sunset.

2

Roderick Hudson:
Tragedy of the Will

I

WHILE *Madame de Mauves* was being serialized, early in
1874, James was writing his first important novel, a work
which seems in so many ways, intellectually and emotionally, to
spring from the same matrix. *Roderick Hudson* was begun in a hot
spring in Florence, continued in Baden Baden, and finished in a
cold bright winter in Boston and New York. In completing it,
James tells us, he clung to 'the illusion of the golden air' of Italy,
where his memorable visit of 1873 had marked the beginning of a
spiritual and sensuous adventure as vivid for him, in its way, as that
of his sculptor-hero.[1] Nostalgia for something lost, and the
excitement of growth and discovery, lie together at the heart of
Roderick Hudson, both in the story of its composition and in its
content. Perhaps this is what has made it seem to be a young
man's book, in a pejorative sense, to disparaging critics in the
past[2]—though its lyrical qualities seem to me not only fine in
themselves but perfectly characteristic of a directness of feeling
that often underlies even the latest of late James. Its humour, too,
is stronger and more buoyant than has been allowed: a little
'literary', no doubt, and consciously well turned, but still with an
energetic openness about it that produces outright laughter.
Further, there is a simplicity in much of the characterization
—Roderick's, for example—that is perfectly compatible with much
in the book that is profound, psychologically and morally. And this,
once again, is distinctly Jamesian, since all the analysis and inwardness of his manner, at its most developed, can accommodate much

[1] The Preface, in *The Art of the Novel*, ed. R. P. Blackmur, New York, 1934,
pp. 6–7.
[2] F. O. Matthiessen, for example, called it 'apprentice work' (*Henry James.
The Major Phase*, London, 1946, p. 153); and F. W. Dupee thought it 'not
much more than a museum-piece . . . being dead in the center' (*Henry James*,
London, 1951, p. 87).

that is theatrical and stark—including the stylized and public note of character. All in all, without something of the *Roderick Hudson* touch even the maturer and more complex of James's novels could not be what they are.

The book's weaknesses lie in specific details rather than in its basic sensibility or technique. Above all, as the later Preface admits, there is a failure fully to realize Rowland Mallet's love for Mary Garland, a sentiment which appears dutifully at certain intervals through the novel, and towards the end with an almost apologetic emphasis. This is clear enough, and important enough: in the author's words, 'The damage to verisimilitude is deep.' But James's stronger apology in the Preface for the portrayal of Roderick's breakdown—for having made it come about 'too fast'—is surely unnecessary. The failure of Roderick's creative powers and moral will is inherent from the beginning—from the first description of his narrow frame and unmasculine voice, and certainly from his first winter in Rome, where his talent shows its fragility on his return from the excesses of Baden Baden, in Chapter 7. James had adequately prepared the ground for his hero's downfall, and, as I shall show, he is unfair to the complexities of his own work when, thirty years later, he regrets the way he made Christina Light the 'well-nigh sole agent of [Roderick's] catastrophe'. She is nothing of the kind.[3]

Apart from Rowland's relation to Mary Garland, the only other flaws of the novel that catch the attention are, on some occasions, the faintly monotonous felicity of its language—the expression is so rich, so regularly metaphorical and clever, that it tends at times to defeat itself—and also the slight excess of similar crises and turning-points in the plot. Perfect scene succeeds perfect scene in too repetitive a rhythm, and the retreat of the main characters northwards, at the end, through Florence, Lake Como, and Engelberg, is somewhat over-prolonged. But this kind of pace and repetitiveness, after all, is perhaps only an essential condition of that total saturation in a subject which is one of the most important qualities of James's writing. And as for the plot-coincidences and contrivances which some criticize in *Roderick Hudson*, there are not many more than in *The Wings of the Dove*—these being a perfectly acceptable feature of James's usual 'heightening' technique.

Consider the typical method of *Roderick Hudson* as revealed in

[3] *The Art of the Novel*, pp. 12–18.

its first four chapters, those set in Northampton, Massachusetts. There is a surface of very formal contrasts, preparatory hints and echoes, recurrent emblems, and debate-like exchanges (as in the early E. M. Forster), with, underneath, a slow growth of impinging characters and felt relationships. The first chapter even opens a little allegorically, with its significant image of combined fruition and deprivation. Rowland Mallet, in the past, when he had seen Cecilia won in marriage by his cousin, 'seemed to feel the upward sweep of the empty bough from which the golden fruit had been plucked'.[4] Further on appears another image that in various guises will appear again: Rowland, reviewing his life to Cecilia, tells her that he is 'groping for the latch of a closed door' (just as he will shortly extol 'living with open doors' to Roderick, and deplore the 'solid blank wall'). And the chapter ends with the dramatically 'placed' moment of Rowland seeing Roderick's fine statuette of 'a naked youth drinking from a gourd': 'There was a loosened fillet of wild flowers about his head, and his eyes, under their dropped lids, looked straight into the cup. On the base was scratched the Greek word $\Delta i\psi a$, Thirst' (p. 30). If this at first seems to promise a superficial antithesis between two types of mankind—the one (Rowland) groping at the closed door, the other (Roderick) quaffing the cup of passionate experience[5]—it eventually becomes clear that the book is exploring the problem far more subtly as it exists inside each of the main characters, and as it exists in a whole society.

Right through the Northampton section of the novel sounds, for one thing, the question of work and leisure. As in *The Ambassadors* and *The Ivory Tower*, James uses the American utilitarian ethos to emphasize the moral problem facing the man with no need to work, the aristocrat born outside an aristocratic society and age: 'You are the first unoccupied man I ever saw', Mary tells Rowland. As with other aspects of the 'international' question in *Roderick Hudson* (and as in *Madame de Mauves* and *Daisy Miller*), national characteristics are used only to point up the more basic

---

[4] *Roderick Hudson*, London, 1961, p. 18. Future page-references are to this edition, which reprints the first English (and revised) edition of 1879.

[5] This is how the book has been most often interpreted as a simple antithesis or allegory, and usually with further reference to James's own psychic dualism—for a useful guide through the plethora and the diversity of interpretations of James, in this case as in the case of all his novels, see Oscar Cargill, *The Novels of Henry James*, New York, 1961.

issues involved. When Rowland contrasts his own uselessness with the widowed Cecilia's practicality, and asks himself, 'in truth, with his means, his leisure and his opportunities, what had he done?' he is touching on the same matter as the lost 'golden fruit', and the enviable boy drinking from the gourd. How can a man express all that is in him by meaningful action in a contemporary world? Even the comic Barnaby Striker, philistine and utilitarian foil though he is, is allowed his passing moment of dignity by the strength of his doctrine of work and application: 'The crop we gather depends upon the seed we sow.' And Rowland, too, has his 'project'—to make an art collection and give it to the nation. All the main characters—these very nineteenth-century characters—need to have a 'project', as we shall see: a nervous urge to justify their lives in significance and happiness. Justification may even lie in unhappiness if that is the truer nature of real experience; for Rowland's desire to believe in 'the essential salubrity of genius' is qualified by an acceptance of strain: 'I nevertheless approve of a certain tension of one's being. It's what a man is meant for' (p. 54). Accompanied by tensions or not, 'true happiness', as he has already explained in an important and premonitory speech,

'consists in getting out of one's self; . . . and to stay out you must have some absorbing errand. . . . I want to care for something or for somebody. And I want to care with a certain ardour; even, if you can believe it, with a certain passion. . . . Do you know I sometimes think that I am a man of genius, half finished? The genius has been left out, the faculty of expression is wanting; but the need for expression remains, and I spend my days groping for the latch of a closed door.' (p. 23)

Cecilia's sceptical answer to this is that Rowland simply wants to fall in love; and clearly, in this story love will be one of the forms that the opening of the door can take. But another of the forms is the creation of beauty. And the relation between the two, art and passion, will show itself to be far more complicated than one of mutual exclusiveness.

Similarly, the relation between the active and the inactive sides of Rowland is a living one, and not a complete dichotomy. There is conscience and passivity in him, certainly, but there is egotism and desire interfused with the others, and sometimes wearing their faces. The main emphasis is on his reasonableness, but the sketch of his forbears prepares us for Rowland's hedonism and assertive emotion that will rise up in him like 'a well of vivifying waters'. His grandfather is present within him: a practical 'do-er', a sea-captain, a sabbath-breaker, and a man who took a plump foreign woman for his wife. Rowland, it should be clear from the first, is no simple caricature (intended or unintended) of the Puritan temperament. Nor is he on the other hand, as some readings of the book suggest, a model figure of intelligence and selflessness. He is closer, I think, to being an everyman: a figure caught up intensely into the drama of any life rather than an exemplar or a rascal. He is a man who feels 'the friction of existence'; essentially an optimist, yet disappointed by life; at times foolish, at times noble; one who finds more to admire in the brave actions of others than in himself; and whose imagination is just strong enough to make him an excited appreciator, but not a maker, of art. We are all, to a degree, frustrated doers, makers, artists, lovers, and we stand very close to Rowland while he takes the lesson of the water-drinker's statue, admiring and envying that power in the unseen sculptor who has 'found it so easy to produce a lovely work'.

Not that the sculptor proves to be the happy incarnation of this power. There will always be much to envy about Roderick, but he, too, contains something of the frustrated everyman. For Roderick is never fulfilled. Like Rowland, he always falls short, seeks for something beyond himself, and in fact perishes in self-contempt. When we first meet him he is 'hopelessly discontented' and without self-knowledge: 'I have done no good' is his complaint, in words almost identical to Rowland's. But out of Roderick, even in his very proper and inevitable distance from the reader, there flows something of a 'sacred fire': a creative but dangerous vibrancy, conveyed in his language, his unstable gestures, his few successful deeds, and not least (what gives him reality for us despite his distance) in his influence on others. The 'well of vivifying waters' is there potentially within all of them, here at the very source of the novel's action—a romantic source, an Emersonian *idée-mère*, that might well have come from nearby Concord rather than Northampton. So that what these opening chapters mainly pick out for both men, and what the book as a whole sustains in its movement and high colour, is the adventurousness of life, the challenge of proving one's identity, and achieving knowledge and contentment. Hence, at the beginning, the narrative bustle of decisive meetings, revelations, confessions, sudden empowering gifts, departures. The prospect of Italy hangs over the early pages like a promise: an imaginative promise for the reader, as well as for Roderick, whose gleeful anticipatory singing of 'The splendour falls on castle walls And snowy summits old in story' breaks through the conservative calm of the Massachusetts night—like the raising of a curtain.

Part of the sense of promise is dependent on another notion that will become important in the story: that of belief. When Roderick and Rowland lie beneath the pine-trees overlooking the curve of the Connecticut River—itself a vista full of alternative promise, that of America—and Rowland reveals his plans for Roderick's European future, the sculptor cries in his delight, 'You believe in me!' (p. 43). And when Mary Garland asks if Roderick possesses 'great powers' that would justify such a gamble, Rowland replies:

'One can't *know* in such a matter save after proof, and proof takes time. But one can believe.'
'And you believe?'
'I believe'. (p. 62)

And a little later, when Rowland and Mary are alone at the picnic, he expresses his regret that she had not believed more fully in *him*. By itself this is not much. But throughout the rest of the novel there is a constant desire in the major characters to believe in someone or something else, and in turn to be believed. Even the egoistic Roderick, informing Rowland of his engagement to Mary as the two men sit on deck, bound for Italy, is moved to declare that 'unless a man is unnaturally selfish he needs to work for some one else than himself'—thereby echoing Rowland's speech about true happiness consisting in 'getting out of one's self'. To be believed in, in the way that Roderick finds his talent believed in by Rowland, is of immense importance. Something essential to life depends on the possession of an individualizing talent, and on the finding of someone who will confirm that talent and encourage its expression. And similarly, the act of believing is itself an act of expression: the opening of a door and the discovery of an external and fulfilling issue.

Roderick's talent is essentially Romantic and idealist, and Christina Light, on her first appearance in the book, in the gardens of the Villa Ludovisi, is the Muse and emblem of his aspirations in art: in his own words, 'a revelation', 'a glimpse of ideal beauty'. A Neoplatonic idea of perfection haunts and exasperates him, and actuality, as he finds it in his models, is only 'a gross degenerate image' (one is reminded of the 'cats and monkeys' of the actual, opposed to the ideality of the painter's dream, in *The Madonna of the Future*). James smiles, and will continue to smile, at the ingenuousness of Roderick's arrogant vision. But equally, he never disparages its power and its traditional appeal to our imagination, and to his. He arranges a formal tableau in Chapter 6 that brings out both of these estimates of Roderick. At Rowland's dinner-party a number of the minor characters (wonderfully etched figures, if a little detachable) are introduced and arranged around a central object: Roderick the idealist. Gloriani the successful sculptor is by comparison obviously corrupt from the beginning; yet he is a figure of some force. He has no trace of idealism or restlessness. He is cynical and perceptive: an infidel amid the credulous. He knows the extent of his talent and exactly how to make it work in the world—and how to make it, in a later Jamesian phrase, work the world, to his own benefit. (There is only one surprise in store from Gloriani: by a cruel irony, at the point where Roderick has lost confidence in himself beyond recall it is Gloriani who tells him, 'I should like to say now that I believe in you' (p. 279). And Gloriani is bewildered to see Roderick's eyes fill with angry, disbelieving tears: a moment of perfect failure in human converse and faith.) The little water-colourist Sam Singleton, on the other hand, while enjoying his own modest talent and knowing how to make it work by patience, is also a dreamer and yearner of a kind. His continual desire to worship Roderick— 'Singleton sat gazing and listening open-mouthed, as if Phoebus Apollo had been talking'—signifies his own pursuit of the ideal vision, which will never quite fade, even at the end. For Sam Singleton's admiration is that of the man, once again, who needs to believe—and in a memorable vignette, we see him hovering excitedly on the edge of the little group of people who have gathered round Roderick's new statue of Eve, while in the middle of the radiant circle the maker himself holds up a lamp, and the cautious Gloriani, head on one side, appraises 'from half-closed eyes'.

And yet, in one of those sudden changes so symptomatic of James's sardonic view, here in the centre of the radiance falls the first real shadow of the book's darker theme: that of the decline of power and belief. Gloriani warns Roderick that 'passion burns out, inspiration runs to seed'; and Roderick's response is that he will make no compromise with his Muse: 'If I break down . . . I shall stay down.' Almost at once, the very next day, Roderick has lost his first creative impulse—that is, before Christina Light has entered his personal life. And as he presses a reluctant Rowland to approve his travelling northwards, we hear beneath their words a hint of the incomprehension and lack of confidence that always threatens their friendship: 'Ah, you don't trust me', Roderick exclaims.[6] Rowland's unease at letting Roderick go is fundamentally connected to their words on the mystery of the human will some months later, after Roderick has demoralized himself at Baden Baden and the two men meet in Geneva (where the statue of Rousseau, the apostle of self-cultivation, makes an ironic companion to their conversation). Now the two of them are split by Rowland's insistence on individual responsibility ('The will is destiny itself') and Roderick's weaker but more realistic admission: 'Who can answer for his will? who can say beforehand that it's strong? There are all kinds of indefinable currents moving to and fro between one's will and one's inclinations . . . It all depends upon circumstances. I believe there is a certain group of circumstances possible for every man, in which his will is destined to snap like a dry twig' (p. 119). James does not endorse either view, to the exclusion of the other. That the will, like talent, is unreliable, is integral to his analysis of personality—as is, on the other hand, the need for a man to continue to act and create as if the will were free and strong: a virtually Conradian incongruity that produces many of *Roderick Hudson*'s ironies, as well as its tragedy.[7]

---

[6] The threat is brought out much more in the revision for the New York edition, where Rowland feels probed to the depths by Roderick's foreign stare, and Roderick's 'Ah, you don't trust me' becomes, more pointedly, 'Ah, that shows you don't *really* believe in me.'

[7] Lambert Strether in his famous exchange with little Bilham in Chapter 11 of *The Ambassadors* has a whimsical perception of this incongruity: 'The affair—I mean the affair of life—couldn't, no doubt, have been different for me; for it's at the best, a tin mould, either fluted and embossed, with ornamental excrescences, or else smooth and dreadfully plain, into which, a helpless jelly, one's consciousness is poured—so that one "takes" the form, as the great cook says, and is more or less compactly held by it; one lives in fine as one can. Still, one has the illusion of freedom; therefore don't be, like me, without the memory of that illusion.'

'What am I to do?' is the despairing question that comes from Roderick in his crisis of will (a question we have already heard from Rowland, and will hear later on from Christina). The answer comes on its cue as Christina enters his studio—and at once Roderick is galvanized and inspired. Here is no mere *femme fatale*, but to an equal degree the opposite: a force that restores Roderick and drives him on, and a force that many others in this Roman society wish to submit themselves to. Perhaps one should see Christina as a catalyst, rather than as being simply baleful or beneficent. In that way, her function would be like the various descriptions of Rome and Italy with which she is so deliberately associated. For example, in the first chapter Italy is described as a place symbolic of deep experience and of life's extremes, where 'the chords of feeling grow tense', either for happiness or for misery. And there is a fine passage at the beginning of Chapter 9 where a parallel is drawn between the history of Rome and the loss of Roderick's creative power. 'There is nothing in one's consciousness that is not foredoomed to moulder and crumble and become dust for the feet . . . of future generations'—that is the lesson Rome offers to Rowland at the same time as the other lesson of *carpe diem*. Christina, with all her contradictions, and with her hair in its classic coil and her 'step and carriage of a tired princess', is very much a Roman Muse. She simultaneously brings out both sides of Roderick's nature, the self-destructive and the creative. And like the city itself, she acts as a zone of power and influence within which certain of the elemental conflicts of living are enacted with new clarity and force.

Christina's lustre and mystery are often described, as in the first visit to Roderick's studio, as qualities of an actress— and this is to become James's favourite way of describing any rich personality whose creativity and moral ambivalence are conveyed through a protean variety of roles, and even through lying.[8] 'Playing a part' can be an expression of the will and the talent to re-create the self (Madame Grandoni later says of Christina, 'when the estimate she may have of herself grows vague she needs to do something to give it a definite impressive form'). She can act in the

---

[8] The list is extensive, from Eugenia in *The Europeans* to Charlotte Stant in *The Golden Bowl*. We shall shortly come upon the full type in Miriam Rooth, in *The Tragic Muse*—and there will be more than a trace in Milly Theale, even, in *The Wings of the Dove*.

way that Roderick sculpts and that Rowland longs to live: from some inner source of personal energy, which is thwarted by the everyday forms of her life in society and can find shape only in the histrionic. On one level there is no contradiction between her wilful exaggerations and her statement, 'I am fond of facing the truth'—sometimes Christina has to invent the truth. Essentially, of course, her bitterness is the mark of the dangerously disillusioned idealist. Her attitudinizing is not only a means of direct self-expression; it is also a way of manipulating a corrupt real world in the light of an egocentric but genuine ideal. In a sharp scene with Rowland in Chapter 20 she reveals the impossible scope of her dream in one of her most stageworthy speeches: the romantic dream of an existence of all-embracing plenitude, where she could live in accord with the luxuriousness of the world *and* with her own heart and spiritual values (which at present, in their frustration, can only torment her for her cynical compromises). Christina at once sees Roderick as her counterpart. 'He is like me', she says, 'he likes to face the truth.' They are both truth-seekers in their way, occasionally ruthless, frequently absurd, and eventually destructive, as such truth-seekers tend to be. And as they both seek something they can believe and worship, so they both desperately—and in Christina's case, despairingly—seek to be believed in. This is one reason why her attitude to Rowland is so demanding and at times so resentful: her existence requires self-respect, but self-respect (like an artist's talent) often needs confirmation from another person. Rowland becomes for her the authority whose faith in her would help to guarantee her inner life. Her acting, too, reflects the importance of belief: 'I think she is an actress', Madame Grandoni tells Rowland, 'but she believes in her part while she is playing it.' She believes in her own roles, and wishes, like the actress in the theatre, to make others believe. Successful aesthetic illusion is one criterion of Christina's private integrity: another paradoxical instance of how, for James, art and life can come together.[9]

[9] Christina's dramatic role-playing is to be continued unabated on another stage in *The Princess Casamassima*, where she will act at politics and at social commitment with the same frenzy and the same destructiveness (Lionel Trilling in *The Liberal Imagination* calls her quest that of 'a perfect drunkard of reality'). I find her later performance much less sympathetic—which is perhaps to be expected from an older, more sceptical author—but also rather less convincingly handled than in the earlier novel.

II

The structural centre of *Roderick Hudson* consists of a group of very dramatic scenes (Chapters 10 to 14) in which Christina, Rowland, and Roderick begin to interact with a new and revealing intensity. The trio's relations of attraction and repulsion are not simple, nor are the ideas that quickly accrue from such heated involvement. At a ball given by Christina's mother—her attempt to penetrate the citadel of Roman society—Christina explains to Rowland why she is so attracted to Roderick, and does so in words that closely echo Rowland's earlier conversation with Cecilia on the nature of happiness and Roderick's own words on the need to work for someone outside oneself: 'I would give all I possess to get out of myself. . . . If a person wished to do me a favour I would say to him, "I beg you with tears in my eyes to interest me. Be strong, be positive, be imperious, if you will; only be *something*— something that in looking at I can forget my detestable self! " ' (p. 167). And the irony of the incident is that Rowland does not recognize the sentiments, and receives them with suspicion and disapproval. Christina and Rowland are always being drawn together uneasily by certain latent and unvoiced similarities, and by a very noticeable current of feeling. But they will never do more than revolve round one another, half-communicating, touching, and drifting apart in anger—a movement that is painfully charac-teristic of many relationships in the world of *Roderick Hudson*, and of the relationship between Rowland and his protégé in particular. For example, we are at once shown the distance between Rowland and Roderick in the scene that directly ensues from the ball, in which Rowland reproves Roderick for becoming attached to Christina, and Roderick sharply asserts his independence. What makes the scene moving is our perception of the strong affection that still exists between them, as a possible bridge. At first we share Rowland's point of view as he upbraids Roderick for his infidelity to Mary Garland and to his art, and despises him for 'standing passive in the clutch of his temperament'. But there comes a sudden turn when we are made to realize that Rowland's view is as far from adequate as anyone else's:

'You are the best man in the world' [Roderick says with sudden affection] 'and I am a vile brute. Only', he added in a moment, '*you don't understand me!*' And he looked at him with eyes of such pure

expressiveness that one might have said (and Rowland did almost
say so himself) that it was the fault of one's own grossness if one
failed to read to the bottom of that beautiful soul. (pp. 176–7)

But one does always fail to read to the bottom—the 'grossness' is
universal—and Roderick in turn understands Rowland no better
than he himself is understood.[10] It is often a mute gaze, as here,
that brings out these moments—like Daisy Miller's stare through
the dark archway in the Colosseum. Christina's eyes have the
same power to tantalize and admonish, with their hint that character
is always unfathomable—and even Mary Garland's, too, in the
glances she casts from *her* distance. At any rate, it is a gaze that
questions our judicial faculties as readers—our instinctive desire
to decide which character is right and which is wrong—and makes
us that much less unsympathetic to Roderick's perpetual demand
that he be left to follow the wayward urges of his inviolable and
inexorable self. And further, it reminds us of the paradoxical fact
that Roderick's reality for us as a character in this novel is partly
dependent on a sense of distance and privacy: on the mystery of
temperament itself, which is no small part of that larger mystery
the book is confronting, the human will to power and creation.

Fittingly enough, the failure to believe, to read to the mysterious
depths of another's soul, at once evokes the theme of the loss of
artistic inspiration. 'Come what come will!' is Roderick's final
reply to Rowland's criticisms. 'If I'm to fizzle out, the sooner I
know it the better. Sometimes I half suspect it.' And he flees to
Frascati from the threatened eclipse of his imaginative powers,
conveyed by an image like that of the door and the wall: 'here I am
face to face with the dead blank of my mind.' This, too, is brought
before us as a human problem of the most general kind, implicating
most other figures in the book. Roderick utters a theatrical monologue on the death of talent—it is smiled at for its obvious excesses,
by Rowland and by James, but, as usual, without being invalidated.
In fact, much of the novel's main refrain can be heard within the
speech's rhetoric. Brought together in this one speech, and in the
dialogue around it—here, half-way through the book—is a

[10] The New York edition emphasizes these aspects of the incident even more
effectively by a bizarre and striking late-James simile: '[Roderick] looked at
him out of such bottomless depths as might have formed the element of a shining
merman who should be trying, comparatively near shore, to signal to a
ruminating ox.'

reminder of the water-drinker in the first chapter, a premonition of the death of Roderick in the mountain thunderstorm of the last chapter, and a vivid expression of life's dependence on action:

'The whole matter of genius is a mystery. It bloweth where it listeth and we know nothing of its mechanism. . . . It's dealt out in different doses, in big cups and little, and when you have consumed your portion it's as *naïf* to ask for more as it was for Oliver Twist to ask for more porridge. Lucky for you if you have got one of the big cups; we drink them down in the dark, and we can't tell their size until we tip them up and hear the last gurgle. Those of some men last for life; those of others for a couple of years. . . . What am I, what are the best of us, but an experiment? Do I succeed—do I fail? . . . The end of my work shall be the end of my life. . . . I have a conviction that if the hour strikes *here*', and he tapped his forehead, 'I shall disappear, dissolve, be carried off in a cloud!' (pp. 182–3)

Christina Light stands out, in her most active role, against this increasing motion towards despair. In the typically histrionic scene in the Colosseum, in Chapter 13, she reviles Roderick for his self-doubts and weaknesses, as the two of them (watched by Rowland) sit perched on a dangerously narrow ledge in the Colosseum's wall. The wall is 'the face of an Alpine cliff'—the chasm where despair will take Roderick in the end. Her high-pitched harangue is a direct attempt to force him to meet the romantic exigencies of both their imaginations. Where Roderick sculpts his Adam and Eve and wishes to do an 'America' that will symbolize impersonal perfection, Christina longs, with a simple but communicated urgency, for 'a great character' who will rise beyond her own miserable frailties, someone 'great in talent, strong in will! In such a man as that, I say, one's weary imagination at last may rest.' When she agrees bitterly with Roderick's suggestion that he is 'incomplete', it underlines how their ideal goal embraces the fullest selfhood and a personal power carried to the degree of impersonal permanence. (The reader remembers with irony that Sam Singleton admires Roderick for his 'beautiful completeness'; and we shall very soon see Rowland writing home to Cecilia about Roderick, 'the poor fellow is incomplete, and it is really not his own fault.') Roderick's near-suicidal attempt to clamber across the Colosseum wall to pick an inaccessible blue wild flower for Christina—Romantic symbol of symbols, even to its colour—is his inevitable response to her taunts: a plunge into arbitrary action. And even if Rowland understandably regards Christina's urgings now as 'sinister *persiflage*', it is an arbitrary plunge that we are to see him emulate later on, and for similar reasons—under the eyes of Mary Garland.

The scene in the Colosseum has its heroic note, despite the absurdity of Roderick's antics and the dubiety as to Christina's motives. But it is succeeded quickly by a darker mood of disillusion, and by an encounter between Rowland and Christina that is notable for its greater inwardness of reach. The encounter is led up to, most effectively, by the transition of a passage where Roderick, disgusted at his own adventures in the chic *demi-monde* of Rome, delivers his Neoplatonic condemnation of this whole society and age, judged against the ideal conception that even his own art has failed to realize:

'I can't describe [*la beauté parfaite*] positively; I can only say I don't find it anywhere now. Not at the bottom of champagne glasses; not, strange as it may seem, in that extra half-yard or so of shoulder that some women have their ball-dresses cut to expose. I don't find it at noisy supper-tables where half a dozen ugly men with pomatumed heads are rapidly growing uglier still with heat and wine; nor when I come away and walk through these squalid black streets and go out into the Forum and see a few old battered stone posts standing there like gnawed bones stuck into the earth. Everything is mean and dusky and shabby, and the men and women who make up this so-called brilliant society are the meanest and shabbiest of all.' (p. 214)

The 'squalid black streets' and 'battered stone posts' lead up to Rowland's excursion through Rome's Trastevere—'a region of empty, soundless, grass-grown lanes and alleys, where the shabby houses seem mouldering away in disuse'. In the church of St. Cecilia there, 'abandoned to silence and the charity of chance devotion', the whole drama of human entreaty and human blankness—the gesturing of the merman to the land-bound ox—is now acted out between Rowland and Christina: the one distrustful but inexplicably excited, the other asking to be believed in and to be changed. The reasonable Rowland is more and more the victim of his bewilderment and the frustrations of his nature; while Christina is basically seeking in him what she seeks in Roderick: to be taken out of herself, out of the shabbiness into the sculptor's imagined state of beauty and reality. 'Prove to me that I am better than I suppose', is her plea. And even her ineradicable lying (Rowland doubts her account of having wished to take the veil) is now seen positively as the attempt to extend her nature through its powers of 'vivacity and spontaneity': 'Rowland felt that whatever she said of herself might have been under the imagined circumstances; energy was there, audacity, the restless questioning temperament.' Though Rowland can rise to such half-sympathy, the two of them diverge over their characteristic attitudes to religion. Christina longs for a religious authority and truth as she longs for other transcendent forces that will be 'eloquent and aggressive'. But Rowland's religion is inarticulate and inward, an inextricable part of himself. And yet, in secular terms, we can see Rowland to be a man of insufficient faith— insufficient faith in Christina, in her hidden but still intuitable qualities. In some ways Rowland betrays Christina, and does much to precipitate the book's tragedy. But his betrayal is venial and perfectly normal. Who *could* believe enough in Christian Light to have confidence in her relationship with Roderick Hudson? And this is what in effect she demands of Rowland, among other things. Throughout this scene, I think, she is implicitly pleading with him to help her to believe in that relationship, even in that possible marriage. And Rowland is clearly wrong when he replies that 'Hudson . . . does not need as an artist the stimulus of strong emotion, of passion. He is better without it.' Roderick's great danger is not passion itself, but the endemic weakness of his own will and his creative faculty. What threatens him is inertia, not the turmoil of strong emotions. Perhaps this is simply to turn one familiar explanation of Roderick Hudson's tragedy upside down, but I can only repeat that it seems less convincing that Christina destroys Roderick through the play of his emotions than that he is destroyed because, for reasons, he fails to be united to her. We are made to feel that they belong together: that there could, just possibly, be a support for the weakness of each in the other's strength. At any rate, we are made to desire it by the book's whole tendency of feeling and idea—which in a novel comes close to being the same thing. They are both romantically conceived characters of latency and strangeness: each of them necessarily further away from us than Rowland, who is the narrative's point of view as well as the nature more typical of our own. They each have the kind of power that expresses itself in posture and in gaze, in rhetoric and in florid crises. And there is an indirect but quite detectable sense of the nervous sexuality that exists between them. This kind of character-drawing has its simplicity, of course, as one has had to accept from the beginning—but it is simplicity rather than *naïveté*. The idea of a personal magnetism is perfectly true to experience, and, as in life, we are impelled in this novel to say that these are characters who are simply driven to one another. Perhaps our sense of their being doomed is a part of it—certainly we sense the threat as one that belongs to the scale of intense feelings and heroic ends. And if one feels throughout the book even a distant promise of the heroic and the fruitful, then Rowland's response to Christina in St. Cecilia's must be seen partially as a betrayal, caused by his failure to comprehend. Christina's eyes are frequently described as being directed fully on him (as are Roderick's in similar scenes), with a silent appeal that goes beyond, and even counter to, what she is actually saying. She needs to be helped to love—this is the pathos of Christina's situation, that she does not fully know her own mind, and is beset by many impulses and many external pressures. Is there not a painful truth in the idea that people often need a friend to tell them whether and how they are in love, just as the artist needs a friend to enter his studio and commend his talent? If Christina receives no such help, it is all the more convincing that her desire for Roderick will at once be diverted into a despairing act of abandonment and renunciation —with the patient Prince Casamassima himself waiting in the wings as her alternative, and as a penance she can cynically take on herself, in marriage. Rowland, to defend his sculptor, encourages her in the direction of 'something magnanimous, heroic, sublime' —and after all, cynical or not, is her 'sacrifice' altogether without its magnanimity?

Christina, her urge for fulfilment momentarily channelled towards self-denial, turns to leave the church on a subtle gesture that is presented without commentary by James. Having discussed her extravagant social timetable with her maid, she then pauses for a second near the church door with 'hastily suppressed tears', to stand 'gazing at an old picture, undistinguishable with blackness, over an altar'. That is all—but the suggestiveness of it, and the thought of what kind of picture it might have been, sink into our minds. And Rowland is left beautifully 'perplexed' and 'ill at ease' in that 'strange decaying corner of Rome', as though half-aware that the truth about Christina, which is something of the truth about himself, has just passed him by.

Christina, after a month, engages herself to the Prince, partly in consequence of Rowland's refusal to support her relationship with Roderick. She is at her most pathetic, her most trapped, when she has her outburst to Rowland at Madame Grandoni's after the engagement: ' "You don't believe in me!", she cried, "not a grain! I don't know what I would not give to *force* you to believe in me!" ' And then, in tears, 'I am weary, I am more lonely than ever, I wish I were dead!' With a characteristic understanding of such tensions, James finally shows the cumulative effect on Rowland of all these dramatic collisions when he withdraws, 'intolerably puzzled', to Florence. Rowland's exasperation at being so used and abused by everyone is associated with his unconscious attraction towards Christina—or at least with his perception that there is a great force in her he must defend himself from, together with Roderick, by his disapprobation. He is tortured by a sense of waste—'life owed him . . . a compensation'— and even the appreciation of beauty fails to console him: 'Raphael's Madonna of the Chair seemed in its soft serenity to mock him with the suggestion of unattainable repose.' His goal of compensation and satisfaction begins to take on the visage of the unattainable Mary Garland (who is as yet too unattainable to the narrative itself to be really convincing as Rowland's goal at this point). Much more compelling, and much more organic to everything we have seen before, is the way in which he faces, and conquers, his hedonistic 'temptation' in the convent-garden at Fiesole. The temptation is to cease trying to save Roderick, to connive at his downfall, and thereby to make his own bid for Mary Garland:

If on the morrow he had committed a crime, the persons whom he had seen that day would have testified that he had talked strangely and had not seemed like himself. He felt certainly very unlike himself; long afterwards, in retrospect, he used to reflect that during those days he had for a while been literally *beside* himself. His idea persisted; it clung to him like a sturdy beggar. (pp. 243-4)

It may be a small matter, but it is interesting that Rowland's desire for once to grasp boldly for himself should be described as the experience of an escape from his normal identity, a kind

of histrionic projection of an *alter ego*. It comes close to many
other expressions given to the idea of self-affirmation in the book
—by Rowland in the first chapter, and above all, perhaps, by
Christina.[11] But Rowland, with an effort, calls such fulfilment the
Devil—and, as always, he is partly right. It is like the appearance
of the fatal boatman with the face of the Baron de Mauves, in
Longmore's dream. And closer at hand, this 'Devil' represents
the debit side of all self-affirmation—and the debit side of a
Roderick Hudson's creative power, which has made him egotistic,
"clear-cut, sharp-edged, isolated'. Its rejection by Rowland in the
garden is not simple puritanism or fear of life—the kind of
interpretation that is so common in criticism of James. It is a
further pointer to what James demonstrated so often and so
forcefully in other places too: that to seek the truth of one's nature
by direct expression in the world of action, while a great and even
necessary aim, is one that is always pursued at someone else's cost
—in the same way that a grand passion, such as Roderick's for
Christina, can also bring waste and sterility.

III

James brings Mary Garland to Rome at a well-judged moment
in the novel. Her arrival brings a very necessary fresh element to
the scene—and the picture of Roderick's mother, her companion,
in foreign parts, is James at his wittiest and best: at once sympathetic to so perfect a 'type' and maliciously observant of her
failings. But as well as novelty, the arrival of Roderick's fiancée
produces the final breakdown of a situation whose tensions have
come to their highest pitch. She fails to save Roderick from his
drifting—he can feel no affection for her, to his own dismay: the
absent Christina is his only fate—and she herself is quickly

---

[11] The strangeness and significance of the moment are emphasized in the
New York edition by an image like the separated merman and ox which James
used earlier to bring out a not dissimilar moment of division (between Rowland
and Roderick in Chapter 11): 'He felt, certainly, very much somebody else . . .
even as the ass, in the farmer's row of stalls, may be beside the ox.'

In Chapter 15 of *Washington Square* Catherine Sloper's first discovery of
her personal will is described in these terms: 'She had an entirely new feeling,
which may be described as a state of expectant suspense about her own actions.
She watched herself as she would have watched another person, and wondered
what she would do. It was as if this other person, who was both herself and not
herself, had suddenly sprung into being, inspiring her with a natural curiosity
as to the performance of untested functions.'

drawn into the whole entanglement and into the centre of the book's concerns. Because Mary becomes at once a figure of restlessness—an angular New Englander ('the daughter of a minister, the grand-daughter of a minister, the sister of a minister') unbending and burgeoning in the warmth of Italy. Mary, too, is given a glimpse in Italy of a fulfilment she has never suspected before, described in the same image used for the desires of Rowland and Roderick: 'I am overwhelmed. Here in a single hour everything is changed. It is as if a wall in my mind had been knocked down at a stroke. Before me lies an immense new world, and it makes the old one, the poor little narrow familiar one I have always known, seem pitiful' (pp. 257–8). Mary has her hidden side, her untapped source, and we are made to sense it in her clear grey eyes in the way we sense Christina's in her dark blue ones—though James, with all his slightly special pleading, never succeeds with her as he does with Christina, and in particular fails to show her in a very convincing relationship with either Roderick or Rowland. There is, nevertheless, a little mystery of pain about Mary: part of her grave essence that one can name but not fully possess. 'To enjoy', she tells Rowland, 'is to break with one's past. And breaking is a pain!' Long before, when we first saw her in Northampton, we were told in an evocative phrase that now returns to us: 'In Mary Garland's face there were many possible [meanings] . . . They followed each other slowly, distinctly, sincerely, and you might almost have fancied that, as they came and went, they gave her a sort of pain' (p. 56). And in a very moving night-scene near the end of the book (in Chapter 22), when Mary looks down over a hot, moonlit Florence, her discovery that enjoyment is a law of her own nature and of all nature is accompanied by an irrepressible grief—a perception beautifully related to the mingled elements of the view, in which the 'shrunken river' and the strangely obscuring moonshine introduce a natural elegy into the signs and smells of the season's fruitfulness. Mary's innate fear now finds a new justification in her premonitions as to the imminent loss of Roderick's love and her sense of the ubiquity of human suffering. And her dual discovery, which is the mark of her maturing, is emphasized by Rowland's sympathetic reply, 'We are made both to suffer and to enjoy, I suppose'—which in its turn echoes his earlier approval of 'a certain tension in one's being. It's what a man is meant for.' Mary develops and grows through her involvement in the specific tensions round which the whole of *Roderick Hudson* is written.[12]

When Mary encounters Christina Light—first in St. Peter's, where the two women exchange stares as foreign to one another as two planets, and next in the magnificent scene at Madame Grandoni's tea-party—our sense of the hidden reality of the great Christina is beautifully matched by our new sense of a very different woman's nature. The book's concern with loneliness has no more striking expression than this encounter at Madame Grandoni's. It is prepared by Madam Grandoni reminding us of Christina's theatrical nature before she arrives (Mary of course is partly defined by her very lack of theatricality). Madame Grandoni, though sympathetic, describes Christina's recent conversion to Catholicism in this way:

'One day she got up in the depths of despair; at her wits' end, I suppose, in other words, for a new sensation. Suddenly it occurred to her that the Catholic Church might after all hold the key— might give her what she wanted; she sent for a priest; he happened to be a clever man and he contrived to interest her. She put on a black dress and a black veil, and, looking handsomer than ever, she rustled into the Catholic Church.' (p. 283)

Rowland dismisses the event as simply a *coup de théâtre* —'the girl is so deucedly dramatic.' And indeed, Christina's entrance to the tea-party is her most staged appearance in the book, a scene in which her beauty is splendidly and wittily projected, and given an almost impersonal quality to her audience:

They were of course observing her. Standing in the little circle of lamplight, with the hood of an Eastern burnous shot with silver threads falling back from her beautiful head, one hand gathering together its voluminous shimmering folds and the other playing with the silken top-knot on the uplifted head of her poodle, she was a figure of radiant picturesqueness. She seemed to be a sort of extemporised *tableau vivant*. (p. 288)

She and Mary meet—James carefully does not let us hear their

---

[12] The New York edition expands Rowland's reply in more normative terms, reminding us of what the withdrawn Euphemia de Mauves had to learn, that 'deep experience is never peaceful': 'We shouldn't be able to enjoy, I suppose, unless we could suffer, and in anything that's worthy of the name of experience— that experience which is the real *taste* of life, isn't it?—the mixture's of the finest and subtlest.'

conversation—and each gains her impression, more or less true, more or less false, of the other. The result of the meeting is only to increase the distance between them. Mary recoils into suspicion and dislike, and even though Christina, in one of her many metamorphoses, feels inspired by Mary's moral beauty, her loneliness is increased: 'I should like to have a friendship with her; I have never had one; they must be very delightful. But I shan't have one now—not if she can help it!... It's too sad. So we go through life. It's fatality—that's what they call it, isn't it? We please the people we don't care for, we displease those we do!' (p. 292).

Thrown back into herself, and into her own conception of herself, Christina's motives for her subsequent volte-face—breaking her engagement to the Prince—remain quite acceptably ambiguous to us. As usual, they are potentially more complex than the motives of any other person in the book—her unreliability being for the reader, too, one measure of her personal charisma. Her explanation to Rowland of the broken engagement is that it represents a moral refusal to enter into a meaningless marriage, and has been inspired by her meeting with Mary ('She in my place wouldn't marry Casamassima'). And James describes her at this moment in high terms that are certainly not mock-heroic: 'The clouded light of her eyes, the magnificent gravity of her features, the conscious erectness of her head, might have belonged to a deposed sovereign or a condemned martyr' (p. 309). But another possible motive, the opposite of the martyr's, at once occurs to the sceptical Rowland: that Christina, jealous of Mary, now wishes to be free to bid for Roderick again, and to give one more chance to the unreliable virility of the sculptor's will. Clearly, both motives, the selfish and the ideal, are meant to be operating as simultaneously as ever in Christina—and in any case, motive-seeking is not the only way we respond to her. Often, we take her inconsequent actions simply as the kind of thing Christina does, the kind of thing Christina is. In terms of our response to the fiction (and this is sometimes how we see living people, too), she tends in part to become her actions, rather than to be the responsible cause of them. That is, at moments we are affected in the same way that Rowland is affected in this very scene (fatefully, he has been asked by Christina's frenzied and mercenary mother to try to save the engagement), when he finds that the desire to judge and to explain Christina

C

falls away when face to face with her. When Christina denies the
charge of breaking her engagement simply to spite Mary, 'Rowland
heard himself answering, "I believe it!" ' And here once again, at
a critical juncture, appears the notion of belief, with the suggestion
that it is sometimes better to submit, and risk delusion, than
always to stand apart in rational suspicion. And perhaps there is an
echo in the fact that Rowland should *hear himself* make his profession of belief. He stands beside himself again for a second, as he
did in Florence—transformed now by Christina's dangerous
magic.[13]

On the edge of this intense confrontation between Rowland and
Christina has stood, all the while, the sadly comic figure of the
Cavaliere, elderly cicerone and parasite of the Lights. Rowland
finds him outside the room with his head in his hands. 'I have
two hearts,' he confesses, 'one for myself, one for the world. This
one is furious with the blessed *ragazza*—the other is enchanted
with her! One suffers horribly at what the other does.' And
Rowland replies sourly, and apparently without irony, 'I don't
understand double people' (p. 315). The old man, of course, is no
more and no less double than any of them, and like the others he
looks on Christina—now revealed to be his unacknowledged
daughter—as a figure of talent and enviable imperviousness far
above the humiliations of his tangled private world. 'At any rate
remember this', are his last words in the scene,'—I delight in the
Christina!' *The* Christina: an emblem and an impersonal force.
And as for the Cavaliere's pathetic love for a daughter who knows
him only as she know her pet poodle; and as for that same daughter
who is now blackmailed into an empty marriage by a mother
threatening to disclose her illegitimacy and the existence of a

---

[13] It is interesting to note an important change in the revised version of this
scene in the New York edition. In the early edition, Christina's theatrical
self-consciousness, which makes her ask Rowland what he thinks of her, is still
seen by him as 'venial', and his answer to her inquiry is to say 'very positively',
'You are an excellent girl'—'And then gave her his hand in farewell'. The later
edition changes this into a complete rebuff for Christina. He makes no answer
to her question—which as before is really a request to be believed in—and
simply notes the beauty of her blush as she recognizes what his silence implies.
Then he turns his back and walks away. So brutal is this that one feels it as
another important betrayal of Christina by Rowland, and the scene in the revised
version (though not in the early one) allows the question to arise of whether
in fact Christina agrees now to go back to the Prince partly because Rowland has
shown such contempt for her, and so closed the way to her escape from the
marriage.

father she can only despise—these things give a new and bitter application in terms of parent and child to those earlier words of Christina, 'I should like to have a friendship . . . It's so sad. So we go through life. . . . We please the people we don't care for, we displease those we do!' This daughter and this father are like the merman and the ox, grotesquely foreign to one another, and yet crying out for the same thing: the same completeness and the same love.

IV

Christina marries her prince, and the last movement of the book begins. Roderick, borne northwards by his long-suffering companions, is in a state of moral collapse, his old passionate egotism reduced to mere flashes of petulance. Typically, he affects us as a combination of tiresome adolescent and fallen Romantic hero. As the former, he is real enough, and James (through Rowland) fully allows for our irritation. And as the latter, he is still capable of moving us by the blatant force of his rhetoric and by the archetypal quality of his fate. On the shores of Lake Como he is the poet who perceives the world's beauty but perishes because his creative sense cannot merge with the world. And the world, as so often, takes the form of Italy. Italy, about to be left behind, embodies Roderick's lost dream—and the lost dreams of more than Roderick. It is 'an Italy that we can never confess ourselves —in spite of our changes and of Italy's—to have ceased to believe in'—*belief* again, as a clue to our survival. It is 'the earthly paradise' of 'iridescent mountains' and 'festooned vines', with a menacing and bizarre metaphor concealed within the description, like a snake:

They followed the winding footway . . . past frescoed walls and crumbling campaniles and grassy village piazzas and the mouth of soft ravines that wound upward through belts of swinging vine and vaporous olive and splendid chestnut, to high ledges where white chapels gleamed amid the paler boskage, and bare cliff-surfaces, with their blistered lips, drank in the liquid light. (p. 353)

As though in recognition of the rocks that break through the paradisal greenery, Roderick pronounces his own splendid and orotund elegy (it is a ceremonial breaking of the water-drinker's goblet). When he speaks of himself in the third person, as if echoing

the last speech of Othello, it is not primarily his self-dramatizing
we recognize (any more than in the case of Othello—*pace* F. R.
Leavis) but a general and transfiguring poetry that James has
uncovered in his material. [14] Roderick declares himself dead to all
that is around him, and he speaks, in a wave of pain, for the whole
romantic-tragic experience that has accumulated through this
novel: the experience of a humanity unable to commit their
intrinsic selves, and entombed from one another (and from life's
greatest reality) in inexpressiveness:

'Dead, dead; dead and buried! Buried in an open grave, where you lie
staring up at the sailing clouds, smelling the waving flowers and
hearing all nature live and grow above you! That's the way I feel!
. . . I don't know what secret spring has been touched since I have
lain here. Something in my heart seems suddenly to open and let in a
flood of beauty and desire. I know what I have lost, and I think it
horrible! Mind you, I know it, I feel it! Remember that hereafter.
Don't say that he was stupefied and senseless; that his perception was
dulled and his aspiration dead. Say that he trembled in every nerve
with a sense of the beauty and sweetness of life; that he rebelled and
protested and struggled; that he was buried alive, with his eyes open
and his heart beating to madness; that he clung to every blade of grass
and every wayside thorn as he passed; that it was the most pitiful
spectacle you ever beheld; that it was a scandal, an outrage, a murder!'
(pp. 354–5)

As a gentle parody of the man who clings to the sweetness of
life, Rowland is presented facing his last chance of diverting
Mary Garland's love away from Roderick to himself, while the
incongruous little party of Americans wends its talkative way over
the Alps. Even when he breathlessly imitates Roderick's folly in
the Colosseum by plucking a dangerously placed wild flower for
Mary—'Will you trust me?' he repeats to her, seeking to be
believed in—James's view of the 'exploit' is not dismissive. For
Rowland, it is a small but genuine self-declaration and a plea for
trust. And the fact that Mary does believe in him for the moment
is in itself a tentative reward. These are the little daily fumblings,
says James, by which people do try to make their declarations and

[14] Richard Poirier, on the contrary—interestingly, though I think un-
convincingly—sees such theatricality of style as Roderick's as a limiting factor,
and as a sign from James that such a character possesses only a fixed 'melodramatic sensibility', as opposed to the 'ideally reasonable attitude' of Rowland
(*The Comic Sense of Henry James*, London, 1960, pp. 11–43).

approaches—there is no despising them. No doubt some readers will continue to feel, like T. S. Eliot, that James is not as exasperated and amused as he ought to be at Rowland in his position of hanger-on, the poor man of conscience at the feast waiting for any stray crumb of feeling to fall.[15] But once again, there is a simple truth in the portrait of Rowland, and a kind of realism that balances well against so much in the book that is stylized and extreme. People do wait at the feast in this way, surreptitiously testing their pulses, thinking about a grand passion, and consulting their sense of decency and duty. Rowland is far from being a perverse specimen of scrupulousness and fear, and is in fact a recognizable man in a recognizable position of difficulty, with very real obligations of honour incurred towards Mary in her relation with Roderick. And an all-important consideration, always brought out by James (and without which the charge of perversity might well stick), is that Mary in no way loves Rowland, for all that Roderick has spurned her. She has nothing to give him but crumbs—and few men would be less inhibited than Rowland when given so little encouragement by so cool a woman. All that Rowland can do is to carry out what will give her pleasure (even though it harms his own chances) and watch carefully for the faintest indication of a response. In any case, James, by a familiar ironic device, frequently raises this very possibility of Rowland's absurdity in order to test it—for example, he quite confidently allows us to hear Roderick laughing at the spectacle of 'a man asking another man to gratify him by not suspending his attentions to a pretty girl'. And the result, I think, is not that we judge Rowland preposterous but that we sympathize with the absurdity and ordinariness of his lot.

As in most tragedies, the hero of this one is allowed his brief surge of energy on the eve of extinction. This is an important part of the book's rhythm—there can be no mere petering out when so much has been at stake. Christina Light, by this aesthetic logic, must reappear, and that she should do so by a chance meeting, here in the mountains accompanied by her inept aristocratic husband, should strain no one's capacity to accept—any more than

---

[15] Eliot says, '[James] too much identifies himself with Rowland, does not see through the solemnity he has created in that character, commits the cardinal sin of failing to "detect" one of his own characters' ('The Hawthorne Aspect', in *The Question of Henry James*, ed. F. W. Dupee, London, 1947, p. 132).

the equally functional reappearance of Sam Singleton with that confidence in his own 'intrinsic facilities' that unconsciously mocks Roderick's loss of power. When Roderick's Muse, the Christina, makes her taunting and vivifying descent at Engelberg, and brings about the last frenzy of Roderick's will ('She makes me feel as if I were alive again'), her appearance is to Rowland as well as to Roderick. 'You have seen me at my best', she tells Rowland, with a look from her tragical eyes; 'I wish to tell you solemnly, I *was* sincere!'—a phrase she repeats (like the last reported message of Daisy Miller), as if to emphasize what Rowland has lost by his failure of belief. But the question of her sincerity, for Rowland, is now as much in the past as Roderick's genius, and the effect of Christina's restored influence is only to make the two men fly apart in a culminating quarrel. Roderick rediscovers the violence of his egotism and turns again to Christina as the only way to gain his salvation as a man and as an artist. All ordinary decency, towards Mary in particular, appears trivial. And we recognize the necessity of it for him at the same time as we share Rowland's outrage against it. This is the moment of utter disruption in the book, when one man, fighting for his whole emotional and imaginative life, sees the recovery of desire as a value in itself; and when the other, equally asserting his personal integrity, believes that 'If you have the energy to desire, you have also the energy to reason and to judge.' For a few pages, Rowland overflows at last in aggression and denunciation, and reveals to Roderick his own love for Mary. The two men confront one another in truth and self-exposure. Their irreconcilable division ironically creates the first complete comprehension between them. And what comes out of this clarity? What comes of this moment when the merman and the ox find a common, unambiguous tongue? Roderick's death, quite simply. Roderick, from being brought to life by Christina's arrival, is shocked and humiliated by hearing from Rowland these harsh truths about himself and by discovering his lack of imaginative insight into Rowland's feelings. It suddenly strikes him as confirming the failure of artistic insight which he had momentarily put behind him. And Roderick, self-centred even in his renewed self-contempt, and consumed by 'aesthetic disgust at the graceless contour of his conduct', walks off ominously into the hills, out of sight—and not in the direction of Christina, waiting for him at Interlaken. Quite unwittingly, it is Rowland, the man of moral sensitivity and honest intentions, speaking out for once, who is the decisive factor in the catastrophe.

The end of *Roderick Hudson* is a heart-break: yet not harrowing or sentimental, and not melodramatic. It makes its perfect tragic sense, and it is all done with a precision of detail, a control of tone, and a perfect swelling measure in the language, which provide a shape to bear, and make bearable, the burden of feeling. The storm itself is essential to Roderick's life and death, in an obvious though not a banal way. The atmosphere of oppression that ushers in the storm is not only a preparation for the immediate disaster but expresses the feeling of black frustration and thwarted powers that has welled up throughout the novel. All through the lamentations of Mrs. Hudson and the high drama of Mary perched on a hill looking for Roderick, James's wit can still vibrate, giving us the picture of the indefatigable Sam Singleton scampering back through the rain as he finishes a sketch of the clouds. In the midst of it, there is another loss: Rowland sees his failure to gain Mary's love confirmed by her wish to sacrifice him, or anybody else, if only Roderick can be saved. And then there is the greater loss: a fall, a descent, and a death that implicates us all. To the sense of utter personal calamity is added the sense of a universal intransigence, as when after the rain comes a morning of derisive splendour: 'The day was magnificent; the sun was everywhere; the storm had lashed the lower slopes into a deeper flush of autumn colour, and the snow-peaks reared themselves against the near horizon in shining blocks and incisive peaks' (p. 396). In a brilliant touch, as Rowland searches 'the stony Alpine void', all this silence and unresponsiveness is suddenly concentrated into the image of a ludicrous, goitrous cretin who grins up at him helplessly from the door of an empty chalet. The book's drama of human search and loss and incommunication comes to its fullness now, at the bottom of a gorge filled with sunlight. Roderick's dead face is still staring (always Roderick's gaze, to the very last), 'upwards open-eyed at the sky'—we are not told whether in accusation or aspiration, only that Rowland now shuts the eyes. The sculptor's handsomeness and strange serenity (one half-remembers the serenity of the Raphael Madonna that mocked Rowland in Florence with its beauty and its 'unattainable repose') are contrasted with the cliff that killed him—'which lifted its blank and stony face above him, with no care now but to drink the sunshine on which his eyes were closed'. In that 'blank and stony face' we have the quintessential image of the wall: the great closed door before which human endeavour fails, and the will, as Roderick always knew, snaps like a dry twig. And when the stony face of the cliff drinks the sunshine, we have a hideous inversion of Roderick's own emblem of the water-drinker—and also a reappearance, in the triumph they always threatened, of those cliffs above Lake Como that 'with their blistered lips drank in the liquid light'. The water-drinker's cup is quite emptied now —the promise of fulfilment betrayed—and even the light of Christina Light has been eclipsed in marriage, with a mere Prince of the Biggest House. Seeing all these things, the witness, whose vision by now is so close to being our own, is overcome:

The most rational of men was for an hour the most passionate. He reviled himself with transcendent bitterness, he accused himself of cruelty and injustice, he would have laid down there in Roderick's place to unsay the words that had yesterday driven him forth on his lonely ramble. . . . Now that all was over Rowland understood how exclusively, for two years, Roderick had filled his life. His occupation was gone. (p. 399)

The echo of *Othello* this time is deliberate enough, though lightly made. But what seizes one even more, as Rowland broods over the body and the cliff-face looks down in 'dumb exultation', is that these words of lament on the novel's last page take us back to its very beginning, where Rowland was in quest of something to fill his existence and to give him, with all his empty leisure, an *occupation*—a work to do, a talent to nurture, a project and a goal to spend himself in. It is something of Rowland, as well as every-thing of Roderick, that lies huddled on the ground before him, like a stone.

As in all tragedy, of course, life—the general life and the general will to live—gathers itself together a little at the very end, and will continue. Rowland is restored to New England and is left there, 'patient' and 'restless', looking for a sign from the bereaved Mary Garland that her gratitude to him might become something more. It offers only a fissure in the cliff-face; but it is enough, and it is consistent, since after all, we remember this youthful novel's celebration of possibility and change as much as its sharp sense of desolation. The Jamesian touch of inconclusiveness at the finish is the very reverse of arbitrariness. For this is the way it does go on, in Northampton and Rome and elsewhere, in fluctuating restlessness and patience: the life of people looking for a sign.

3

The Price of Power in
The Aspern Papers

H ENRY JAMES in the 1880s means James the realist—the
mature creator of *Portrait of a Lady*, *The Bostonians*, *The
Princess Casamassima*, and *The Tragic Muse*. That is our usual
emphasis, and a perfectly proper one. But James had many styles
in each period of his writing, and it is important to take a reminder
from *The Aspern Papers* (published in 1888) that James was also
a master of the grotesque fable, and could use it, characteristically,
to parody the theme he treated elsewhere with more obvious
gravity.[1] It is a very modified grotesque, of course, and an essentially positive form of parody. A note of the bizarre and even of
the playful is always compatible with the most serious activity of
James's imagination: the slightly rococo can quickly pass without
incongruity into effects that are, as it were, fully human, fully
implicative, and even tragic. (In this sense, as well as another,
James is a writer of wit—the sense that applies to the poetic wits
of earlier centuries than his own.) Sometimes the transition does
not occur, or occurs unsteadily or too late. *What Maisie Knew*,
for example, is to my mind weakened by a failure to expand the
social comedy and the rather elbow-nudging Restoration jokiness
which characterize it up to the change of scene to Boulogne. The
poetry, the suggested profundity, begin to emerge at that stage,
but the change of tone is puzzling, and a little arbitrary. When the
blend is successful the result is a fine story like *The Pupil*; or,
much greater, as we shall see, *The Spoils of Poynton*. The successful
fusion of modes in *The Aspern Papers* is clearly achieved by James
using a first-person narrator who is himself something of a wit
and something of a grotesque. The question of the author's attitude
to this narrator is one that has long vexed critics, and Wayne Booth,

[1] Another very similar, though slighter, parodic version of this theme of the
baffled search for power—aesthetic, intellectual, and sexual power—is *The
Figure in the Carpet* (1896).

in *The Rhetoric of Fiction*, provides one useful account of that debate—though with conclusions most unfavourable to the story itself. Says Booth: 'We have, then, three distinct narrative voices in this story: the narrator's self-betrayals, evident to any careful reader; his efforts at straightforward evocation of the past, which taken out of context might be indistinguishable from James's own voice; and the passages of mumbling, as it were, that lie between.' And the result is 'a vague, realistic, unjudged blur'.[2] Some of the difficulties, one suspects, have been created by the critics themselves. Having failed to be drawn into the deeper feelings and poetry of the tale, they have been left to look with too scrupulous an eye on a narrating figure who is not meant to bear continual judicial scrutiny from outside, or to be 'placed' definitively in any fixed category of value, and certainly not meant to offer an individual 'psychology' as the tale's main purport. There is an important duality in James's use of him, but a duality that is not the same as a 'blur'. This is a narrator who is at once reliable and unreliable, objective and subjective. We can stand outside him with one part of our minds, judging his selfishness and irresponsibility, aided by moments of obviously 'loaded' irony against him and also by moments where the narrator expressly judges himself. This allows us to resist full illusion and to see around the dangerous subjectivity of his narrative. It also helps us to read a meaning into his motives and his experience that goes far beyond his conscious understanding of them. And yet in another respect we are identified with the narrator—drawn into illusion by the traditional persuasions of literary rhetoric, and made to experience directly that which we will subsequently interpret. The narrator's words become an immediate means of entry into certain 'truths': truths of our own experience which we are now 'tricked' into re-creating in our imaginations. There may be a strictly logical contradiction between these two aspects of the narrator, but there is no contradiction in terms of how we actually experience his story. What we experience is a perpetually dual and moving thing: we are always moving into the narrator, and moving out of him. At moments his 'character' is individualized and judgeable. At other moments it is

---

[2] Wayne Booth, *The Rhetoric of Fiction*, Chicago, 1961, pp. 354–64. There is a valuable (and sympathetic) analysis of the whole narrative problem of the story in Ora Segal, *The Lucid Reflector: the Observer in Henry James's Fiction*, New Haven, Conn., 1969, pp. 74–92.

not important—we accept it and pass on into what he is undergoing. This kind of interplay between distance and identification is absolutely intrinsic to the nature of art—and it is perhaps intrinsic to human perception outside the aesthetic field, too, one's whole perceptional apparatus being surely the most devious (and Jamesian) of narrators. To suggest, as a general preliminary to reading *The Aspern Papers*, that any aesthetic experience is a fluid thing, yet can come with a self-authenticating authority and coherence; that we experience illusion and forgetfulness, yet watch ourselves as we do so; that we can participate imaginatively in a narrator's life, yet see the meaning of that life in a wider context; that we lose ourselves in art in order to rediscover ourselves—to suggest these things is only to restate a set of paradoxes that have determined much of the history and the energy of aesthetic theorizing, and will continue to do so.

A further paradox that emerges from ssking where the reader stands in relation to this narrative is that we are drawn closer to the narrator's experience by features in his portrayal that can only be seen as non-realistic. He is too obsessive to be 'natural', too feverish, too mannered in his expression; too literary by half. And yet the result is that this Nabokovian figure draws us straight into his fantasy-realm, where 'reality' unexpectedly seizes us in the form of powerful and almost hallucinatory images, which lose nothing of seriousness for their comicality. By refinement, artifice, and caricature, James is always able to touch on the actual at least as intimately and revealingly as can a more naturalistic art. His fictional characters—even in works much less distorted than this one—are often not quite human, and yet are utterly full of life. This is particularly true of the late novels—it is true, for example, of two we shall come to, *The Spoils of Poynton* and *The Wings of the Dove*. A modicum of distortion in literature, such as we have in the action and the language of *The Aspern Papers*, is only another means of implicating the reader's imagination— exciting it to participation and entry into the work by reminding it directly of its own transformative powers. An image of life that a creative mind has twisted a little, to please itself, is always a challenge to an audience. The result can be that experience of intensity—sparked off by the meeting of two minds, the author's and the reader's—which is the prerequisite of all 'truth' of effect in literature. Thus the convincing 'reality' of *The Aspern Papers* is

partly brought about by its elements of unlikeness and exaggeration
(and partly, of course, on another level, by its elements of mimetic
accuracy). The reader, for all his intervals of detachment and
disapproval, is enticed into the editor's self-conscious style (let us
call him the editor now, since that is how he regards himself):
the deliberate ponderousness, the strangely attractive self-
parodying wit, the over-ripe hyperboles and mock-epic extrava-
gances. We will surmise certain things about the kind of man who
would use such a style; but more importantly, at first, we join in
the actual *play* of the story's surface—so often a vital factor in
our approach to James. This is a sophisticated game of style that
contains its seriousness of import, and leads gradually towards
revelation as the end of the game. The hyperboles are affected and
infectious in themselves, and they are also, at a deeper level,
sincere: sparks from a distant fire. The Papers are continually
'buried treasure' or 'sacred relics'; the editor is a 'minister' of a
'temple'; and the presence of the dead Jeffrey Aspern in the
surviving Juliana Bordereau makes it seem 'as if the miracle of
resurrection had taken place for my benefit'. Even the editor's
confidante, Mrs. Prest, is given the exalted note: 'One would
think you expected to find in [the Papers] the answer to the riddle
of the universe', she tells him—though he needs no telling. 'One
doesn't defend one's god', he intones about Aspern: 'one's god
is in himself a defence. Besides, to-day, after his long comparative
obscuration, he hangs high in the heaven of our literature, for all
the world to see; he is a part of the light by which we walk.'
These phrases make us smile a little, this early in the narrative.
They even make the editor smile a little: suavely, half-depre-
catingly. But later on they will lose some of their irony.

The *palazzo*'s little garden and its flowers (perfect for Gothicism
—Hawthorne's garden-Gothicism in *Rappaccini's Daughter*, say)
are pressed into service in a particularly lurid and revealing way
in a passage (in Chapter 4) that is a good example of the story's
method. It begins with some traditional spookery: the editor
pausing with his candle in the dark echoing *sala* to sniff the air
for impressions and to stare at the inner door as if 'attempting
some odd experiment in hypnotism'. It passes into a bizarre
image of the house as a kind of blank face (like that of Juliana
herself) hiding its secrets from the editor as he stares at it over the
top of his book from his seat in the garden: '[The two ladies']

motionless shutters became as expressive as eyes consciously
closed, and I took comfort in thinking that at all events though
invisible themselves they saw me between the lashes.' Then the
observer's growing frustrations are expressed in the stratagem
of his 'horticultural passion' and in the swelling figures of speech
by which he describes it: 'by flowers I would make my way—I
would succeed by big nosegays. I would batter the old women
with lilies—I would bombard their citadel with roses. Their door
would have to yield to the pressure when a mountain of carnations
should be piled up against it.'[3] And the scene sinks down into the
sunlit serenity of his endless waiting and imagining in his arbour,
as he muses on the 'mystic rites of ennui the Misses Bordereau
celebrated in their darkened rooms', and gives himself up to the
magical Venetian sunset—'while the golden hours elapsed and the
plants drank in the light and the inscrutable old palace turned
pale and then, as the day waned, began to flush in it and my
papers rustled in the wandering breeze of the Adriatic'. As a
description the thing is monstrous and self-indulgent and quite
luscious. The passage combines the obvious delights of a kind of
minor decadence, both literary and living, with the pleasure of
seeing that decadence just sufficiently 'placed' by irony. And the
language is not only to be savoured in itself, for its exoticism—it
also declares and elucidates something, a particular sensibility,
certain desires and resistances, and a personal dilemma of growing
significance.

   Or look, again, at how the editor's tendency towards the over-
wrought leads us deeper into the possibilities that are contained in
Juliana's perpetual green eye-shade: 'I believed for the instant
that she had put it on expressly, so that from underneath it she
might scrutinise me without being scrutinised herself. At the same
time it increased the presumption that there was a ghastly death's-
head lurking behind it. The divine Juliana as a grinning skull
—the vision hung there until it passed' (p. 291). Here is a tiny
exercise in Gothic transformation, made more effective if we see
it in connection with everything else around it. The editor's
'vision' suggests the power in Juliana that will always tantalize
and frighten him, the power that we can see comes from a

---

[3] *The Complete Tales of Henry James*, ed. Leon Edel, vol. 6, 1963, p. 307.
Future page-references are to this edition, which reprints the first book-form of
the story, published in 1888.

former passion, from history, and from the timeless poetry of the dead poet who had seen and celebrated her now concealed eyes. The eyes cannot be revealed any more than the Papers—any more than the past can be relived, or the wells of heroic passion and poetry can be retapped. The eyes are a force that can inundate and destroy, as well as attract, by virtue of all they have seen and inspired. When they *are* revealed—only once, at the climax of his felonies—it is to annihilate the unfortunate editor with their glare (in contrast to the words of Mrs. Prest, Juliana has warned him of the danger of what he seeks from her: 'The truth is God's, it isn't man's; we had better leave it alone'). The death's-head is not a trivial image in a story that imitates, in its ironic way, the Romantic quest for potency and forbidden knowledge (as in many of the tales of Poe, for example). And when the image appears, at this point, it is entirely characteristic and entirely effective that James should quickly turn its latent seriousness into comedy. When the death's-head speaks for the first time, instead of the Delphic oracle we hear the wonderfully incongruous tones of the estate-agent's brochure: 'Our house is very far from the centre, but the little canal is very *comme il faut*.' It is as though James is manipulating his material in every way, from the topographically precise to the macabre to the Wildean—jostling it till it begins to shine with unexpected life, like a symbol.

The very movement and arrangement of the plot—like the style—is a subtle vehicle for these suggested meanings. Above all, I think, its movement combines the excitement of pursuit with the stress of frustration. The story progresses, like a siege, through stages of approach—some lingering and gradual, some directly aggressive—towards a dimly seen centre of alluring and menacing power. The stages are physical, room by room, box by box, as well as figurative. And repelling the approach, creating the pressure of the narrative, are the many obstacles: walls, veils, masks, locked doors, locked cabinets, tests and trials, a silent statue, a mocking picture. Mrs. Prest, who belongs to the outside world of factuality and scepticism, serves as the initial and most external stage, and her gondola, in which the editor comes to the Bordereaus' *palazzo*, marks the first reconnoitring. Then comes an entry— as far as the *sala*, as far as Juliana's niece, Miss Tita. Then an inner room, where Juliana herself receives the editor. The editor takes up residence, and prowls through the *sala* and the garden, staring up at the blank wall that conceals the *palazzo*'s treasures. He confesses his intentions to Tita in the garden at midnight, worms himself closer to her private feelings and therefore to the forbidden Papers—and so on, around and around, closer or further, until at last he is defeated and expelled. The baroque style, the comically or disturbingly overdrawn images, add to our sense of incipient violence, and even the pauses are filled with portentous watching and lingering—'I had never encountered such a violent *parti pris* of seclusion; it was more than keeping quiet —it was like hunted creatures feigning death.' It creates an extreme narrative tension, in which the climaxes of plot come with a release of bottled-up feeling—a sense of strain, obsession, and claustrophobia that reminds one once again of Poe, and of his whole Gothic-psychological tradition. The tension, just as in Poe, moves towards a crisis where something is disclosed or triumphantly possessed. What is desired is to posses the past, to achieve 'esoteric knowledge', and to defeat time ('[the Papers] made my life continuous, in a fashion, with the illustrious life they had touched at the other end').[4] The past is hoarded away like a treasure, in the person of Juliana—in her hidden eyes, her memories, her Papers. Compared with the extraordinary link she represents, all the other editorial researches of the narrator and his colleague are 'phantoms and dust, the mere echoes of echoes': she alone offers the living reality of the past, which is a touchstone of present and future realities. Both Tita and Juliana, for the editor, 'went back, went back'—the vista stretches out over three-quarters of a century in an almost physical way, like the secret door at the end of the *palazzo*'s main *sala*, and like the whole vista of approach that determines the shape of the plot. Even the American origin of the two women is something that opens out, rather than closes, the vista. They have lost all national characteristics, are classical *déracinées*, undefined and ungraspable. The editor evokes

---

[4] As so often, James in the Preface indirectly restates something of the book's effect and subject, as he begins by talking of his thwarted desire as a novelist to possess the whole secret of Italian life: 'we peep at most into two or three of the chambers of their hospitality, with the rest of the case stretching beyond our ken and escaping our penetration. . . . So, right and left, in Italy— before the great historic complexity at least—penetration fails; we scratch at the extensive surface, we meet the perfunctory smile, we hang about in the golden air' (*The Art of the Novel*, p. 160).

the period of 1820: its heroic quality, its poetic peaks, its adventurousness, compared with the safe staleness of modernity. And Aspern's having been a true American of that era is a further touch (an acceptable one, despite James's worries in the Preface as to the verisimilitude of suggesting there could have been any great poet in America in 1820), in that it adds a note of republican openness and pristine creativity to all the other qualities clustered within that magic compendium and totem, the Aspern Papers: 'His own country after all had had most of his life, and his muse, as they said at that time, was essentially American . . . he had found means to live and write like one of the first; to be free and general and not at all afraid; to feel, understand, and express everything' (p. 311).

The totem of the Papers is also a sexual one, though not pre-eminently so: sexuality being implied throughout the story as only one of the expressions of human vitality and imagination. From the first, the editor establishes the enviable virility of Aspern, which shines up at him tauntingly in the eyes of the poet's portrait clutched by Juliana. 'I . . . had not the tradition of personal conquest', he confesses; and again, in a snickering parenthesis when describing Aspern's sexual adventures among so many Maenads, 'if I could imagine myself in such a place!' This power, too, has its possible channel to the present (or its reliquary, rather) in the hand, eyes, and voice that the poet-lover had known so intimately—those of Juliana, whom the editor jocularly compares to such historical *demi-mondaines* as Mrs. Siddons, Queen Caroline, and Lady Hamilton, and around whose name there still hovers 'a perfume of reckless passion, an intimation that she had not been exactly as the respectable young person in general'. And within the swelling hoard of the Papers there is, of course, poetry: almost as a part of passion. Even the editor is a little bit of a creator in his vicarious way. He is one of James's figures of the collector and appreciator; an uncoverer rather than a mere journalistic spy (like Flack, in *The Reverberator*); one who longs to reveal the depths of Aspern's poetic achievement 'by opening lights into his light'. 'We are terribly in the dark, I know', he tells Juliana. 'But if we give up trying what becomes of all the fine things?' And the ambiguity with which we view him in this respect is like that which surrounds the narrator of *The Sacred Fount*: he is one of those offenders against privacy who stand on the verge of the

novelist's own act of creation-by-intrusion.[5] Certainly, the editor's
leisurely word-spinning is reminiscent at times of a man inventing
his plot and his dramatis personae, with the arbour in the garden
as his study. And it is striking when some of his fancies prove to
be correct—'I on the other hand had hatched a little romance
according to which [Juliana] was the daughter of an artist . . .', etc.
—as though the editor has after all succeeded for a moment in
penetrating the 'temple' of the past by his imagination, if not yet
by his stealth of hand.

The Papers are also Venice: Venice, in its ubiquity through
this story, being the summation of many things, bringing
together past and present, vanished power with present beauty,
land and sea, *piazza* and *sala*, grandeur and intimacy, its publicities
and its arcana, richness and dilapidation, all in one vision of
harmony and light. The city becomes the imagined voice of the
great poet himself, as he interprets the message of Venice for the
consolation and inspiration of his editorial disciple:

It was as if he had said, '. . . Meanwhile are we not in Venice together,
and what better place is there for the meeting of dear friends? See
how it glows with the advancing summer; how the sky and the sea and
the rosy air and the marble of the palaces all shimmer and melt together'. My eccentric private errand became a part of the general
romance and the general glory—I felt even a mystic companionship,
a moral fraternity with all those who in the past had been in the service
of art. They had worked for beauty, for a devotion; and what else was I
doing? That element was in everything that Jeffrey Aspern had written
and I was only bringing it to the light. (p. 305)

Such moments of equipoise come only at intervals amid the
editor's increasing frustrations. But sometimes he finds release
of a more active kind—as happens at the half-way point of the
story when he meets Tita in the garden at night, and under the
pressing sense of closeness to her, for the first time reveals his
true aim of securing the Papers, and creates the first crisis of the
plot. We have gradually been growing aware of the fact that this
is the story not only of the editor and the Papers, but of the editor

[5] This approach to the editor dominates Laurence Holland's analysis in
The Expense of Vision: 'James's act in writing *The Aspern Papers* . . . is analogous
to the deeds of the Publishing Scoundrel who narrates it' (Princeton, N.J.,
1964, pp. 135–54). Holland handles such analogies brilliantly, if a little gym-
nastically.

and Tita Bordereau, with Juliana as the guardian of both niece
and Papers manipulating and watching them all (just as her chief
adversary in his turn manipulates and watches). Tita is caught up
in this machinery of their personal contest, and our awakening to
the reality of her own frustrated nature is vital if we are to grasp
the full meaning of the story and the firmness of its basis in
character and feeling. She is created for the reader by the merest
wisps of suggestion. And what James suggests, as he can always
do so well, with a delicate blend of laughter and sympathy, is a
woman with a spiritual self, and with the potentialities of an
emotional life: an *animula vagula blandula*, feeble, mild, faded,
totally innocent and transparent, awkward and shy, but on the brink
of discovering and declaring herself. She has much to undergo
in this small space: the growth of her first and misplaced affection;
the first flurry of a vital self-seeking; then shame, and forgiveness.
And in the end she discovers, for the briefest flash, a luminosity
of spirit that shines straight through the intrigues of Juliana and
the editor and is a hint to us that the Aspern power itself, so
aggressively profane, may be neither comprehensive nor ultimate
in itself. But this flash comes only once, as we shall see. And for
most of the story Tita is clearly before us as an oppressed and
dingy spinster, clenched in the 'strange, soft coldness' of her aunt,
and only beginning to learn (as Catherine Sloper learned, in
Washington Square) that the authority even of well-intentioned
guardians can be resented and resisted. Her one passion, for
flowers, could begin to flow into other channels—towards a whole
world of experience, and towards a man who listens and talks to
her intently in a garden. Venice is what she has been denied, in the
shut-up *palazzo* of her dilapidated life—just as the historical and
visionary Venice has been denied to the scholarly man who is
paying such disturbing attentions to her. The section begins
significantly with an evocation of St. Mark's Square, the footsteps
and voices, the tables, the social bustle of Florian's, and as part of
it all, 'The wonderful church, with its low domes and bristling
embroideries, the mystery of its mosaic and sculpture, looked
ghostly in the tempered gloom, and the sea-breeze passed between
the twin columns of the Piazzetta, the lintels of a door no longer
guarded, as gently as if a rich curtain were swaying there' (pp. 311–
12). Set against this richness and openness is the bathos of the
editor thinking he will take home to Tita, as a token, an ice-cream

from Florian's—and set against the thought of Romeo, and of
Aspern himself, each making love in a garden, the editor comes
back in the darkness to stumble through a sad parody of the great
lover. Before, he had smiled at the idea of being in Aspern's place,
a man assaulted by Maenad-like women, but now this seems for a
second to be his fate: 'She came out of the arbour almost as if
she were going to throw herself into my arms.' But of course to
his un-Aspern-like relief, 'I hasten to add that she did nothing of
the kind.' And though he consciously pushes his gallantries in
conversation as far as he dare (the memory of the Venice of
Casanova even floats into his mind), his freshly aroused excitement easily diverts itself—from so unseductive a woman, it must
be admitted—into his old rapacity for the relics that are the mere
emblems of power. But he does open himself to Tita—he takes a
gamble of sorts, frankly revealing his plan to her. And Tita, too,
is beginning to open and unfold in the darkness. James can catch
with such accuracy, as well as humour, the desolate lives of im-
mured women like Tita Bordereau:

I asked her what people they had known and she said, Oh! very nice ones
—the Cavaliere Bombicci and the Contessa Altemura, with whom they
had had a great friendship. Also English people—the Churtons and the
Goldies and Mrs. Stock-Stock, whom they had loved dearly; she was
dead and gone, poor dear. . . . These people came to see them without
fail every year, usually at the *capo d'anno*, and of old her aunt used to
make them some little present—her aunt and she together: small things
that she, Miss Tita, made herself, like paper lamp-shades or mats for
the decanters of wine at dinner or those woollen things that in cold
weather were worn on the wrists. (pp. 317–18)

Released from such a grey world by the editor's presence, Tita
talks as presumably she has never talked before. There is a flow, a
loosening, a communication. It helps to bring about the editor's
own unexpected confession—which, ironically, passes into an
attempt to use Tita's self-exposure for his own purposes. Each
confession is elicited and yet cheated by the other—cheated to
such effect that Tita flees back into seclusion, all communication
ends, and the editor, returning to his petty siege, cuts off the
supply of flowers.

But Tita is to have her excursion—one comes more and more to
understand that this is the story of her adventure almost as much
as the editor's. She has her 'immense liberation', her 'revelation

of Venice', when the editor, obeying her aunt's order, takes her out in a gondola, and her childlike reliance and intimacy suddenly bloom into a hurtful ecstasy at the world she has missed. She lies 'receptive' on the gondola's cushions; she is all 'appreciation', agitated by 'impressions' (those very honorific words in James's vocabulary). And yet all the time we see the editor throbbing with an equal but adverse excitement: that of learning from his increasingly pliable friend that her aunt 'has got everything' he has dreamed of. It is the mixture in Tita of passivity and efflorescence, the sense of youthfulness appearing in middle age, that makes her so affecting a character—especially when seen against the unyouthful worldliness and cunning of the other two. She affects the editor even now. Her 'extreme limpidity' exasperates him, but also makes her almost charming. He recognizes in her eyes 'a kind of confession of helplessness, an appeal to me to deal fairly, generously'. And he feels 'almost as one who corrupts the innocence of youth'. Tita, herself growing in a direction she can barely understand, makes something grow strangely within the editor— not quite an answering affection, but the faculty of shame. And that is one faculty presumably little recorded among the Aspern Papers.

The editor forces Tita, whose affections he only just suspects, to be his accomplice against the ailing Juliana. Juliana in turn tries to force Tita into the editor's arms—into the financial security which she knows her niece will need before long. It is revealing to watch how James, as always, uses money as one of the central principles of power, both for itself and for what it can represent. Tita is one of the impoverished and the meek. But Juliana makes the world pay, with a vengeance. The extortionate rent she charges the puzzled editor is an indicator of her price in ways that are also non-pecuniary. He finds such greed embarrassing in a woman of heroic associations, but it does suggest the way in which so many other sources and ends of human energy are concentrated in the Papers. Money becomes, as it were, the residue of passion and poetry for Juliana, and it, at least, can still trickle into her hoard. Her cupidity is a love of power and an appetite for survival, and it turns the superbly dramatic scene where she and the editor haggle over a 'price' for Aspern's portrait into a real battle to the death. Here is a desperate power game between them, full of bitter duplicity, gibes, and *doubles entendres*, and it is being played, figuratively speaking, for the highest possible stakes. Of course the money question is not all figurative—it is based very realistically on the uncomfortable facts of Tita's need for provision in the outside world. And Juliana's malevolent covetousness is not all a symbol of that ravening quality that so clearly attaches to the power of the Papers—she is also a merely stubborn and greedy old American expatriate, playing a bizarre game of hide-and-seek. Nevertheless, such an encounter cannot fail to touch on the important concept of paying and spending in wider terms. The story of the editor is the story of a man prepared to 'pay' so much, and no more; a man who expects sacrifices of others but who cannot expend himself. And he is a man, somewhere in his nature, who wishes to spend: who can at least invoke a world where great poets, lovers, and warriors spent greatly and dangerously, and had, in consequence, a great return. Juliana's greed is not only a vestige of the vitality that still flickers behind her mask; it is also, in the way she applies it, an instrument and a judgement against her enemy, the editor. The high 'price' she sets is to show her withering contempt for this unheroic and contemporary man, whom she sends scurrying to his bankers in a vain attempt to find a cash value equivalent to her life and her memories of Aspern. And the 'price' is so high for Juliana herself, and calls for such expenditure of emotional force in the defence of it, that it drives her into her last illness.

The climax of *The Aspern Papers* is one of the most exciting and unexpectedly revealing in any of James's shorter works—only *The Turn of the Screw* can compare with it from this point of view. It is in fact a double climax, and takes place between the editor and each of the two women. Juliana on her sick-bed becomes more and more witchlike: 'the upper half of her face was covered by the fall of a piece of dingy lacelike muslin, a sort of extemporised hood which, wound round her head, descended to the end of her nose, leaving nothing visible but her white withered cheeks and puckered mouth, closed tightly, and, as it were, consciously' (pp. 351–2). Her still-hidden eyes become objects almost apart from herself: things to be spoken of in hushed voices by Tita and the editor at the bedside, protected objects of price and magnificence, catalogued in Aspern's verse. And set directly against the 'treasure' of the hidden eyes are the equally emphasized eyes of the editor, who is always the intent observer, spy, and robber, and has now at last reached the *palazzo*'s *penetralia*. A complete little ocular drama (of an almost surrealist kind) is played out through this scene: 'I turned my eyes all over the room, rummaging with them the closets, the chests of drawers, the tables'. Juliana's eyes have been carefully prepared for us right through the story: it will soon be their moment. But before the editor sees them he has to run another gauntlet, that of his reluctant entanglement with Tita. Both aspects of his fate are closing on him. The hidden Papers are nearer than ever before—unless the old woman has burned them—and he prowls with unbearable anxiety and concentration through the darkened garden, behind the glowing tip of his cigar. Tita, too, comes nearer and nearer to him, revealing more of her hidden expectations—willing to help him to his wishes yet inadvertently pulling in another direction. She has gone so far as to search for the Papers in the old woman's trunk, and speaks now 'with a strange, unexpected emotion': 'I don't know what I would do [for you]—what I wouldn't!' The effect on the preoccupied editor is to make him feel 'reprimanded and shamed'. And the direct result of shame is, in a splendid touch by James, to make him tell her for the first time his true name. He laughs with relief at rediscovering something honest and essential of himself—his own identity. And Tita, who has unconsciously brought it about, insists on the importance of his confession: 'I feel as if you were a new person, now that you have got a new name.' But the humanizing moment of relief passes. The editor escapes in facetiousness, and is only exasperated by her Fleda Vetch-like injunction, 'You must wait—you must wait.' Because poor Tita, after all, is no more completely an angelic figure than is Fleda Vetch (as we shall see). Her quiet human desires have made her into the editor's accomplice, no matter how something else in her nature inspires conscience and shame in him. And even though the editor feels this shame when he decides to rifle Juliana's secretaire—'I think it was the worst thing I did'—it is precisely the thought that Tita by now wishes him to steal the Papers, and has prepared the way for him, that is the decisive pressure on his will. (It is a tiny version of that major Jamesian situation of a redeeming figure who also acts for disruption and loss.) And so the editor comes to his revelation. As the button of the secretaire is touched, it is not the lid that opens and reveals. It is, for the first and last time, the 'extraordinary

eyes' set in the white withered head of Juliana Bordereau, accusing
him, extinguishing him, from the doorway. And if their power
immediately drives the editor out of the house, and out of Venice,
stammering in dismay and humiliation, it is important to realize
that revelation has also worked the other way. Juliana has looked
for the last time into a little vignette of modern pettiness and
degeneracy at work in her own parlour—'Ah, you publishing
scoundrel!' is her denunciation—and she is killed by what she sees.
It is as if two of this story's cherished 'treasures' have been revealed
as the two gazes meet—a vision, for the editor, of outraged power;
and a vision, for Juliana, of dust and mortification. And the
narrative flashes with the irony and fatality of their collision.

That first part of the book's climax is successfully melodramatic:
very condensed, and with a grotesque, mirthless humour. The
second, that between the editor and Tita in Chapter 9, is marvellously different in kind and tempo, for all its kinship and logical
consequence. After the explosive heat of that crisis with Juliana
comes, within a few days, the first elegiac, sea-borne coolness of
the Venetian autumn. There is a quick change, also, in our sense
of these two characters, the editor and Tita. There is a new
inwardness, a new seriousness, and a brief achievement— of
intensity, of feeling, of mystery—that can only be called a poetic
one. After a bout of self-analysis and self-justification, the editor
palpitatingly returns to Venice out of two contradictory motives:
a hesitant charity for the feelings of Tita, and an undimmed and
selfish greed for the Papers. Will there be a way of reconciling
these two? Charity seems to act, even to his own eyes, as a mask
for his greed; and his whole ambivalence to himself is expressed in
the reason he offers for his return—'I wanted to put myself on a
better footing.' Juliana, the keeper of Tita and the Papers, has died,
and the gates are almost open. We see into Tita through the
editor's descriptions, but much further than he. In her utterly
transparent weakness and total dependence on him (the only
other people she has left in the world are a few old Venetian ladies,
an old doctor, an old lawyer), she has at last expressed her feelings
of grief before she sees him, weeping 'simply, satisfyingly,
refreshingly, with a sort of primitive, retarded sense of loneliness
and violence'. And now, unselfconscious, unproud, even amazingly
unreproachful, she waits to encounter the editor, with her long
white face framed in a mantilla—'standing there in the first dusk

with her hands full of flowers smiling at me with reddened eyes'
(there is no mawkishness in the picture: only realism and tenderness). Against the plainness of Tita's naïve behaviour the complicated self-awareness and archness of manner in the editor stand
out like the branches of a contorted and stunted tree. And then,
suddenly, her simplicity changes. Tita, too, is forced into knowing-
ness and into having a manner. She discovers that she has a strong
bargaining counter in the Papers that she might use to secure her
personal happiness—a discovery that forces duplicity on her and
humiliates her. There is nothing more pathetic in the story than
to see her here, obliged by her position and by her new fearful
liberation to adopt indirectness for the first time—and to see the
distraught editor, faced by the 'extraordinary expression of
entreaty in her eyes', fail to save her embarrassment by himself
making the required offer of marriage. To protect Tita would
require the editor to take too great a gamble by any standards—
far greater than the one that faced Winterbourne while he watched
Daisy Miller, in *her* difficulties, adopt more and more of a manner.
Tita's mind is not directly revealed to us. But what we surmise by
her awkward gestures and words is, on the one hand, a wish that
the editor might marry her for herself, taking the Papers as a
dowry; and on the other, a sense of shame at having this desire,
and at herself having to take the initiative—and even at possessing
so violent a source of power and attraction as the Papers. She
could almost wish him to go away and leave her, virginal and
alone with the Papers as a kind of charge. And when she withholds
them from him (he thrills in acquisitive delight to learn they are
still accessible, and voluminous) she does so with a bizarrely
mingled modesty and enticement. The painfulness that runs
through their conversation is that of two people caught in a
situation that is partly of their own making, and yet is now out of
control; the pain of seeing a very imperfect man forced to face the
enormous responsibility of being loved; and above all, the pain of
Tita emerging so late in life into so troubled a womanhood.

Tita gives the editor 'a precious possession'—the portrait of
Aspern. It brings back at a very crucial point the memory of Aspern
(assaulted by his Maenads!) and all the associations of money:

'I may have it—do you mean you give it to me?' I questioned, staring,
as it passed into my hand.
'Oh yes'.

'But it's worth money—a large sum'.

'Well!' said Miss Tita, still with her strange look. (p. 371)

Will the editor pay up? Dare he pay in such currency? In his predicament he consults the oracle of his hero, whose portrait he holds —and Aspern's eyes (*eyes* once again) only look up with unhelpful mockery. The memory of Juliana's eyes is evoked for both Tita and the editor in their present oppression. 'Lord, they were fine!', says the editor, who had of course cringed at the glare of them. 'I see them—they stare at me in the dark!', cries Tita, who had been their victim, too. The two of them, shuffling through this little labyrinth of their relationship, are united at least by their puniness underneath the larger gaze of such passionate lovers as the dead Aspern and the dead Juliana.

The editor's way out of the labyrinth is the opposite of 'spending' —'I must renounce', he says; and Tita moans in obscure 'desolation'. Then at last, in her 'heroic way', she brings it out, her extraordinary 'offer': 'Anything that is mine—would be yours.' They are both overcome with the shamefulness of what they have come to. The editor is filled with compassion—quickly followed by a panic that sends him in flight once more, scurrying to his gondola ('That was the price—that was the price!'). And as for Tita, her cry of 'I would give you everything—and she would understand, where she is—she would forgive me!' is that of a very simple human voice echoing back through all the other stages and other styles of this story.

The editor's flight proves to be a brief journey into self-knowledge. This at least will be something he has gained from the whole affair, and from the sound of Tita's cry. On the sands at Malamocco he undergoes the pains of inner scrutiny: 'there were moments when I pacified my conscience and others when I lashed it into pain.' Because of this pain, and this new seriousness, we follow his extenuating arguments more sympathetically than before: 'I could not accept. I could not, for a bundle of tattered papers, marry a ridiculous, pathetic, provincial old woman.' He has at least come to the point where he can curse the Aspern relics as 'crumpled scraps', and see himself undergoing a deserved punishment for having 'unwittingly but nonetheless deplorably trifled', and for 'that most fatal of human follies, our not having known when to stop'. He wishes to escape, but without brutality. And at such a moral turning-point, the editor finds himself wandering confusedly beneath a culminating image for that same elemental power which has lain beyond him all the time in those Aspern scraps:

> I only know that in the afternoon, when the air was aglow with the sunset, I was standing before the church of Saints John and Paul and looking up at the small square-jawed face of Bartolommeo Colleoni, the terrible *condottiere* who sits so sturdily astride of his huge bronze horse, on the high pedestal on which Venetian gratitude maintains him. The statue is incomparable, the finest of all mounted figures, unless that of Marcus Aurelius, who rides benignant before the Roman Capitol, be finer; but I was not thinking of that; I only found myself staring at the triumphant captain as if he had an oracle on his lips. The western light shines into all his grimness at that hour and makes it wonderfully personal. But he continued to look far over my head, at the red immersion of another day—he had seen so many go down into the lagoon through the centuries—and if he were thinking of battles and stratagems they were of a different quality from any I had to tell him of. He could not direct me what to do, gaze up at him as I might. (p. 378)

Verrocchio's statue of the *condottiere*, which brings together so many of the story's motifs, represents the unconfused man of action: it is specified as not being the statue of Marcus Aurelius, the imperial stoic and philosopher. It indicates the glories of the Venetian past. It indicates the secularity and humanistic beauty of the Renaissance. And it is as potentially inspiring in its way as Christina Light to her sculptor,[6] or, as we shall see, the sight of Notre Dame to the men of sensibility in *The Tragic Muse*—though, unlike those cases, it strikes the beholder dumb, and merely throws him back into his personal chaos. We feel a reluctant and partial kinship with the editor in this. The *condottiere* is a vision of splendour to our imaginations; but the editor's reactions have an ordinary human dimension that the bronze hero does not afford, on his high pedestal. And as if reflecting this, the picture of the great statue is at once followed in the same paragraph by a vision of everyday human society—this passage, too, must be quoted in full—a Venice not heroic but communal and intimate, within the

---

[6] We remember Roderick Hudson, on a visit to Venice, expressing his own gargantuan aspirations to power and beauty, declaring 'that the only thing worth living for was to make a colossal bronze and set it aloft in the light of a public square' (Chapter 5).

warm solidarity of whose life a wanderer might well hope to find a more sympathetic response. It represents this wanderer's last and delusive opportunity. For on the words, 'And somehow', the description of Venice-as-family subtly pivots and becomes Venice-as-theatre, with the editor just as much excluded as he was by the *condottiere*, and condemned (by his nature, by his lost chance) to play the desolate bystander until all of this rich, promising reality fades into the ungraspable figments of scenery and masked comedians:

I don't know why it happened that on this occasion I was more than ever struck with that queer air of sociability, of cousinship and family life, which makes up half the expression of Venice. Without streets and vehicles, the uproar of wheels, the brutality of horses, and with its little winding ways where people crowd together, where voices sound as in the corridors of a house, where the human step circulates as if it skirted the angles of furniture and shoes never wear out, the place has the character of an immense collective apartment, in which Piazza San Marco is the most ornamented corner and palaces and churches, for the rest, play the part of great divans of repose, tables of entertainment, expanses of decoration. And somehow the splendid common domicile, familiar, domestic and resonant, also resembles a theatre, with actors clicking over bridges and, in straggling processions, tripping along fondamentas. As you sit in your gondola the footways that in certain parts edge the canals assume to the eye the importance of a stage, meeting it at the same angle, and the Venetian figures, moving to and fro against the battered scenery of their little houses of comedy, strike you as members of an endless dramatic troupe. (p. 379)

James, as we have seen elsewhere and will see again, has an imaginative feeling for human glory that is equalled only by his feeling for desolation. It is the movement between the two that creates his tragic sense; and there are few places where we can catch that movement more precisely than in this one paragraph.

It follows by an unspoken logic that the editor, having seen with clarity into the nullity that awaits him, should that same night suffer an 'odd revulsion' of spirit and find himself swinging back 'to a passionate appreciation' of the Papers—back, that is, to something he has made into his *raison d'être*, and dare not abandon now. There is a new despairing 'ferocity' in his 'desire to possess them' by some means that will still let him escape Tita's condition. The ferocity of his desire comes from his recent vision of exclusion from *condottiere* and from city. His desire to possess is now simply his instinctive desire to *be*: to be admitted, to avoid the exile from reality with which he is threatened. And—so symmetrical are the ways in which even breakdown and disunity can declare themselves —Tita has had in the night *her* revulsion of spirit after *her* experience of exclusion and humiliation the previous day. The editor is transformed back into his old 'concupiscence' for the Papers. But her transformation is more profound. Tita's growth towards a fuller life has been driven back on itself, and she has discovered her 'force of soul' and her soul's isolation in the same moment: 'Poor Miss Tita's sense of her failure had produced an extraordinary alteration in her . . . Now I perceived it; I can scarcely tell how it startled me. She stood in the middle of the room with a face of mildness bent upon me, and her look of forgiveness, of absolution made her angelic. It beautified her; she was younger; she was not a ridiculous old woman' (pp. 380—81). This 'phantas-magoric brightness' dazzles the editor. It is an 'optical trick' that is no mere trick but essentially a true thing, or several true things: a complex real event taking place in Tita, and at the same time an event taking place in the editor. The latter event is something of the nature of an unexpected moral insight on his part into the soul of another person—blurred as always by the presence of some concupiscent self-delusion: his desire to *find* beauty in the face of the Papers' new owner. Even if coloured by egotism, his perception allows him at least a glimmer of what could truly save him, so that he suddenly feels 'ready to pay the price' for what he wants: the price of commitment to another human being. 'I heard a whisper somewhere in the depths of my conscience: "Why not, after all—why not?" ' But in practical terms it is all irrelevant now. The transforming brightness and infinite gentleness in Tita, that might have saved him, has been brought about by the painful finality of her separation from him, and also by her painful birth into an independent and lonely identity, free from the aegis of her aunt and now from her aunt's onerous legacy. Gently, she an-nounces the destruction of the Papers; and a darkness descends upon the editor. 'The transfiguration was over.' And despite the fact that he will never forget the long look she pauses to give him now from the doorway, as she turns her back and leaves—it is not a look like the one her aunt had given—it does seem as if, for him, the transfiguration is quite over. He returns and withers, as he must, into his dingy self, and is welcomed back from his adventure by the astute and ironical Mrs. Prest, who stands significantly at the beginning and at the end of such a narrative, as a very contemporary and mundane lady. He sends payment for the portrait to Tita as a kind of conscience-money—instead of the other payment of himself that he could not and can never make. And he is left with a sense of loss which, since he can explain it only as 'the loss of the letters', is clearly too great and too comprehensive a loss for him ever to be able to assess.

There are for us two measures of what the editor lost: one is moral, one in the widest sense aesthetic. One is expressed by Tita's forgiving 'soul' and his own not quite defunct conscience; the other by the power of poetry and love and Venice. The two worlds of value, though perennially different, have almost come together to offer the fullest of all fulfilments to this half-conscious Jamesian quester—Tita representing the chance of goodness, gentleness, affection, and marriage; *and* the quite other tradition of the Papers which she alone, symbolically at least, can transmit. To have suggested issues of such amplitude, and to have touched on the sense of a larger existence towards which all separate insufficient people are impelled—this is the achievement and final justification of that witty grotesqueness of method which we began by considering. The method has been only another way of catching normal life off balance, through comedy, stylization, and exaggeration, revealing glimpses of what Longmore glimpsed in *Madame de Mauves*: 'the world's great life' that lies within and around our individual lives, and comes to our knowledge only in moments of illuminating disturbance, spiritual or sensuous, self-abnegating or self-affirming. The editor, absurd and bungling human being that he is, is left with these two different but complementary glimpses of the power of this greater life that he has failed to purchase. One lies in his memory of Tita's long look of beatific farewell. And another view of it, we imagine, will continue to stare down at him from the worldly derisive eyes in the one thing he *has* purchased—the portrait above his desk of that latter-day *condottiere*, creator, and man of passion, Jeffrey Aspern.

4

The Story of the Talents in
The Tragic Muse

I

ANY account of *The Tragic Muse* still seems to require an opening note of apology and defence. Modern criticism has been even less generous to it than to *Roderick Hudson*; and yet each novel could quite properly be seen as a major and fully representative work from James's early and middle periods. *The Tragic Muse* is even more than that. In its complexity and unity, and its general sense of an author at ease with himself and totally in command of many of his most characteristic powers, it is a greater work than either of the two novels usually associated with it—less black and white than *The Bostonians*, and far more sure of its material than *The Princess Casamassima*. *The Tragic Muse*, in 1890, stands chronologically at the mid-point of James's writing career, and if it has left behind something of *Roderick Hudson*'s lyrical quality at one end of the scale, and, at the other end, does not offer the poetic-analytic synthesis of the late style, it nevertheless provides the most complete compendium of his qualities as a novelist in the realist mode. James never wrote a more mature or, in its own way, more fully satisfying book.

The sign of its maturity that strikes one most immediately is its air of assurance. From the start the reader is given a sense of absolute confidence in his author: that security of tone, almost classical in effect, that is the criterion of James's best writing. For example, could there be anything more controlled and purposeful, anything more full of subtle exposition, humorous evaluation, and sheer play of tone than the opening paragraph of Chapter 13, where Nick Dormer has just won his by-election, under Julia Dallow's patronage, and the two of them return in triumph to where Lady Agnes Dormer awaits in noble expectation?

The drive from Harsh to the Place, as it was called thereabouts, could be achieved by swift horses in less than ten minutes; and if Mrs. Dallow's ponies were capital trotters the general high pitch of the occasion made it congruous that they should show their speed. The occasion was the polling-day, the hour after the battle. The ponies had worked, with all the rest, for the week before, passing and repassing the neat windows of the flat little town (Mrs. Dallow had the complacent belief that there was none in the kingdom in which the flower-stands looked more respectable between the stiff muslin curtains), with their mistress behind them in her low, smart trap. Very often she was accompanied by the Liberal candidate, but even when she was not the equipage seemed scarcely less to represent his pleasant sociable confidence. It moved in a radiance of ribbons and handbills and handshakes and smiles; of quickened intercourse and sudden intimacy; of sympathy which assumed without presuming and gratitude which promised without soliciting. But, under Julia's guidance, the ponies pattered now, with no indication of a loss of freshness, along the firm, wide avenue which would and curved, to make up in picturesque effect for not undulating, from the gates opening straight into the town to the Palladian mansion, high, square, gray and clean, which stood, among parterres and fountains, in the centre of the park. A generous steed had been sacrificed to bring the good news from Ghent to Aix, but no such extravagance was after all necessary for communicating with Lady Agnes.[1]

Criticism of *The Tragic Muse*, when criticism has bothered about it, has usually emphasized its 'public' aspect. Here is James, we are told, investigating the problems of philistinism, aestheticism, and politics in nineteenth-century England, and writing a panoramic novel that tends to become a loosely handled debate—in Leon Edel's words, 'a cold discursive novel'.[2] James's own remarks, in the Preface for the New York edition, would seem in places to confirm such a description, and even such derogation; but as usual with the Prefaces James's later views need to be treated with great care. The Prefaces seem to me to be a unique and inestimable pot-pourri of misguided depreciation, over-honeyed complacency, and intermittent dazzling acuity, all of which can

---

[1] *The Tragic Muse*, London, 1948, p. 185. Future page-references are to this edition, which reprints the first English edition of 1890.

[2] In a review by Edel in *Nineteenth Century Fiction*, xxvi, 1971–2, 499. J. I. M. Stewart calls the book 'inert' and 'disastrous' (*Eight Modern Writers*, 1963, p. 98). For a brief survey of typical negative criticism of *The Tragic Muse*, from such names as Joseph Warren Beach, Edmund Wilson, Michael Swan, Quentin Anderson, F. W. Dupee, and R. P. Blackmur, see—as always—Oscar Cargill, *The Novels of Henry James*, New York, 1961, pp. 182–202.

mislead just as easily as it can assist. What the Prefaces often reveal most helpfully is not a comprehensive theory of fiction, as is sometimes claimed, but something of the essential mood that prevailed at each novel's inception, and something, re-created in different words, of its original inspiration. And from this point of view the Preface to *The Tragic Muse* is full of suggestions. James describes in it how in the autumn of 1889 he was struggling hard over the last chapter of the book in a Paris hotel room (it was the Hôtel de Hollande—and he made Julia Dallow stay at the same place). As usual, he tells, he had succumbed to the vice of over-preparing his subject, leaving too little space for his conclusion. The 'confounded irreducible quantity' of his subject was an exasperation and a challenge to his powers of 'economy' and 'organic form'. And the twin plots of Nick Dormer and Julia Dallow, Peter Sherringham and Miriam Rooth, threatened to remain apart, and called for a mighty compositional effort of fusion, after the example, he hoped, of 'certain sublime Tintorettos'. Meanwhile, as if offering a paradigm of his plight, his room was 'impregnated' with 'the rich rumble of the Rue de la Paix', at once 'auspicious' and 'fatal': auspicious to the artist by the richness of its life ('The "plot" of Paris thickened at such hours beyond any other plot in the world'); yet fatal by the depressing lesson he could draw from its natural lack of composition, foreshortening, and revealed meaning.

James thus describes the interplay of 'form' and 'life' during the composition of the book in a way that dramatizes its actual subject, the subject he was to call 'the conflict between art and "the world" ', and which he regarded as 'one of the half-dozen great primary motives'. The Prefaces often present this same picture of James, in a room, striving to extract significant from insignificant life by the power of form, and being assailed by the seductive and formless sound of footsteps on bridges, cries, water-noises, the sounds of living cities: Venice, Rome, Florence, London. The situation occurs for his characters, too—as when Strether, in *The Ambassadors*, becalmed within Madame de Vionnet's 'beautiful formal room', where it is like living in a 'high clear picture', hears coming in from outside, 'as if excited and exciting, the vague voice of Paris', which is the disruptive voice of harsh reality. At worst, for James, the sounds below the window distract and depress. At best, they pass into the book being written, shorn of their randomness

D

and waste: life making art possible, art making life meaningful. It was a union between the 'animation' of reality and the 'harmony' of art—presided over by a 'consistent tone'—that James wished to present in *The Tragic Muse* as an effect, and also as a theme. And it is imaged for us not only in the hotel room above a street where the novel was finished but in the fourth-floor Kensington study, admitting the voice of another great city, where it was begun: 'by a wide west window that, high aloft, looked over near and far London sunsets, a half-grey, half-flushed expanse of London life'.[3]

An expanse of life within a high, shapely window: not many critics have been prepared to allow any such success to this novel, and most have been only too prepared to accept James's self-critical remarks about the balance of its two halves, or the lack of characterization in Nick Dormer, or to conclude from his own over-schematic account of the book's 'motive' that it is fundamentally essayistic, and that 'the values asserted are far ahead of the values rendered.'[4] The issues of *The Tragic Muse*, as the Preface confirms both overtly and between its lines, are of the deepest personal concern to James, and engage his intelligence and feelings in a thoroughly dramatized way. This is very far from the rather allegorical and contrived treatment of similar topics in the short stories about artists in the eighties and nineties. Through diversified characters who make us share in their lives; through the gradually revealed interconnections among all of them; through a plot that is leisurely but full of life and change; through a fine use of gesture, pause, and glance; through richly constituted scenes and settings; and through a language that is deliberate and witty and decorative and perfectly accurate: through all these things and more, James ensures that *The Tragic Muse* is drama and not just debate or panorama—outward and inner drama of the subtlest kind. Only by creating the individuality of its characters does it establish their general humanity. And only by our seeing each of them in continual relation to the general structure and meaning of the novel can we grasp their individual natures and predicaments. That is, this novel is more particular in its psychological and moral exploration than has usually been

---

[3] *The Art of the Novel*, pp. 79–88.
[4] The phrase is R. P. Blackmur's, in his essay on James in *Literary History of the United States*, ed. R. E. Spiller *et al.*, New York, 1948, vol. 2, p. 1053.

accepted and also, by that fact, more truly universal. It should be approached as a performance and a fiction, not just as an exposition of ideas, for we can possess its significance only if we take delight in its manner.

The Tragic Muse is a story about talent—the word itself being in constant evidence. Primarily, there is Nick Dormer's talent for painting, as against politics; and Miriam Rooth's for the theatre, as against a conventional marriage. But we soon realize that the concept of 'talent', in its wider meaning of 'power' and 'natural disposition', and even in its Biblical meaning of a characterizing strength that it is our duty to use and develop, is eminently at work in the stories of others: in Peter Sherringham, Gabriel Nash, Julia Dallow, and even in minor figures like Lady Agnes and Biddy, or old Mr. Carteret and Mme Carré. The 'talent' of each of them is very close to the secret of what makes them unique individuals. To achieve one's talent is to be fully realized as a person: to stand on one's bedrock. It is not to be found in some isolated spiritual value or in withdrawal of any permanent kind, but in action and in a chosen mode of living and working. Their individual 'styles' may afford a clue to their essential 'talent'; but some of them will discover that style itself is not enough. They will discover that art, which is a part of life, must be and can be as viable a form of action as politics or diplomacy; and that these latter careers are not necessarily closer to reality, but are just as prone as art itself to decline into falsity and the equivalent of aestheticism. A man, in any career, has to *make* it real, from within himself. For some—the minor figures—their talent has already taken on its form of expression, and can hardly change. For the others, it is a desperate matter to find it and understand it, among forces that pull them in contrary ways. And even when it seems to have been found, or perhaps only glimpsed in the distance —on a stage, say—it is as elusive as any other profound truth. People may be individually defined by their talent; but they are also, in part, defined as human beings by the fact that they tend to drift away from their talent.

We identify with Nick Dormer, for example, as much through his uncertainties and his ordinariness as through his triumphant vindication of his true talent. Roderick Hudson's was a different case. Though his talent—his selfhood and his flair as a sculptor—

always had something a little absurd and petulant about it, he was very firmly endowed by James with the heroic note, and we entered into even his eventual failure as into something on a grand scale. It is strange that James should have worried in the Preface to *The Tragic Muse* about the degree of our identification with Nick, and strange that so many subsequent critics have accepted his point that since the artist 'in triumph' is necessarily impossible to portray, Nick is therefore too 'simple and flat' as a character.[5] Nick is precisely what James apparently goes on to criticize him for not being: a 'hero' who evokes our admiration and compassion because he is also a 'comparatively floundering *person*'. The opening description of him—placed uneasily among the women of his family at the annual art exhibition in the Palais de l'Industrie—prepares for this ordinariness by emphasizing the combination in his appearance of a certain muscular English conventionality with an artistic side that is rated as yet no higher than 'dreaminess'. Nick's talent always has to be nurtured very carefully by himself and by his friends. And it is easier for us— especially in a novel that is on the whole unromantic—to enter into the unsure man with an ounce of true talent than into the large artist-hero of doomed genius. By a dramatic appeal not uncommon in James, and one that is of the utmost importance in this book, Nick comes to represent the hidden artist in all of us: the inarticulate and shamefaced painter or novelist or poet, whom most people cherish or laugh at inside their daily selves. Because of this, Nick is, for our imaginations, the most immediate point of access to the plot— the more acceptable for the comparative lack of fuss or emphasis that surrounds the early portrayal of him. And his subsequent battles with himself and with daily circumstances will continue to invite this deep, instinctive recognition on the part of the reader, a recognition that not only creates his verisimilitude as an individual character but his successful generality as a type. A further advantage of this closeness is that it helps to keep us untroubled by the lack of external detail in the references to Nick's political activities—another point on which the book has been criticized. What matters for the story is clearly

---

[5] *The Art of the Novel*, pp. 96–7, Even W. W. Robson, in a quite sympathetic essay, thinks Nick unconvincing in a manner that gives away the whole novel's essential weakness, that of being somewhat 'constructed' and 'arbitrary' (*Critical Essays*, 1966, pp. 225–40).

Nick's personal reaction to politics and to art: how each of the two worlds affects him, not how he votes in the division lobbies or how he cleans his brushes. We see quite enough of the externals to suffice—in the case of his painting we see a considerable amount. The rest we are made to assume, drawn as we are into the arena of Nick's own awareness, where the real drama is taking place: the drama between the sense of sterile constriction and the sense of creative release.

Another distinctive method by which James takes us into Nick's story, and into the deeper issues of *The Tragic Muse*, is represented in Chapter 9, where Nick and Gabriel Nash talk as they walk by evening across Paris and along the banks of the Seine. Here is one of the many chapters of fully dramatized discussion in the book, one in which Nick questions and qualifies, while Nash expounds a blithe Pateresque philosophy of self-culture through style, and of personal hedonism in defiance of society. The dialogue is very alive, full of turns and contradictions, its ideas always presented as part of the shifting attitudes of each speaker, and even as part of the Parisian scene around them. We can take unconstrained pleasure in Nash's dazzling exaggeration and his own super-Jamesian figures of speech, and yet we can detect the way James is using him to parody some of the tenets of Aestheticism—and at the same time to establish some others. And where the talk suddenly passes into something more than talk—passes into one mastering image that draws both men's ideas to a focus and confers on their meeting the quality of an emblematic crisis—is where they come face to face with the Cathedral of Notre Dame:

They had come abreast of the low island from which the great cathedral, disengaged to-day from her old contacts and adhesions, rises high and fair, with her front of beauty and her majestic mass, darkened at that hour, or at least simplified, under the stars, but only more serene and sublime for her happy union, far aloft, with the cool distance and the night. Our young men, gossiping as profitably as I leave the reader to estimate, crossed the wide, short bridge which made them face towards the monuments of old Paris—the Palais de Justice, the Conciergerie, the holy chapel of Saint Louis. They came out before the church, which looks down on a square where the past, once so thick in the very heart of Paris, has been made rather a blank, pervaded, however, by the everlasting freshness of the great cathedral-face. It greeted Nick Dormer and Gabriel Nash with a kindness which the centuries had done nothing to dim. The lamplight of the great city washed its foundations, but the towers and buttresses, the arches, the galleries, the statues, the vast rose-window, the large, full composition, seemed to grow clearer as they climbed higher, as if they had a conscious benevolent answer for the upward gaze of men.

'How it straightens things out and blows away one's vapours—anything that's *done*!' said Nick; while his companion exclaimed, blandly and affectionately:

'The dear old thing!'

'The great point is to do something, instead of standing muddling and questioning; and, by Jove, it makes me want to!'

'Want to build a cathedral?' Nash inquired.

'Yes, just that'. (pp. 139–40)

The effect of the moment extends over several pages, as the two men prowl around the building appraisingly, then cross to the right bank and continue their conversation in a small café there. It is one of those Jamesian episodes in which an art-object is used to crystallize the many suggestions and ideas around it in the book —and as art-object is itself significantly drawn into the life that is being pictured. Notre Dame is a very solid symbol of harmony and inclusiveness, founded deeply within a real city, yet rising above it as a 'composition' and an 'answer'. It is shown to bring together the history of Paris—from Saint Louis to Madame Roland—and the modernities of the boulevards. Within its 'wide and bright domain of art' it comprehends 'the perpetual click on the neat bridges', the 'drippings of watery beer' in the little café, and the voices of the two friends arguing beneath it—just as James, in the Preface, described his efforts to reconcile aesthetic form with the vitality and shapelessness of a city's life going on beneath his window. And not only does the great structure of the church—'a great ship of stone, with its flying buttresses thrown forth like an array of mighty oars'—embody the idea of beauty that has been the subject of debate. It also makes that idea fully active and, as it were, incarnate, in terms of one man's private life. The sight of a beauty that has been so realized and so *made* at once stimulates everything in Nick that drives him towards the 'wide and bright domain of art', rather than the House of Commons. And for a moment the force of his essential 'talent' is free to flow. The sense of release is great, in that James has already built up a wonderfully complex structure of pressures in the book—pressures on Nick from the Dormer family and its intense political traditions; pressures from his expected betrothal to Julia Dallow, with her strong social and political ambition, and her possessiveness; all of them intensified by the fact that Nick fully recognizes the just claims that many other people make on him. And our awareness of Nick's tension is sharpened by our having seen a not dissimilar conflict building up in Peter Sherringham, too, confronted by *his* inspiring and tempting Notre Dame in the person of Miriam Rooth, and by our perception of the strains within such figures as Julia, Lady Agnes, Biddy—and even in Nash himself. That is, our own sense of excitement at the vision of Notre Dame goes a little beyond Nick's, in that we recognize it as a symbol that already governs many lives in the book and stands on the apex of a whole converging system of stresses and desires.

Notre Dame, Paris, and the onset of Gabriel Nash (Gabriel, the announcing angel of the Beautiful) have acted together in their liberating influence on Nick. But one last thing to observe about Notre Dame is that it has helped to put Nash firmly in his place, and has emphasized the important fact that James does not use him as a spokesman in this novel any more than he uses him as a simple butt: there is, instead, an interplay of attitudes to Nash which is very characteristic of the book's general sophistication and lack of fixity. On this occasion, Nash has been an inspiration; but it is Nick who has responded more deeply to the church. 'Dear old thing!' is how the former addresses it—facetiously, but a little fatuously, too. Nash has been arguing airily that the 'style' of beauty he wishes to live by can be an active one, and can embrace those moral values that are only meaningful in terms of action. But nevertheless he is always abashed and rendered impotent when faced by beauty that has become actual, constructed by the hands of men, as in the case of Notre Dame. For all its attractiveness when contrasted with the philistinism that surrounds Nick, Nash's idea of doing one's duty to one's own talent, and his whole concept of personal 'style', are gradually revealed to be lacking in certain respects. They retain their truth, but they are seen to be essentially preliminary to the truer endeavours of the artist in action. And beside those later endeavours by Nick, Nash's style, for all its gaiety and wit, strikes us as flimsy, and at times as a little invidious. He is a self-styled artist of life; but what the book eventually reveals is that such a person is committed neither to art nor to life, but remains merely an amateur at both. Real art—professional art—depresses him by the little compromises on which it is dependent; and as the plot develops he begins to fade away —not only as a character in the book dropping into the background, but also in the allegorical incident at the end, where Nick, professionally, tries to paint his portrait and place him *in* art, and Nash disappears abroad in fear and embarrassment at the same time as his portrait literally begins to fade. Art itself seems to reject the devotee who is so prone to convert it into talk and fetish. At best, however, Nash is more than this: he is the appreciator and the idealizer, while Nick is the creator who falls short of the ideal. Each man needs the other, and each, to the end, will be one measure of the other's falling short.

Notre Dame offers Nick only a brief moment of certainty and clarity: his full liberation is not to come till half-way through the book. For the extent of the forces ranged against him—which include certain aspects of his own temperament, too—is revealed in the immediately subsequent episodes at Harsh and Beauclere. These five chapters—Chapters 13 to 17—comprise the finest large-scale section in the entire novel, and are in themselve an anthology of James's technical skills and of the specifically sympathetic capabilities of his dramatic imagination.

Nick's destiny at Harsh Place is embodied in the handsome, demanding person of its proprietor, Julia Dallow, who is also becoming something of Nick's proprietor. But an important intermediary to be encountered first is Nick's mother, who forces her son to see the attractions of the place, and of its owner, through her eyes. Lady Agnes Dormer is one of the minor triumphs of *The Tragic Muse*, and not least by the way in which the theatrical comedy of so *grande* a *dame* (there is 'rather a clanking chain' on the lorgnette she interposes between her vision and the un-English horrors of Paris) is quickly refined by the perception that she, too, has a destiny at stake, and a very appreciable inner nature. Her philistinism is thoroughly vitalized by her supreme practicality, her acute sense of 'things as they are' (she is certainly free from the falsities and self-delusions of a mother like Mrs. Rooth). Her troublesome family require, in her judgement, not only the glory of following in the deceased Sir Nicholas's tradition of political eminence, but, more desperately, the financial security which

Nick's marrying Julia would provide. Her hostility to art is part of a general worldly pessimism and suspicion ('This competent matron, acquainted evidently with grief, but not weakened by it') which reinforce her stratagems for preserving the family's dignity and survival (no one knows better than she how to order a good economical meal in Paris). She is an admirable as well as impossible woman: perceptive as to many of the characteristics of her son and daughters, and not unintelligent in the pursuit of certain specific and restricted ends. And her practicality and defensive rigidity have been imposed over an emotional and wilful personality, and purchased at the cost of much bitterness—such as comes out, for example, in the 'strange, quick little flare of passion' with which she tells Nick how his father had been broken and killed by his lack of funds.[6] When we see her in Chapter 13 waiting, with such high tone and style, for Nick's triumphant return to Harsh Place from the hustings—'she had evidently been walking to and fro, the whole length of [the drawing-room], and her tall, upright black figure seemed in possession of the fair vastness like an exclamation-point at the bottom of a blank page'—she is obviously a very considerable force, in whose presence the lesson of Notre Dame and Gabriel Nash begins to lose much of its distinctness. The grand view from the windows of the drawing-room, over all those 'level lands' and rich symmetries, becomes the view of the particular possibility she wishes Nick to seize—'With a single word . . . you may have it all.' And there is a note of desperation in Nick's attempt to cling to the principles that Nash outlined, of independence and 'personal experiment', when he tells her: 'I love my freedom. I set it far above everything'—especially when his mother's answer is so complete: 'What freedom is there in being poor?' One aspect of the book's whole dilemma is here, supremely and tensely dramatized: the collision in one family, in one drawing-room, between practical means and an ideal end. Actual survival

[6] Chapter 5 offers a marvellous introductory account of Lady Agnes. It is notable how James can get so much simple fun out of such a character and yet can allow her to take on an estimable 'life' of her own behind the ironic pomposities of the language he describes her in. And she remains a force to the end of the book—there being two particularly memorable scenes, one (Chapter 34) where we hear by report Nick's confession to her that he has resigned his seat and broken with Julia; and another (Chapter 39) where Peter Sherringham, one lunch-time, is suddenly perceived by her to be a disappearing asset who must be snapped up quickly for Biddy.

in a world of money and position is set against the high goal that only responsibility to one's self can achieve; and James's respect for freedom is set against his recognition that freedom is always qualified by the claims of others and the pressures of circumstance. The drama in the drawing-room reaches its climax when Lady Agnes humbles herself to her son, and makes a high tragic appeal to him (almost as high and tragic as Miriam, later on, reciting Queen Constance's tirade from *King John*) to save his family—herself, Grace, and Biddy—from a very real social desolation: 'We are three dismal women in a filthy house. What are three dismal women, more or less, in London?' The reader feels the genuine shock of her 'unexpected rage of self-exposure' as she reduces herself to 'a poor woman crying for a kindness': the sudden intensity rising up, typically, within a chapter that begins and ends with the language of urbane comedy.

Significantly, and even ominously, Nick responds to such a scene through his dramatic sense. He is moved towards his mother's position—which is one that would nullify his talent for art—by precisely that sympathetic mind that impels him towards portrait-painting: 'He had the gift, so embarrassing when it is a question of consistent action, of seeing in an imaginative, interesting light anything that illustrated forcibly the life of another: such things affected a union with something in *his* life . . .' (p. 198). Here is one of those double-edged swords in human nature that James is so adept at revealing: in Nick's case, the dangerously protean adaptability of the imagination. Nick is pushed towards Julia and a political career in various ways—even literally, when the scene with his mother ends comically in her thrusting him like a sacrificial offering through the French windows to where Julia's 'long shadow' awaits him on the terrace. He is driven by the unspoken pressure of Julia herself, by her intermittent attractiveness to him, by his sharp sense of owing a debt of honour to her, by a recognition of there being some slight 'fun' in politics, and very strongly by his sense of his family's expectations, needs, and traditions. But not least, his own aesthetic capacity lays traps for itself by making the world of Harsh seem viable to him—more viable than it can ever really be in terms of that essential self and talent which we are now beginning to recognize. His mother's arguments move him to the degree that he has a vision of Harsh that is delusively close to his earlier vision of Notre Dame, in which the authoritative virtues of family and state are somehow blended into the power of beauty:

> Julia's wide kingdom opened out around him, making the future almost a dazzle of happy power. His mother and sisters floated in the rosy element with beaming faces, in transfigured safety. 'The first house in England', she had called it; but it might be the first house in Europe, the first house in the world, by the fine air and the high humanities that should fill it. Everything that was beautiful in the place where he stood took on a more delicate charm; the house rose over his head like a museum of exquisite awards . . . (p. 198)

But this is a trap—almost like the trap Isabel Archer's imagination sets for itself when she fills out the unseen side of Gilbert Osmond's character to fit her ideal conception. But James never dismisses Julia or what she aspires to, as he dismisses Osmond. He knows that the world of public affairs does have a genuine appeal to the imagination, and he can allow it its own value for those who belong to it. This is not a book that rejects the world for the sake of a private or ethereal 'art', but one that emphasizes how art can properly *be* 'the world' for certain people. For these people—
—people like Miriam Rooth as well as Nick Dormer—art is a very genuine form of human action and commitment; and the alternative to their art is in fact a life devoid of meaningful action. Politics will always be rather a sham for Nick—attractive to him at best 'because it was amusing and slightly dangerous, like playing football or ascending an Alp'. To embrace it in these circumstances would even be a kind of aestheticism, since the man himself would not be fulfilled in his politics, but only wearing politics as a superficial style (as Miriam Rooth would wear the character of a diplomat's wife). Another way of putting it is that Nick would remain an amateur at politics; and as we have already indicated with regard to Gabrial Nash, professionalism in this book is an important touchstone of the fulfilled life.

Nick still does not know these facts about himself, and only later will he discover faith in his true bent (encouraged, as was Roderick Hudson, by his friendly connoisseur). At present, the novel's vivid subject is the way he is caught in turmoil between both worlds. As he goes out one morning into the Park to propose to Julia, it seems for the while that she is his reality. Even if his recent dip into political affairs was mere play-acting, she undoubtedly stands out as 'of all the queer phantasmagoria, the most substantial thing that survived'. She is more real than the shadowy aesthetes who moved in Nash's circle in Paris, and her substantiality may be a promise of some potential reality that waits for him in politics: 'She *was*, indeed, active politics.' And once again, his self-betraying artist's mind converts her—for all her noted animosity towards the aesthetic—into a painter's subject, an 'impression' within a 'frame':

> what had happened met his eyes as a composed picture—a picture of which the subject was inveterately Julia and her ponies: Julia wonderfully fair and fine, holding her head more than ever in the manner characteristic of her, brilliant, benignant, waving her whip, cleaving the crowd, thanking people with her smile, carrying him beside her, carrying him to his doom. (p. 207)

But it *is* a doom—his suspicion of it always breaks through the delusively composed picture. For Nick's personal attachment to Julia is still dependent on the more 'public' matter of his political career—such connections between the private life and the life of work being one of the most vital concerns of this novel—and their relationship is to that extent still built on an unreality and a lie.

Julia Dallow is a portrait that reminds us in several ways of Olive Chancellor in *The Bostonians*. In each woman we sense a profound emotional strain—though to the degree of neurosis in the case of Olive—caused by some violence being done by herself against her natural feelings. Each has devoted herself to 'public affairs' at the cost of some perversion to the private self and its demands. Each is unstable, alternately aggressive and fearful. Each is passionate in a selfish, overpowering way. Each is shown contemplating, at a critical juncture, the desert of her life: Olive, with the lapsed Verena at her feet, in the darkened room at Marmion, or walking on the shore there; Julia, more briefly, as she rides alone through the winter gloom of Hyde Park. The differences, of course, are also striking—not least that Julia remains to the end a woman who very much wants her particular man, and that we remain much more sympathetic to her, in her quandary, than to the invidious Olive Chancellor. Nevertheless, we are made to feel that Julia could conceivably move towards the position of an Olive Chancellor, and that this is a crossroads in her life as well as in Nick's. James nowhere in this book explicitly judges the life of politics as such, or suggests that it is absolutely incapable of providing fulfilment to those who choose to take part in it. He is concerned, rather, with the predicament of specific individuals. And Julia's predicament is this: that the field she has chosen for the expression of her personal ambition is at odds with the nature of the man she loves, and if she forswears the man for the ambition then there is a risk of emotional atrophy or distortion on the scale of an Olive Chancellor, since her politics do not seem to contain any equivalent to Nick as a lover—only the amusing shadow of Mr. Macgeorge. Politics, that is, are not necessarily abstract and delusive; but a Julia Dallow, deprived of the passion for Nick which represents one essential truth of her nature, could easily make them so (once again, it is a case of the individual having to confer reality on the career). For Julia is not the merely cold and haughty Englishwoman, though she can fill that historic part perfectly, to the aggrieved admiration of a snubbed Gabriel Nash: 'She is the perfect type of the object *raised*, or bred, and everything about her is homogeneous, from the angle of her elbow to the way she drops that vague, conventional, dry little "Oh!" which dispenses with all further performance. That sort of completeness is always satisfying' (p. 134). Julia is also a woman with a very physical and sexual presence: she causes as much stir when she enters a room as Miriam Rooth, and her charm operates on Nick 'in a very direct, primitive way'. And in addition she is a person of considerable inner perturbation, whose brusqueness to others comes from a peculiarly self-vexing awkwardness, a mixture of pride and shyness, and from an inability to deal with feelings rather than from a lack of them—traits as archetypally English, in such a social class, as her hauteur. She may seem to be all of a piece, even mechanically so—not just to Nash but to her companion, Mrs. Gresham, who praises her 'constitution' to Nick in alarming terms: 'The surface so delicate, the action so easy, yet the frame of steel.' But Nick has seen the other side of Julia. He has seen, in Paris, how she could surprise by her unexpected freedoms and nervous unconventionalities as well as chill and impress by her imperiousness and by the smothering, possessive note in her affection for him. Her awkwardness and unease are innate, but they are also the direct expression of her particular relation to Nick, which is continually humiliating for her. She is obliged always to distrust him and the state of his feelings for her—very rightly.

And she is driven therefore more and more to distrust herself and her own strong feelings for him. This comes out even in the nervous gestures that mark her return with him from the poll to her own drawing-room at Harsh, where she abstractedly adjusts her hat before the mirror, and is inadvertent and preoccupied while the Dormer clan celebrate. Like Christina Light she is seeking for someone more powerful than herself, who might nevertheless be moulded by her according to her own imagination: which is a familiar enough human inclination, and not just one that afflicted the career-less and frustrated nineteenth-century woman of talent. No doubt Nick is correct when he tells her she has no intellectual sense of politics at all; but the power she desires, and which would accompany a husband's political eminence, is a genuine one. She is to be taken seriously when she warns Nick, in Paris, that if he is so pusillanimous as not to win Harsh for the Liberals she will never see him again (it is like Christina haranguing a self-doubting Roderick in the Colosseum). Two passions are at variance in her, since the object of one of them refuses to bend to the shape of the other. But since the bias of the book is clearly towards the relation between people, rather than the relation between a person and a cause or an idea, we feel that her passion for Nick is on balance rather more intrinsic and vital to her than the other, and that therefore some at least of her 'political' arguing against him is her desire for him speaking in disguise. When she wishes he would 'change', and throw himself into his political career with determination, she is *also* expressing in that wish her desire simply that he would love her more directly and strongly.

Julia Dallow is bitter against the art world; but she has her 'aesthetic' side, too, in that she is a woman with deep feelings and with a repressed imagination. It is the existence of this side of her that adds to the sense of truth in the ending, where James hints that she and Nick will come together again, in a mutual compromise. Nick by that stage will have had time to discover himself in his painting, far away from her interference—and only if a man has first discovered his real self can he love fully (a principle we shall see Fleda Vetch apply, when she leaves Owen Gereth to his own devices). In this way, a man confers reality on his loving just as he must confer reality on his chosen career, from within himself. And Julia in her turn, it is fair to surmise at the end, can approach an independent Nick more confidently herself, with the cause of her nervous imperiousness removed, and with the prospect of emotional release and stability. But that is far in the future: at present, the hidden 'artist' in Julia can only add violence to her inner strife. Some of the violence is attributable to her life with her first husband; and the references to the late George Dallow add a small but highly provocative item to the sum of our knowledge of Julia. 'Why should [art] always be put upon me?', she cries. 'What have I done? I was drenched with it before!' Her first marriage, it seems, has been an impotent immurement in a House of Beauty, and 'art' at present evokes for her not the experience of the true artist, who is a truly active man, but only aestheticism, which is very different from art. The aestheticism of George Dallow has had about it a kind of sexless and sickly passivity:

George Dallow had made it [the interior beauty of Harsh], caring for these things and liking to talk about them (scarcely about anything else); so that it appeared to represent him still, what was best in his kindly, uniform nature—a friendly, competent, tiresome insistence upon purity and homogeneity. Nick Dormer could hear him yet, and could see him, too fat and with a congenital thickness in his speech, lounging there in loose clothes with his eternal cigarette. 'Now, my dear fellow, *that's* what I call form: I don't know what you call it'—that was the way he used to begin. The room was full of flowers in rare vases, but it looked like a place of which the beauty would have had a sweet odour even without them. (pp. 187–8)

No wonder such a man's widow recoils from Gabriel Nash with a shudder of reminiscent aversion that goes beyond mere social snobbery. And no wonder she is so dismayed when the very different man she wishes to marry next, and whom she idealizes as a great statesman (perhaps even as the equivalent of Colleoni in *The Aspern Papers*, that virile and political man of affairs!), shows apparent signs of drifting towards that former world of flowers in rare vases. Julia is a repressed woman, and paradoxically it is 'art' in its decadence—art as supine connoisseurship—that has frustrated the genuinely 'aesthetic' and passionate side of her. It is characteristic of the density of this novel that James can thus dramatize within Julia's life those same contradictory aspects of the artistic impulse which he sets out in the contrast of Nash's 'style' and Nick's 'doing', and in the contrast between Peter Sherringham in the stalls and Miriam Rooth on the stage.

All this restless self-delusion and resentful attraction between

Julia and Nick is magnificently caught in the proposal scene itself, in Chapter 15, where Nick walks with Julia in the Park, and rows her to the little temple on the lake. Nick, as we have seen, approaches his decisive step almost as a self-induced event of the imagination, and sees Julia for the moment as an essential feature of an idyllic landscape. The painter in him seems determined to connive at his own immolation (in yet another of those contradictory aspects of the artistic impulse). Their conversation vibrates with undertones: all the distortion and intensity of the false position each is placed in. Julia is suddenly reluctant and apprehensive, only too aware that Nick's affection is somewhat forced, and that it partly comes from his sense of an unpaid debt. Nick is overtly bland and confident, having decided to do the honourable thing and the politically sensible thing; but behind his teasing words he is at moments aggressive and taunting. It is an unlikely approach to a proposal; and both of them know instinctively that in such a marriage, and on such terms, they are going to their deaths. She responds to his banter with bitter and inadvertent remarks which Nick recognizes, only half-adequately, as coming from her 'odd shyness—or perverse stiffness at a moment when she probably only wanted to be soft'. 'How nasty the lake looks!', she says, all at a tangent; while her wooer says three times he could 'kill' her for making a reference to politics, his violence only thinly veiled by its facetiousness. With painfulness Julia haltingly reveals herself—'Well, kill me!'; and again, 'Why do you hate me so?'; and in a word abandoning her political self, 'What do I care for candidates?' And James unsparingly discloses Nick trapped in a situation that can only corrupt him, and corrupt him even into some of the detached aestheticism that lies in wait for artists: '*He* was not shy now, for he considered, this morning, that he saw things very straight and in a sense altogether superior and delightful. This enabled him to be generously sorry for his companion, if he were the reason of her being in any degree uncomfortable, and yet left him to enjoy the prettiness of some of the signs by which her discomfort was revealed' (p. 209).

On the little lake, in a dilapidated temple of Vesta (much liked by George Dallow, irony of ironies), Nick forces his 'love' on Julia. The scene is one of a kind of violation: a violation, morally at least, of Julia's long-preserved virginity, and a violation of various honesties as well. She is afraid to leave the boat, where she clutches a political periodical. Julia, with the 'frame of steel', is now all fear behind her vestal haughtiness, and suspects 'malice prepense' in being taken into so enclosed a spot. She shrinks as Olive Chancellor shrank, more than once, from Basil Ransom's assertive masculinity; but from disbelief in Nick's love more than from sexual shame. The interior of the little temple, with its other-worldly elegance, adds strangeness and luminousness to their encounter—which has its pathetic comedy, on top of everything else:

Mrs. Dallow sat on the edge of a sofa, rolling her parasol and remarking: 'You ought to read Mr. Hoppus's article to me'.
  'Why, is *this* your salon?' asked Nick, smiling.
  'Why are you always talking of that? It's an invention of your own.'
  'But isn't it the idea you care most about?'
  Suddenly, nervously, Mrs. Dallow put up her parasol and sat under it, as if she were not quite sensible of what she was doing. 'How much you know me! I don't care about anything—that you will ever guess'. (p. 213)

The opening of the parasol inside the room is a wonderful touch (the parasol has been referred to several times already in the chapter: we are very aware of it). The gesture is partly inexplicable, of course, and this is its rightness—an unpremeditated and entirely nervous spasm. But also, it is as much a dark hint and a *double entendre* as her remark, 'I don't care about anything—that you will ever guess.' Julia opens the parasol to protect herself, desiring the security of the open air against Nick's attractiveness and against his sexual animosity. Before, she had criticized Nick for his lack of will. But now, when he acts, with masculinity and committment (and Nick is now tender, and by his own lights sincere, for all his earlier gibes), she detects and fears the unreality of his actions.

Julia accepts the marriage offer of the man she loves with reluctance—'I wish I didn't adore you'—and as they leave the island she returns Nick's kiss with a blind and slightly desperate violence: 'He was close to her, and as he raised his head he felt it caught; she had seized it in her hands and she pressed her lips to the first place they encountered. The next instant she was in the boat' (p. 217). For all that the two are now informally engaged, the scene ends, as it began, in a blur of doubt, and with the hollowest of echoes beneath their brave words about the future. Their talk of

their marriage is full of surreptitious challenges, ironical concessions, and inadvertencies. Still they attack one another,
circuitously. Their love is acknowledged now but still has no basis
on which it can stand—the essential basis of two individuals,
understanding and accepting one another's 'talent', and fulfilling
something of themselves in independence as well as in concert.
Julia can relax to the extent of talking about Nick's artistic habits
(acceptable in a statesman as a hobby). She confesses to having
some liking for 'poor George's treasures' (including his 'Vandykes
and Moronis'), and even hopes that Nick will paint her. But Nick's
insulting and unexplained 'Never, never, never!' comes out of the
chasm that truly separates them. And in fear again, fear of the
foreseen failure of it all, Julia refuses to return to the temple alone
with him, and flees to the house—'Because I'm so happy'. There
is so much good feeling between this pair, so much pressure to be
united, so much strength for successful living in both of them:
and it is all going astray, in a charade of happiness that could have
been designed by the muse of tragedy herself.

A last phase of Nick's full charade, which is the charade of all
people untrue to themselves, is acted out on his memorable visit
to Beauclere, the home of old Mr. Carteret, patron of his political
career and colleague of his deceased father. The close juxtaposition
of the two places is important, to begin with, for the way in which
Nick's impression of Beauclere, as of Harsh, becomes an artist's
impression. Only a man of imagination could respond in this way
to the town, the Abbey, the associations they have with English
society and history; and to the life of English politics, of which
Mr. Carteret is the retired doyen: all of which fuse as one to produce an intoxicating vision. But if the way the vision is made
reminds us again of Nick's true talent, the vision itself is one that
entices him further away from his talent—like the vision of Julia
as a framed picture. Beauclere brings together Nick's personal past
and his fancied future. The vital bonds of family continuity, in the
shape of his father's friend, his father's memory, and the remembered visits of his own childhood, together with the prospects of
eminence at Westminster and wealth through Mr. Carteret's
promised benefactions, are all much more warmly evoked than at
Harsh. Every detail of the description has its function, as well as its
immediate local solidity. The town itself is an amalgam of man-

made and natural: the countryside interpenetrates its huddled lanes and square red houses with greenery and the smell of new-mown hay, while in Mr. Carteret's the garden seems even to come into the room through the wide windows. Mr. Carteret's life—this is one of the most superb minor portraits in the book, rich in detail, feeling, and subdued laughter—is one of unostentatious but fixed ceremony; determinedly unaesthetic and even ugly, but solidly human; enriched by little privacies, and presided over by an immortal butler (Chayter, who always advances to receive guests in exactly the same spot in the middle distance, 'like a prime minister receiving an ambassador'). The lesirely order of it all, and the predictable nature of every dinner-party, evoke the political past:

> . . . the conversation would incline itself to public affairs. Mr. Carteret would find his natural level—the production of anecdote in regard to the formation of early ministries. He knew more than any one else about the personages of whom certain cabinets would have consisted if they had not consisted of others. His favourite exercise was to illustrate how different everything might have been from what it was, and how the reason of the difference had always been somebody's inability to 'see his way' to accept the view of somebody else—a view usually, at the time, discussed, in strict confidence, with Mr. Carteret, who surrounded his actual violation of that confidence, thirty years later, with many precautions against scandal. In this retrospective vein, at the head of his table, the old gentleman always enjoyed an audience or at any rate commanded a silence, often profound. Every one left it to some one else to ask another question; and when by chance some one else did so every one was struck with admiration at any one's being able to say anything. Nick knew the moment when he himself would take a glass of a particular port and, surreptitiously looking at his watch, perceive it was ten o'clock. It might as well be 1830. (p. 228)

The whole meaningful ensemble is completed by the brooding presence of Beauclere Abbey's vast bulk on the hill (like 'the ark left high and dry upon Ararat'). Here is a very vivid counterpart to the 'stone ship' of Notre Dame, and for a little while at least the life of politics seems to come under its transforming influence—though the realities of politics, in the person of Lord Bottomley and the other mechanical committee-men invited to meet Nick that evening at dinner, will very quickly reassert their charmless-ness. Nick's vision, we can detect, is just a little too sweet in tone, a little passive and self-indulgent, and though it has some of the true power of art it is not to the same extent as Notre Dame's the power of something 'made' and 'done', or something that stirs the beholder with the desire to create:

there was another admonition that was almost equally sure to descend upon his spirit in a summer hour, in a stroll about the grand abbey; to sink into it as the light lingered on the rough red walls and the local accent of the children sounded soft in the churchyard. It was simply the sense of England—a sort of apprehended revelation of his country. The dim annals of the place appeared to be in the air (foundations bafflingly early, a great monastic life, wars of the Roses, with battles and blood in the streets, and then the long quietude of the respectable centuries, all cornfields and magistrates and vicars), and these things were connected with an emotion that arose from the green country, the rich land so infinitely lived in, and laid on him a hand that was too ghostly to press and yet somehow too urgent to be light. It produced a throb that he could not have spoken of, it was so deep, and that was half imagination and half responsibility. These impressions melted together and made a general appeal, of which, with his new honours as a legislator, he was the sentient subject. If he had a love for this particular scene of life, might it not have a love for him and expect something of him? What fate could be so high as to grow old in a national affection? What a grand kind of reciprocity, making mere soreness of all the balms of indifference! (pp. 228-9)

Significantly, when Nick is to return some time later to Beauclere, to announce to a stricken Mr. Carteret his final breach with politics, he will visit the Abbey again, and this time feel 'comforted and confirmed by its beauty'—confirmed in his decision to embrace beauty rather than politics. And this is perhaps a truer measure of the Abbey's meaning for Nick. The rest is unavoidable delusion—as delusive as the engagement to Julia which he is now able to announce to his approving patron. And the falsity that sounded so discordantly through the scene of that engagement echoes again through Nick's whole closing conversation with the old man. Mr. Carteret, eminently at one with himself and firmly based on his own fixed life, now watches the squirmings and evasions of the younger man with increasing unease and disappointment. To live as falsely as Nick Dormer, and to be so influenced by a personal imagination made treacherous through its lack of proper outlet, is to cause disruption and pain in many other lives, and not just one's own.

II

Nick's falsity must be broken, and the break is made, at the exact half-way point of the book, by the entry of the Tragic Muse herself into his studio, in the person of Miriam Rooth. It is Gabriel Nash who ushers her in; and it is Nash who importantly prepares for her arrival by being the first person to discover on the spot the real quality of Nick's artistic talent, like Rowland Mallet finding the signs of genius in that basement studio in Northampton. Julia, doing the rounds of country houses, has left her fiancé to potter at his painting, and while she is away Nick is brought to discover his own soul. It comes with a great stir and a great sense of excitement for the reader: the casting-off of an incubus, the unlocking of a door. Nash is enthusiastic and discriminating over Nick's paintings, and urges on him a step that we recognize as heroic: to stake everything on the chance of finding his true self in the action of creating some beauty for the world (putting Parliament aside, and Mr. Carteret—and even Julia): 'To be what one *may* be, really and efficaciously . . . to feel it and understand it, to accept it, adopt it, embrace it—that's conduct, that's life'. And Nick is able at last to throw off shamefacedness and articulate his ambition to paint portraits:

'There it is', said Nick at last—'there's the naked, preposterous truth: that if I were to do exactly as I liked I should spend my years copying the more or less vacuous countenances of my fellow-mortals. I should find peace and pleasure and wisdom and worth, I should find fascination and a measure of success in it: out of the din and the dust and the scramble, the world of party labels, party cries, party bargains and party treacheries—of humbuggery, hypocrisy and cant. The cleanness and quietness of it, the independent effort to do something, to leave something which shall give joy to man long after the howling has died away to the last ghost of an echo—such a vision solicits me at certain hours with an almost irresistible force'. (pp. 311–12)

At this point, Nash describes Miriam's success on the London stage—*her* achievement of beauty, *her* heroic possession of her talent and her soul. And when he brings her to be painted next day, James achieves a climactic sense of connection: two separate lives touching in a way that will change the direction of both of them (Nick's more than Miriam's), and will change or illuminate the lives of others (Julia's, Peter's, the Dormer family's, even Gabriel

Nash's). It is an important moment for the structure of the novel, too, since its two plots, proceeding up till now in parallel, one in England and one in Paris, very much need a dramatic fusion of this kind, for all the complex interconnections of character and theme that have kept them related so far. Miriam, as a portrait-subject, is a catalyst for Nick's private strength:

> the idea—the idea of what one might make of such material—touched him with an irresistible wand. On the spot, to his inner vision, Miriam became a magnificent result, drawing a hundred formative instincts out of their troubled sleep, defying him where he privately felt strongest and imposing herself triumphantly in her own strength. He had the good fortune to see her, as a subject, without striking matches, in a vivid light, and his quick attempt was as exciting as a sudden gallop—it was almost the sense of riding a runaway horse. (p. 320)

And equally, she serves almost impersonally as a justification for the whole enterprise of art, including Nick's particular branch of it—the art of portrait-painting being one in which, like Miriam's own art-form, the actual and the formal flow very closely together. Nash, for example, having seen his protégés meet, eulogizes portraiture in terms that are very significant for the book's general bearing:

> ... the possible greatness of the art of the portraitist—its reach, its range, its fascination, the magnificent examples it had left us in the past: windows open into history, into psychology, things that were among the most precious possessions of the human race. He insisted, above all, on the interest, the richness arising from this great peculiarity of it: that, unlike most other forms, it was a revelation of two realities, the man whom it was the artist's conscious effort to reveal and the man (the interpreter) expressed in the very quality and temper of that effort. It offered a double vision, the strongest dose of life that art could give, the strongest dose of art that life could give. (p. 328)

This is not the end of Miriam's immediate impact. If she brings energy and confidence to Nick, and a general sense of life and art in harmony, she also drives Julia from the scene. Nick is happily released from falsity, but Julia's release is humiliating and painful. To find the Tragic Muse in Nick's studio, slightly *déshabillée*, is the final proof to Julia that she is about to marry a man utterly foreign to her. She flees from an art that so compromises itself, and from the sexuality she recognizes in Miriam and now distrusts more than ever in herself. In the April dusk, in fog and cold, Julia perversely drives in her carriage round and round a deserted Hyde Park, facing what she calls 'the ugly truth' about her own ambitions and needs, and Nick's failure to realize them for her. It is an indirectly presented scene, an image in Nick's mind; but it suggests a deep despair and exclusion. Julia excluded means Julia thrown back on her pride; and in the tempestuous scene that follows, where she breaks with Nick, she takes on a stature that for the last time appeals to Nick's dangerous imagination. He detects in her words of rejection 'a personal passion . . . held in check, with a tension of the cord . . . of which he could still feel the vibration'. And he is typically so moved by the nobility of a woman sacrificing her love, as it seems, for the ambitious ideal of playing a part in 'great affairs', that the ideal itself appeals to him; and he pleads vainly to be allowed to join her and to reject his artistic self, in words and in a tone reminiscent of the special pleading of his 'vision' at Beauclere:

'I'm inextricably committed and dedicated. I was brought up in the temple; my father was a high priest and I'm a child of the Lord. And then the life itself—when *you* speak of it I feel stirred to my depths: it's like a herald's trumpet. Fight *with* me, Julia—not against me! Be on my side, and we shall do everything. It *is* fascinating, to be a great man before the people—to be loved by them, to be followed by them. An artist isn't—never, never!' (p. 346)

This is what James calls 'the heavy penalty of being a man of imagination', that he should be so open to 'wondrous communications', and so capable of 'disloyalties'. But thanks to the disruptive effect of the true and dedicated actress, this has been the last disloyalty, and the last scene of Nick and Julia's long charade.

Of all James's major heroines, Miriam Rooth is one of the least close and 'personal' to the reader, and yet one of the most alive. She is not one of those distinguished by their superlative intelligence and their moral discrimination, and thereby used as the narrative's 'centre of consciousness'; but she is no less truly a heroine than any of them. Her living effect is actually dependent on her distance from us—on the 'indirect vision' of her to which James knew he was committed—since her particular powers of mind and personality are best conveyed not by analysis of motive but by showing her charismatic effect on others. (It is a more developed and subtle version of the 'external' approach to characterization used to create Roderick Hudson and Christina Light.) 'Character', for James, is always in part what other people make of you; and our response to the evidences of 'character' in real life, as in art, often involves an act of imagination and of willed illusion: 'Her character was simply to hold you by the particular spell; any other—the good-nature of home, the relation to her mother, her friends, her lovers, her debts, the practice of virtues or industries or vices—was not worth speaking of. These things were the fictions and shadows; the representation was the deep substance'[7] (p. 378). From her very first appearance Miriam is a force as much as an individual. In the salon of the Palais de l'Industrie she strikes a nervous Biddy Dormer (who very much wishes and needs to be struck) as being a dancer who can transform her observer into an element of her dance: 'Biddy had a momentary sense of being a figure in a ballet, a dramatic ballet—a subordinate, motionless figure, to be dashed at, to music, or capered up to. It would be a very dramatic ballet indeed if this young person were the heroine' (p. 25). She has her immediate effect on Nick Dormer, long before her critical intervention in his London studio. And above all she acts as a Cleopatra-figure on Peter Sherringham, the repressed side of whose nature is inflamed every time he sees her. Time and time again, once she has learned the mastery of her art of acting, and once she has come to London, Miriam takes on the role of an uplifted and glorifying emblem—'Something that one may turn to for glimpses of perfection, to lift one out of all the vulgarities of the day'. All around her in the book we see people in their uncertain pursuit of happiness, while Miriam rises above them as a 'priestess of harmony', and as a reality that is 'monstrously definite' amid the mere 'shining confusion' of their lives. Miriam appears as an art-object in herself, a perfect Notre Dame of the stage—'She was beauty, she was music, she was truth.' And in

---

[7] The 'external' characterization of Miriam is yet another feature of *The Tragic Muse* which has caused offence to many critics. Edmund Wilson, for example, writes: 'One trouble with "The Tragic Muse" is that James does not show us the inside of Miriam Rooth; and if he fails to do so, it is because, here as elsewhere, he does not know, as Tolstoy did, what the insides of such people are like' ('The Ambiguity of Henry James', *The Triple Thinkers*, London, 1939, p. 153)—a point and a comparison that are exactly repeated in Gorley Putt, *A Reader's Guide to Henry James*, 1966, p. 209.

one of the most exalted moments of the novel, one magical Sunday at her house in Balaklava Place, her acting, which is her life, and which is her completeness and beauty as a person, transports the watching Peter Sherringham into an almost paradisial state—'something which had no reason but its sweetness, no name nor place save as the pure, the distant, the antique'. Almost inevitably for James, this state of exaltation before a perfect living work of art produces the image of a kind of balcony or terrace (like the window from which he looked out over London as he wrote *The Tragic Muse*): 'It made of the crooked little stucco villa in St. John's Wood a place in the upper air, commanding the prospect; a nest of winged liberties and ironies, hanging far aloft above the huddled town. One should live at altitudes when one could—they braced and simplified; and for a happy interval Sherringham never touched the earth' (p. 397).

Miriam, however, has never really left the earth. As well as being an art-object, she is a creator of art: a combination that the painter, who cannot be a painting, might well envy in the actress or the dancer; and certainly an advantage that helps to explain Miriam's status in this novel. Her acting pervades her everyday life, to Peter Sheringham's moral perturbation; and as with any created work of the imagination, her acting seems to bear its own seal of truth, as opposed, say, to the trivial role-playing of her dreadful mother: '[Mrs. Rooth] made even the true seem fictive, while Miriam's effort was to make the fictive true.' Far from hiding an inner emptiness, Miriam's daily performance underwrites and confirms the real, and represents, at its very highest, the mind of the artist in intimate and strenuous encounter with the stuff of experience:

To say she was always acting suggests too much that she was often fatiguing; for her changing face affected this particular admirer at least not as a series of masks, but as a response to perceived differences, an intensity of sensibility, or still more as something cleverly constructive, like the shifting of the scene in a play or a room with many windows. Her incarnations were incalculable, but if her present denied her past and declined responsibility for her future, it made a good thing of the hour and kept the actual very actual. (p. 447)

If Miriam's external 'representations' are so real as to seem to deny the existence of any consistent personal identity behind them

—if she seems to be all 'effects' without a 'cause'—then this, too, must be seen as part of the paradoxicality of art, and of her life as an artist. Because there is no doubt that Miriam, for all her distance from us, and for all her position as an art-object, also affects us as being a very real person—the more real, even, for being so difficult to know and pin down. Her acting transforms her into a symbol and an image; but she can act only because she draws her energies and her talent from her own life and from the life about her. Her art, which means imitating characters foreign to herself, essentially expresses her own nature as truly as Nick Dormer's portrait-painting expresses his. The artist finds his true self by active submission to what is outside himself; and there is much in Miriam to be found and to be revealed in action. 'In action': perhaps this is a key to the whole novel's presentation of the artist. Art is action, as much as politics or diplomacy are action. Art means commitment and striving and difficulty. It is not rewarding to consider it for very long as a divine afflatus, or as the nimbus around some 'priestess of harmony'. The priestess lives in St. John's Wood, and is a phenomenally hard-working and self-disciplined young woman. We see her progress from crudity to perfection of performance: not stage by stage, of course, but in quite enough detail for us to accept the development without demur. And such progress bespeaks Miriam's strong ambition, determination, patience, and common sense. We see her force of will in the way she can impose herself on so sceptical a judge as old Mme Carré.[8] To the end of the book, even when she has arrived at eminence, she retains a distinctive note of her early vulgarity and breezy vigour. And further, we can see one reason why she drives herself so unsparingly when she describes to Nick and Peter the squalid-genteel poverty of her life with her mother, and 'with a flare of passion' throws out the question, 'Do you wonder that I should want to do something so that we can stop living like pigs?' This is an unexpected similarity between Miriam and Lady Agnes: both women, from their very different points of view, consider themselves living on the

[8] The brilliant sketch of Mme Carré, retired doyenne of the French theatre, also confirms how an inner identity—conveyed here only by flickers of 'deeper expression' in her eyes—can coexist with an outer life of perpetual polished theatricality: a 'sincerity' of faint envy and puzzlement at the youthful phenomenon of Miriam beneath a 'falsity' of perfect manner and method—the method that she can use, for example, to reveal Miriam's technical imperfections by imitating, for her benefit, Miriam's inadequate imitations of *her*!

edge of the social abyss, and both aspire bitterly after material security as well as glittering success. And like Lady Agnes, Miriam has learned much of her practicality and self-control through the force of a family's economic circumstances.

Miriam's practicality also takes the important form of a desire to understand herself. As we saw before in Nick's case, this is a prerequisite for the artist (and for the lover): it is part of his adventure and of his commitment. It is especially important for the actress, who needs to preserve a kernel of selfhood somewhere at the heart of so much self-extension and self-parody through the playing of parts. 'I know what I am!', she replies to Peter Sherringham when he accuses her of being 'an embroidery without a canvas'. Miriam is aware of a distinction between her 'true self' and the roles she enacts both in her social relations and on the stage. But she accepts the distinction happily, and is able to use her roles to extend or modify or tactically conceal her nature as she moves through the complexity of her outer life, rather than allowing them to fragment her nature or obscure it to her own understanding. By her perceptiveness and her force of will she can maintain some kind of healthy dialectic between her private self and her public roles—an ideal towards which Nick Dormer has to move by abandoning the false play-acting of his politics, which would have separated him fatally from himself. Nick, of course, is under very much more pressure than Miriam, and moves more haltingly at first. And it is ironic that the actress, the creature of many disguises, strikes the reader as being from the beginning the most balanced person in the book, contrasted with so many who are in a state of division that they cannot understand.

The relation between the 'true' Miriam and the roles she plays is one of the main points at issue between her and Peter Sherringham. Peter, who is himself so helplessly divided a man, is quite unable to reconcile himself to the true artist's protean capacities, and (like Rowland Mallet) vexes himself with the question of the moral identity of an attitudinizing woman. Does such a woman have *any* truth or selfhood? Or is it in fact mistaken ever to aim at knowing the absolute truth about another person? When he is at his most negative and rationalistic—and when he is thereby most self-protective—Peter sees Miriam as a walking illusion, 'a female gymnast, a mountebank', and 'a kind of monster': 'her existence was a series of parts assumed for the moment, changed for the next, before the perpetual mirror . . . of spectatorship.' And there is 'nothing to like, because . . . nothing to take hold of'. At other times, as on the Sunday at Balaklava Place when he is transported into 'a place in the upper air', Peter's suspicions fall away before the actual power of the performance—which is the power of her inner life, as well as of her adopted art. It is an issue that clearly fascinated James, not just through his own interest in the theatre, and in women of the theatre like Fanny Kemble and Elizabeth Robins, but because it touches on the whole enormous question round which so much of his work is written: the relationship between the artificial and the natural, between 'form' and 'life', 'art' and 'the world'. In a general way, it is *The Tragic Muse*'s main issue, too, of course; which is why Peter Sherringham, who interests us as a person rather less than either Nick Dormer or Miriam Rooth, is nevertheless kept close to the centre of the book. Almost everything we see of his life is spent caught up in the very mill of the paradoxes of art and nature. He can resolve nothing, yet all the energies of his being are bent on achieving some kind of resolution. His perpetual switches of position and of mood afford a dramatization of ideas that we have already seen at work in the book's other plot, and produce from James a dazzling proliferation of sustained ironic analyses, which at times offer a mild foretaste of the later feats of dissection that will fill the pages of *The Golden Bowl*.[9]

[9] Here is one example, out of dozens, each as clever as the last (at times a little too clever), and each offering a slightly different view, or a different tone. Peter has arrived in London, determined to display his lack of involvement with Miriam:

'He waited after breakfast but a very few minutes before jumping into a hansom and rattling away to the north. A part of his waiting indeed consisted of a fidgety walk up Bond Street, during which he looked at his watch three or four times while he paused at shop-windows for fear of being a little early. In the cab, as he rolled along, after having given an address—Balaklava Place, St. John's Wood—the fear that he should be too early took curiously at moments the form of a fear that he should be too late: a symbol of the inconsistencies of which his spirit at present was full. Peter Sherringham was nervous, too nervous for a diplomatist, and haunted with inclinations, and indeed with purposes, which contradicted each other. He wanted to be out of it and yet he dreaded not to be in it, and on this particular occasion the sense of exclusion made him sore. At the same time he was not unconscious of the impulse to stop his cab and make it turn round and drive due south. He saw himself launched in the breezy fact while, morally speaking, he was hauled up on the hot sand of the principle, and he had the intelligence to perceive how little these two faces of the same idea had in common. However,

Peter is very much Julia Dallow's brother. He has an impulsive, emotional self, which strongly inclines towards the aesthetic; Julia's is more hidden, but it does at least produce a passion for one man, who is a painter. Like her, he has a practical and reflective self that aims at success in a career which involves public affairs and social eminence. And each of them has chosen as an object of devotion an artist whose integrity as a person is hopelessly incompatible with that social and political world. Peter is a bad actor and an indifferent artist, with much, however, of 'the celebrated artistic temperament'; an *aficionado* of the theatre, but a perpetual if inconsistent rationalist who can despise his own *afición*—a Jamesian tragicomic man, in fact, with a will too weak and ordinary to surmount his own antinomies. As a divided man he can also be seen in relation to his cousin, Nick, another young man torn in different directions and enmeshed in difficulties that are sexual, familial, political, and artistic. Each of the cousins is trying to push to fulfilment (in Nash's words) his 'personal experiment', and to master that unique 'instrument that each of us . . . carries in his being'. For each of them it is the full happiness and 'truth' of his life that is at hazard; but the diplomat is in the end less fortunate than the portrait-painter, in that he is more essentially and irremediably divided. His truth does not lie clearly in the direction either of Miriam or the Foreign Office. The latter is almost never shown to appeal to all of his nature, despite his single desperate attempt, during a last meeting with Miriam, to convey the imaginative possibilities of such a career. He never attains to a Beauclere vision of the diplomatic life. And equally, on the artistic side we always feel a fatal lack of something in his attitude to the theatre and to its 'priestess'. He cannot emulate Nick's sacrifice of a career for an art-form because he has only the 'artistic temperament' and none of the artistic activity. And he cannot sacrifice the career for the woman because his view of her, like his view of art, is fatally idealistic: too idealistic, too tinged with aestheticism in a way, ever to be saved by a straightforward passion. Strange as it may seem, Peter Sherringham, for all that

---

as the sense of movement encouraged him to reflect, a principle was a poor affair if it remained mere inaction. Yet from the moment it turned to action it manifestly could only be the particular action in which he was engaged; so that he was in the absurd position of thinking his behaviour more consummate for the reason that it was directly opposed to his intentions.' (pp. 355–6)

he belongs to the world of affairs, is a little touched by Gabriel Nash's debility. He is another amateur, straying into a world of professionals. Among those who make art, he is a talker and an appreciator. And like Nash he bitterly resents and despises the practical necessities of art. Despite his desire for Miriam and his admiration of her, he cannot accept her own imperfections and her socially compromising relations with the everyday world of the theatre—even though these are the very conditions of her art, and therefore the conditions by which alone her true nature can ever be expressed.

At times—in this debate between Peter and Miriam that ebbs and flows through the length of the novel, in anger and in good humour, and in all the self-contradictions of so tentative a relationship—Peter does recognize and respect the mixed nature of the art of acting, though he remains reluctant to apply this to *his* actress. He recognizes that acting is above all (like any art) a fusion of instinct with reflection, and of 'talent, desire, energy' with self-disciplined technique. And one can see in that case why acting should so fascinate him, a man congenitally unable to balance these very faculties. The key to Miriam's success as an actress is that she works hard (it was Mme Carré's wisest lesson) and suffers no personal illusions in her search to perfect *the* illusion, that of the theatre. She can always stand aside from her performance, a fact which guarantees its excellence, as in the exciting and triumphant scene where Peter hears her recite Constance from the Third Act of *King John*: 'the cold passion of art had perched on her banner and she listened to herself with an ear as vigilant as if she had been a Paganini drawing a fiddle-bow'[10] (p. 261). 'Cold passion' is one of James's richest oxymorons. The passion is there just as much as the essential coldness, in a perfect fusion of mind and feeling, abstraction and substance, art and life: 'the application, in other words, clear and calculated, crystal-firm as it were, of the idea conceived in the glow of experience, of suffering, of joy'.[11] The passion is not just for the fictional Con-

---

[10] We are just about to hear Gabriel Nash urging Nick to master his own fiddle: his talent that is 'a regular Stradivarius'.

[11] The paradoxical relation of the actor to his part—one of coldness or one of identification—was a controversial topic during the years before James wrote *The Tragic Muse*, and Diderot's *Paradoxe sur le comédien* was a key text in the debate. For this, and for a study of other points at which the novel touches on

stance: part of it is the creative heat of Miriam's first complete self-expression and self-discovery: 'Her finger at last had touched the right spring, and the capricious casket had flown open.' And Miriam's indirectly released inner life, the technique of its utterance, and what it means emotionally to Sherringham the onlooker, are all brought together in the image of the transfigured actress, who is the meeting-point of heat and coolness:

she seemed now like the finished statue lifted from the ground to its pedestal. It was as if the sun of her talent had risen above the hills and she knew that she was moving, that she would always move, in its guiding light. This conviction was the one artless thing that glimmered like a young joy through the tragic mask of Constance, and Sherringham's heart beat faster as he caught it in her face. (p. 261)

But the image of the finished statue applies to Miriam's effect, and not to the processes behind the effect. No matter how transfiguring Miriam may be, or how transfigured, her power is deeply rooted in material things and in perpetual struggle. The actress always requires to be committed to the life around her, the life of the streets as well as the life of the theatre, even if it means her being 'compromised' in the eyes of drawing-room society:[12]

'I have learned a great deal that way; sitting beside mamma and watching people, their faces, their types, their movements. There's a great deal goes on in cafés: people come to them to talk things over, their private affairs, their complications; they have important meetings. Oh, I've observed scenes, between men and women—very quiet, terribly quiet, but tragic! Once I saw a woman do something that I'm going to do some day, when I'm great—if I can get the situation. I'll tell you what it is some day; I'll do it for you. Oh, it *is* the book of life!' (p. 159)

Apart from her study of life at close quarters, it is also her commitment to hard work and to the perfecting of a rigorous technique that preserves her sense of the real—the mastering of an art being thus seen once again as the very opposite of dilettantism. To master Miriam's particular art means accepting to a large degree the

---

issues of the day, see D. J. Gordon and John Stokes, 'The Reference of *The Tragic Muse*', in *The Air of Reality: New Essays on Henry James*, ed. J. Goode, 1972, pp. 81–167.

[12] Somewhat out of character, it is Gabriel Nash who confirms this necessity to Peter, reminding him that 'you can't make omelettes without breaking eggs'; and, 'you can't be a great actress without quivering nerves' (p. 439).

circumstances and drawbacks of the contemporary stage: only in this way can the idea take on substance, even if an imperfect substance. Undoubtedly James detested many of these circumstances in real life, and put many of his own criticisms of the London theatre into the derogatory words of Gabriel Nash and Peter Sherringham; but the profound realism of the book's total vision does in the end enforce a kind of acceptance of them.[13] Miriam herself is able to see the theatre's deficiencies very sharply, but she responds to them as a practical challenge to her powers. The artist may be none the worse for having to fight against restriction. In this she is again linked to Nick Dormer, who is always very properly bound to the earth and to his art's day-to-day requirements: 'I must just peg away here and not mind', is one very English expression of his aesthetic credo. It is Peter Sherringham, the non-artist and civil servant, who is least able to accept the worldliness of art. When he is carried away by Miriam's triumph on the London stage, he does, it is true, realize that 'he had never seen her before; he had never seen her till he saw her in her conditions . . . they were paltry enough as yet . . . but . . . the uplifted stage and the listening house transformed her.' But these are the conditions of the stage that he always balked at—along with the actress's unsanctified position in society, which seems to be a part of these conditions. For example, it is typical of the self-defeating extremeness of Peter's vacillating attitudes that he should launch one of his most violent attacks against the theatre on the occasion when he takes Miriam behind the scenes at the Théâtre Français (Chapters 20 and 21). There, in the drama's sanctum sanctorum, to which he has a very privileged entrée, amid the evoked history and majesty of the French stage that acts as a clarion call to Miriam's ambitions, Peter chooses to urge her to 'give it up' in order to marry him and to enter his world of social respectability and diplomatic receptions. Yet it is not as easy as it might seem to deride him in such a scene, because, typically,

---

[13] Cf. Alan Bellringer: 'James lets us view Miriam without enchantment, objectively. It is more difficult, as we read, to pay respect to what looks like her point of view. . . . If one cannot help thinking of her as culpable, it is James himself who has condemned her to this exhibition, because of his fundamental idea of the nature of actresses and his opinion of the virulently vulgar and intellectually degenerate condition of the English stage, to which Miriam's genius will have to accommodate itself' ('*The Tragic Muse*: the objective centre', *Journal of American Studies*, iv, 1970, 81–2).

James allows us to see some force in Peter's criticisms. On the visit to the Théâtre Français he certainly allows for the ambiguities that surround such well-sketched figures as the worldly Mlle Voisin, with an 'abyss' beneath her 'inimitable surface', and Mlle Dunoyer, that ageless *ingénue* of the stage, for ever rippling, for ever gay, for ever vapid and false. It is difficult to blame Peter entirely for finding it impossible to reconcile the supreme values of Miriam's art with the Voisins and the Dunoyers, the Fanny Rovers and the Basil Dashwoods, and 'all the twaddle of the shop' on which those values are propped up—though James in the end does seem to suggest that the 'twaddle' cannot easily be detached from those other practical rigours of art, hard work, serious intention, and technical expertise, that produce the 'cold passion' in which a Juliet is acted, or a Notre Dame is built.

The idealism that prevents Peter accepting the imperfections of the theatre is thoroughly mixed up with straightforward folly and egotism on his part. He is patently blind to Miriam's rights as an individual, and pushes his suit with little regard for the fact that Miriam, though interested, is far from being overcome by a passion for him. She can always see into him very calmly and very sensibly: 'He wants to enjoy every comfort and to save every appearance, and all without making a sacrifice. He expects others —me, for instance—to make all the sacrifices' (pp. 523–4). Miriam is well able to take care of herself and to guard against disappointment where a man like Peter Sherringham is concerned; but someone who is more likely to suffer is Biddy Dormer. Her relation to Peter, which is so admirably handled by James, is a further link between the two main plots, and is a very valuable adjunct to the Peter–Miriam affair: a part of the book which begins to suffer slightly from the fact that James, having got Peter into his quandary, can do little other than let him spin round and round in it. All along, we have cleverly been kept aware of the slight but real charm of the ingenuous Biddy (emphasized by the exasperating, self-righteous angularity of her ill-named sister, Grace). We have seen her loyal attachment to Nick in the pursuit of art, which she herself pursues in an amateur way. We have seen the intentness that comes over her demeanour whenever her handsome cousin Peter comes on the scene. And we feel for her in her being so eclipsed by the splendid Miriam, whom she half-likes and fears. By

E

the slightest of touches—even in the way she will lean forward to
look for Peter while Grace sits rigidly—James has managed to
create a little inner life in her as a character, a little unfulfilled
'talent' and desire of her own, and a susceptibility to affection and
to hurt. She is drawn into the centre of our attention and of the
book's concerns only after we have seen the disappointed figure
of Julia urging her brother to marry Biddy to protect himself:
'Then you would be quite in shelter, you would know the worst
that can happen to you, and it wouldn't be bad.' And from here on,
Peter uses Biddy as the second string to his bow, acting with a
patronizing gentleness that develops towards affection as Biddy
herself begins to change and reveal herself.

There is one very moving scene between the two of them
(Chapter 29) that is full of awkward movements, gestures, and
false tones—a scene that is exemplary in its use of dramatic detail.
Peter, calling to see Nick, is embarrassed to find Biddy alone in
the studio, and they both make conversation about Julia and Nick
and Miriam above their silent awareness of the fact that they are
each a suitable and half-expected match for the other: 'While they
both thought of it, they sat looking into each other's eyes.' Peter is
trapped by his awkwardness into facetiously raising the question
of what Biddy would do—all very hypothetically, and just between
cousins of course—if he were to ask her to marry him. It is quite
intolerable of him: we can read Biddy's agony between the lines.
Biddy, who feels she has no rights to anything, tries to let him off
lightly: 'her smile conveyed, at the expense of her own prospects,
such a shy, generous little mercy of reassurance.' James himself is
less merciful: 'It did not occur to him that she might have a
secret small irony to spare for his ingenious and magnanimous
impulse to show her how much he liked her in order to make her
forgive him for not liking her more.' But the deepest irony of the
scene lies in the fact that Biddy's description of Nick's heroic
sacrifice of Julia and the House of Commons for the sake of art
inspires Peter with the sudden thought of emulating such heroism
by marrying Miriam (rather than Biddy, therefore). It comes in
one of the most shining moments of connection in the novel. Here
in Nick's studio, looking at Nick's half-finished portrait of Miriam,
Peter hears 'the sudden blare of a trumpet'—just as, a few pages
before, Nick has had a similar inspiration when Nash brought
Miriam to the same studio. The aesthetic man in Peter is released

by what his artistic cousin, Nick, has created in a painting. Before the portrait, the artistic fineness of which he at once perceives, Peter experiences 'a quickened rush, a sense of the beauty of Miriam'—as he does whenever he sees Miriam framed by the stage. That is, the work of art, with its formal 'composition' and its 'look of life', at once irradiates life, his own life of unexpressed feeling, imagination, and sexuality (the same work of art that has blighted his sister's happiness when she found the model for it posing in that room). And—this is the ultimate touch—the portrait is displayed at his urgent request by Biddy. Her eyes 'plead' with him with 'a gleam of anguish', but he is too enraptured to read them. And she is made to stand there holding up for him the image of her rival. ' "Oh anything for art!" said Biddy, smiling': that is her last brave remark, thrown after a preoccupied Peter. In all that it secretly expresses of her feelings and her situation, and in the ironic way it deflates the novel's serious vindication of art, that simple phrase makes a valuable addition to James's whole complicated commentary on the relations of art to the world.

But Biddy is not out of it yet (apart even from being taken by Peter that night to the theatre to see Miriam, and to see him seeing Miriam). Her darkest moment comes after a later encounter at Nick's studio, when the prudish Peter takes her away quickly to spare her the impropriety of meeting Miriam Rooth, the professional actress, in such a place. Peter's only thought is then to dispose of Biddy with decent haste. His fumblings produce a revealing nervous tic that will occur in more and more situations towards the end of the book—'For the twentieth time Peter referred to his watch.' As he talks of Miriam, then labours out the compliment to Biddy that she, too, will be a 'charming impression' for him to remember, she walks faster and faster along the pavement—'She seemed almost to be running away from him.' He wants to dispatch her in a cab, to end the painful scene; and her sudden tiredness, and a desire for a hansom, saves him:

They were in a straight, black, ugly street, where the small, cheap, gray-faced houses had no expression save that of a rueful, inconsolable consciousness of its want of identity. They would have constituted a 'terrace' if they could, but they had given it up. Even a hansom which loitered across the end of the vista turned a sceptical back upon it, so that Sherringham had to lift his voice in a loud appeal. He stood with

Biddy watching the cab approach them. 'This is one of the charming things you'll remember', she said, turning her eyes to the general dreariness from the particular figure of the vehicle, which was antiquated and clumsy. Before he could reply she had lightly stepped into the cab; but as he answered: 'Most assuredly it is', and prepared to follow her, she quickly closed the apron.

'I must go alone; you've lots of things to do—it's all right'; and through the aperture in the roof she gave the driver her address. She had spoken with decision, and Peter recognized that she wished to get away from him. Her eyes betrayed it as well as her voice, in a look—not a hard one however—which as he stood there with his hand on the cab he had time to take from her. 'Good-bye, Peter,' she smiled; and as the cab began to rumble away he uttered the same tepid, ridiculous farewell. (pp. 512–13)

The little vignette is almost emblematic. It is the way London might have struck a lost and wandering Hyacinth Robinson in *The Princess Casamassima*. It is all a vista of frustration and 'want of identity': Biddy's and Peter's, as much as that of the 'grey-faced houses'. Everything in the scene before this has been grey and desolate: a dreariness of clumsy, ugly incomprehension between otherwise charming people. Like the picture of Julia Dallow driving in the foggy park, or the whole scene of Nick Dormer's proposal, it is part of that general encroachment of falsity and disappointment against the vision of a life of truth and beauty that makes for the large-scale tensions of this novel, and keeps us aware of the darker possibilities contained in its title.

It is a similar grey vista, in effect, that marks the close of Peter's adventure with Miriam—a revenge for Biddy, if she could have seen him face it. In a splendidly dramatic *scène à faire* (Chapter 46), in the garden and in the drawing-room at Balaklava Place on the night of Miriam's greatest theatrical success so far, Peter, inspired by what he has seen on the stage, makes his last bid for happiness. 'I'll marry you to-morrow if you'll renounce; and in return for the sacrifice you make for me I'll do more for you than ever was done for a woman before', is Peter's plea. It is now that for the only time Peter makes an imaginative appeal on behalf of the career for which he is asking Miriam to give up her art—'the responsibility and the honour of great affairs'. When she argues that without her talent, which is only for the theatre, she would be a mere 'third-rate woman', Peter's reply has great cogency, and much of the book's weight seems to be piled behind it: 'Your talent is yourself, and it's because it's yourself that I yearn for you . . . You were made to charm and console, to represent beauty and harmony and variety to miserable human beings; and the daily life of man is the theatre for that.' It seems, in its way, as impassioned a plea as any in the book for the amalgamation of art and life. But for a person like Miriam it is sadly a sophistry and a mirage: a Beauclere-vision to delude her. She can see as well as we can the impossibility of her personal talent fully expressing itself within Peter's social round. And her 'theatre' just as much as his—perhaps more than his— belongs to 'the daily life of man'. She can support herself by referring to Nick's sacrifice as against Peter's perpetual demands. And she answers him memorably in his own words, as James makes his people do so often, using the same terms to establish opposed conclusions: that her husband would be ennobled by *her*, and by his opportunity to marry her art even more fully to experience. Miriam's contemplation of the idea of marriage produces 'a splendid vision' of harmony and completeness that is at once the ideal for art and for the private life. The great thing about acting, Miriam says, is—

'the way we simply stir people's souls. Ah, there's where life can help us', she broke out, with a change of tone, 'there's where human rela- tions and affections can help us; love and faith and joy and suffering and experience—I don't know what to call 'em! They suggest things, they light them up and sanctify them, as you may say; they make them appear worth doing'. She became radiant for a moment, as if with a splendid vision; then melting into still another accent, which seemed all nature and harmony, she proceeded: 'I must tell you that in the matter of what we can do for each other I have a tremendously high ideal. I go in for closeness of union, for identity of interest. A true marriage, as they call it, must do one a lot of good!' (pp. 554–5)

Peter drops back in defeat from the Tragic Muse's bright vision— excluded from her 'perfection of perfections'—into the opposite, which is like the fragmented desolation of Biddy's street of grey- faced houses:

gazing defeatedly, doggedly, into the featureless night, into the little black garden which had nothing to give him but a familiar smell of damp. The warm darkness had no relief for him, and Miriam's histrionic hardness flung him back against a fifth-rate world, against a bedimmed, star-punctured nature which had no consolation—the bleared, irre-sponsive eyes of the London heaven. For the brief space that he glared at these things he dumbly and helplessly raged. What he wanted was something that was not in *that* thick prospect. (p. 555)

In the garden, left alone with the twittering, parodic encourage-ments of a still-hopeful Mrs. Rooth—'All you've got to do is to be yourself—to be true to your fine position . . . we must take a still firmer hold of the *real* life, of the true anchor'—Peter utters his final execration and denial of one half of his own nature: 'Art be damned.' And in this phrase, which is the offset of her own 'Oh anything for art!', Biddy, somewhere off stage, has her little triumphant *quart d'heure*.

Considering ways by which he might bring together his two main plots, James resisted one very obvious temptation: that of making his two committed artists, Nick and Miriam, fall in love, while the two 'politicians', Peter and Julia, were left to wither on the branch. He tells us in the Preface that he would have liked to show show Nick and Miriam at least becoming lovers, but was inhibited by the restrictions of periodical publication. And he remarks that Miriam would easily have given up her life in the theatre for Nick, since he is a fellow practitioner.[14] But both points—if we are to take them as more than whimsical—are peculiarly incongruous with the details and the general tenor of these two characters as he actually created them. Nick hangs around Balaklava Place from time to time—frequently enough to make Peter jealous. But he is always detached from that scene, and is always a little surprised himself at how unattracted he is by Miriam as a woman: 'He could paint Miriam, day after day, without any agitating blur of vision; in fact the more he saw of her the clearer grew the atmos-phere through which she blazed, the more her richness became one with that of the flowering picture' (p. 570). If this is an example of the 'cold passion of art' in operation, it is not to suggest in general that art and sex are basically opposed. The main reason for Nick's predominantly aesthetic interest in Miriam is that his sexual feelings for Julia have never really disappeared, and are now —as he paints Miriam and becomes firmly engaged in his new career—in the very process of coming to a fuller and more confi-dent expression than ever before (Julia is brought back to the story

14 *The Art of the Novel*, pp. 96, 93.

at the first moment that Miriam and Nick could really have been free enough to develop their relationship). It is mainly the unreliable Gabriel Nash who spreads the idea—for example, to Peter and to Nick himself—that Miriam is secretly in love with the painter. Miriam obviously cherishes an inclination of a kind. She is struck by Nick and takes a different tone with him from the one she uses with all the others of her set—mainly because he is so detached, so apparently complete in himself, so very different from his attentive and exhausting cousin Peter. But it remains an inclination only, and a flash of possibility in the plot that is quite quickly extinguished. The idea of Miriam abandoning the stage to be a painter's helpmate is laughably unconvincing, even to Gabriel Nash who envisages it.

The temptation to marry off Nick and Miriam is also the reader's. There is inevitably a curiosity and a desire on our part, no matter how repressed, to see two such luminaries in conjunction. But in keeping them apart the book is true to its basic inspiration—much more true than the author's remarks in the Preface, years later. This is a realistic novel in several senses: realist in technique, realist in attitude. And by disappointing our faint and facile expectations about Nick and Miriam it forswears the high romantic line—the Christina Light–Roderick Hudson line—and holds us to the point that life is anticlimactic by nature. In addition, as has been said, there is much in the detailed development of each character that we recognize as preventing such a resolution, in terms of motivation and consistency. And when each has had to bear the burden of separately representing the destiny of the rising artist, the two being brought together, one feels, would be too much of a good thing: one fire would put out the other. But on top of that, even, the failure of Miriam and Nick to marry fits the book's whole presentation of the artistic life as a battle, a discouragement, and a perpetual struggle with detail. Art, the book says, has its heroisms and grandeurs, but it is also very largely based on sacrifice and niggling compromise. And a grand rewarding passion between two such toilers would not be the culmination this view suggests—nor would it be a dénouement in keeping with the whole tone of the ending, which is the very Jamesian tone of a rueful and ironic acceptance of the mundane.

It is the way Nick and Miriam converge, in the latter part of the novel, consider one another speculatively, exchange ideas, and

then go their entirely separate ways, that paradoxically confirms
the final unification of James's plot-scheme. It satisfies our sense
of form, our sense of the fitting, that the two most successful and
active people in the book should be seen close together near the
end in several intense scenes; and it confirms our reading of the
coherent ideas behind the book's double plot that Nick and Miriam
should separate. For one thing, the two characters are connected
at this stage by that fear of failure that is always, for James,
integral to the experience of the practising artist (as we saw in
Roderick Hudson). At the same moment in the plot that Peter is
discarded in the dark, dank garden in St. John's Wood, Nick begins
to slide into the doldrums. His technical facility threatens to take
him over—he sees himself as being 'too clever by half'[15]—and
inspiration begins to fail with his loss of confidence. He visits the
National Gallery and is perversely overcome by the futility of all
artistic effort, compared with the practical achievements of the
politics he has abandoned: 'The force that produced [the paintings]
was not one of the greatest forces in human affairs; their place was
inferior and their connection with the life of man casual and slight.
They represented so inadequately the idea, and it was the idea that
won the race, that in the long run came in first' (p. 488). It is only
a passing phase, and the National Gallery will soon convey to him
a very different lesson of reassurance. But the mood of it is important. It is a mood that goes beyond the question of art. For
example, it moves Nick to discover that the 'freedom' he has
attained by breaking with Julia is far from complete; that the
pressures of family and friends in his new situation in life are as
great as in his old life, and that existence in general clamps down
on any individual's aspirations:

though only asking to live without too many questions and work
without too many disasters, to be glad and sorry in short on easy terms,
[he] had become aware of a certain social tightness, of the fact that
life is crowded and passion is restless, accident is frequent and community inevitable. Everybody with whom one had relations had other

---

[15] This is exactly the danger James had seen awaiting that real-life prodigy
of portraitists, John Singer Sargent, in 1887: 'It may be better for an artist',
James brooded, 'to have a certain part of his property invested in unsolved
difficulties'—at the same time as he expressed the belief that 'There is no
greater work of art than a great portrait' (*The Painter's Eye*, ed. J. L. Sweeney,
London, 1956, pp. 223, 227).

relations too, and even optimism was a mixture and peace an embroil-
ment. (p. 490)

'Relations' is usually a very positive concept for James, signifying
the internal structure of art and also (as we have seen in this
novel) art's connections with everyday life. And it is part of the
very realistic view of the artist being propounded here that we
should now have a hint of 'relations' being invidious, and of those
same connections on which art relies also being a cause of its
decline.

Miriam has fallen into the same temporary doldrums, even at
the height of the London season and of her own success in it, and
describes them as she sits to Nick, having another portrait painted.
It is the last important encounter between them, and a scene (in
Chapter 48) that is a model of how well James handles their
tentative relationship. Each envies the other: Nick silently, as he
contemplates his own 'wasted youth' and uncertain 'fruition'
compared with the actress's more immediate glory; she with a
histrionic forcefulness, as she dismisses her own 'successful
crudities' and 'screeching', laments the pressures of the box-office
compared with Nick's solitary dedication, and (as Nick has just
done in his own case) disparages her tendency to the merely clever.
It is a moment of very real, if very ironic, communion between
them, each of them finding in the other a momentary image of a
richer fulfilment than he or she has yet achieved. The communion
is also very personal, on a level below the surface generalities of
their talk about art, and below Miriam's slightly feverish banter—
Nick has never seen her so inconsequential and nervous, though
he has several times before seen her as sardonic at her own
expense. It is that different tone she often takes when in his
company—self-disparaging yet attention-seeking; but this time it
is even more suggestive of her private inclination for him, in that
she has really come to make a farewell of a kind. It is all between
the lines—marvellously so—even to her casual allusion to her
dream of having a perfect manager who would allow her to develop
her technique. Because as we have already seen, Basil Dashwood,
that supremely practical if mildly asinine young manager, is very
much a member of her retinue, and is presumably in her mind at
this moment as a convenient husband, while she comes (a little
speculatively, perhaps) to tell Nick she will not sit for her portrait

any more. Little gestures aid the expressiveness of the encounter: Miriam arranging her hat before the glass as she asks Nick about his other models and alludes disingenuously to Julia Dallow; Nick non-committal on that subject, with his hands in his pockets; Miriam playing with her parasol at the door; and then her bravely nonchalant exit, 'floating away to her victoria' with a laugh, as she finally abandons the field to Julia. It is done with perfect lightness: an approach and a separation; a brief and wistful *pas de deux* between them. And its very last movement is one of the author's cleverest. Nick is apparently so affected by the undertones of the scene that he suddenly shows a 'strange' candidness to her, just as she leaves, about his mixed feelings for Julia: only a moment before, he had thought it would be arrant tastelessness if he so much as mentioned that question. In its more hidden way it is like the unhappy Biddy being asked to hold up Miriam's first portrait for Peter to admire. Nick has been sufficiently touched by his conversation with one woman for the image of the other to loom up more clearly in his mind, and for him virtually to ask Miriam for her advice about Julia. But a 'supervening candour' sees the two artists through at the last: she advises on the side of his Mrs. Dallow; he watches her go off in the direction of her Mr. Dashwood; and the personal link between them dissolves into the theatrical radiance of Miriam's departing smile and the colder passion of art which they must separate to pursue.

Miriam's marrying Basil Dashwood is of course a considerable anticlimax: he is incongruously trivial, and she seems to know it as clearly as anyone else. But being a prosaic compromise, it is congruent with that general movement of the book towards accepting the contingent and the half-perfect. And it is lifelike, too— gifted women having been known to marry beneath them. Her art seems to require it, and perhaps her personality does too. 'Doesn't it look as if we should pull beautifull together?', she asks Nick later, when the news comes out: 'What will you have? It seemed simpler! It was clear there had to be some one.' If it is on the stage, rather than in a diplomat's drawing-room, that Miriam will fulfil herself and create some beauty for the world, then a Basil Dashwood, self-effacing and a born 'arranger', a man of his time, will be one of the enabling conditions of that success. Though certainly not offering the perfect union that Miriam so eloquently described to Peter, Dashwood is far from being the most fatal form that the contingent and the imperfect can take. For Nick and Miriam are able to be active artists to the end only because they believe in making your beauty out of what you can get, and in coming through your doldrums by recognizing that though it is bad to fall short of an ideal anything is better than ceasing to *do*. There is no excellence without action, in art or in life, and there is no action without shortcoming.[16] The London stage, and Basil Dashwood, are what they are, but something not too bad might possibly be done with them. The only alternative to such realistic compromise is to be a Peter Sherringham or a Gabriel Nash. And significantly, Nick and Miriam's exchange of beliefs about art, in the scene between them we have just discussed, involved a dismissal of Nash. He set both artists in train, as it were, but they both now accept his disappearance into limbo—his charming, greenery-yallery limbo—with the superiority of the practitioner over the mere intelligent critic and theorist. And the latter is primarily distinguished in this case from the practitioner by feeling discomfort—as Nick sardonically tells Miriam—at mere vulgar 'applications' and 'consequences' as opposed to 'the reasons and the essences of things': 'to come down to the little questions of actions—the little prudences and compromises and simplifications of practice—is for the superior person a really fatal descent.' Miriam's sharp response to this is the striking of a key-note. ' "The simplifications of practice?" cried Miriam. "Why, they are just precisely the most blessed things on earth. What should we do without them?" ' (pp. 584–5). Basil Dashwood will be one of her 'simplifications'—a risky one, as all simplifications and practical compromises have to be. Nick's helpful 'simplifications' include the facility of technique that depresses him on occasion, and results in several works of art that Peter, looking round the studio, privately considers to be 'unpromising productions'. But then Peter is, like Nash, a man menaced by inanition and impotence through refusing to risk the imperfect—as he recognized in himself, early on, when he 'took up' Miriam as a tyro: 'He had fine ideas, but she was to do the acting, that is the application of them, and not he; and application

---

[16] James himself writes quite characteristically, in *The Lesson of Balzac*, in 1905, 'there is no art at all, we are often reminded, that is not on too many sides an abject compromise. The element of compromise is always there; it is of the essence; we live with it, and it may serve to keep us humble' (*The House of Fiction*, ed. Leon Edel, London, 1957, p. 80).

was always of necessity a sort of vulgarization, a smaller thing than theory' (p. 180). And in that difference between Peter and his protégée on a question of art lay the roots of the personal, even the passional, failure on his part. Despite the lack of a passion between the two most dedicated artists of all—Nick and Miriam—it is worth remembering from the case of Peter Sherringham, and even from the cases of Gabriel Nash and the late George Dallow, that the pragmatic 'vulgarizations' of the active artist are essentially more compatible with sexual involvement than are the attitudes of the uncommitted theorist. Sexual passion is not, at any rate, as straightforward an enemy of art, in this book, as a reading of some of James's short stories about artists might suggest; and it is always accepted by Miriam herself, for example, as a feature of art's contingency—one of its necessary 'relations' with the world of emotions and with 'the book of life'.

The sense of broad reconciliation in which this novel ends is based on such acceptances of compromise—and of the compromising. Its realism of attitude and its commitment to the idea of personal fulfilment through action and struggle provide the solidest possible underpinning to its worship of the beautiful. Even philistinism itself is not castigated. James takes great pleasure in the little group of blatant philistines who assemble at Beauclere, for example, and sees in someone like the lovingly sketched Mrs. Lendon, sister of Mr. Carteret, a real and lasting value: 'the goodness of these people was singularly pure: they were a part of what was cleanest and sanest and dullest in humanity.' Philistinism seems even to blend into that early vulgarity and lack of refined 'good taste' which remain among the sustaining strengths of Miriam's nature, and by which her artistic achievements are supported. Perhaps even Nick's survival as an artist will be helped by that very slight touch of the muscular conventionality of his race and class which we saw on his first appearance, in the Palais de l'Industrie, and which will help him to accommodate himself and his art to the country-houses in the end. Nick and Miriam did both agree, with ironic delight, that in their so prizing the 'simplifications' of art they made a pair of 'awful Philistines'.

Peter Sherringham will be supported in his disappointment by his 'immemorial compact formation' of this very same philistinism; though quite properly it is art that has the last word with him, and with the others. When he comes back from his posting to Central

America to see Miriam's long-awaited triumph as Juliet—and, absurdly, to try his luck once again, too late—it is the perfection of Miriam's performance that at last affects him with 'assuagement'. Art restores life, at least to the extent of recalling Peter to what is sensible, and making him turn to Biddy Dormer with a decent if modest affection. His marriage to her may be prudential, but it is also perfectly approvable and convincing—another very natural compromise, and one that is at least an action, and far better than his former helpless indecision. And as for Nick and Julia, they seem to be borne on the same current. It is the current that Gabriel Nash prophesied for the two of them, and which he has himself finally rejected by fleeing from the ordeal of having his portrait painted by Nick—since in the actual processes of painting, as in life's foreseeable compromises, there has always lurked for Nash the threat of time, old age, and mortality: so bound is art in the long run to the conditions of common experience. This had been his sardonic prophecy to the rising painter:

'Your differences with the beautiful lady will be patched up, and you'll each come round a little and meet the other half-way. . . . She'll put up with the palette if you'll put up with the country-house. . . . You'll go about with her and do all her friends, all the bishops and ambassadors, and you'll eat your cake and have it . . . and everything will be for the best in the best of worlds.' (pp. 592–3)

And indeed, Nick, having made 'conditions' with the lady, paints Julia, who in return forfeits the faith of her highest political friends; and on the other side of James's closing question-mark the couple will probably marry in the end, in a mutual compromise almost as fraught with hazard for the future as Miriam's marriage with Dashwood. It is far too much to say that James gives us, at the last, the best in the best of worlds. For all these people it is a world that has not quite matched up to what it promised, and we feel a qualm at the forms it has finally provided for all that talent and energy and thought and feeling. But nevertheless our sense of reconciliation is a very profound one, as profound as at the end of all great comedies; and the profundity is that of James's eventual submission to life and its limiting conditions. The harmony of the ending rises out of the whole book's harmony of tone, plot, and motif, as James himself claimed in the Preface—a perfect harmony between technical means and imaginative ends, and between an author's personal vision and his fictional material. It is also a harmony of language: a sustaining and unifying style balanced between wit, scrupulous sensitivity, and magisterial weight. But the harmony, on another level, is one that emanates from James's decision in *The Tragic Muse* that there are no simple conclusions as to the relative merits and truths of 'the world' and 'art', the free 'expanse' of life and the shaping window of the mind. The conclusion he offers is only this: that truth itself lies in relationship and movement, including the movement of decline; that art is very worldly and very human and exceedingly onerous; that the world, to be our world, must go on being painted and staged, as well as being legislated for or merely endured; and that to be true to oneself and one's talent, in the practice of art or in other ways, is to be in the most intimate and fulfilling relationship with the world's daily life of circumstance, and also with that deeper, creative life of the world in which James believed. Talent, which it may be death to hide, is a man's or a woman's private creativity; but ultimately it is the world's creativity, too.

5

The Passion of Fleda Vetch

THERE is no greater contrast between any two consecutively written novels by James than between *The Tragic Muse* and *The Spoils of Poynton*. The contrast is between the broad, humane realism of the one and the other's more mannered concision and concern with extremer reaches of motivation and moral value. And though the differences never obscure from us the common origin of the two works, which is evident in both style and theme, they are pronounced enough to indicate a turning-point, even a lacuna, in their author's career. After the completion of *The Tragic Muse* came the most troubled decade in James's life as a writer: the ill-starred theatrical ventures of the mid-nineties, six years without a full-length novel, and then the search for a new mode in his fiction that would satisfy the urge for compact dramatic projection that his writing for the stage had stimulated and yet in the end had so dismally frustrated. This is when the sureness of James's writing most faltered, and the period of what is perhaps his most controversial group of novels: *The Spoils of Poynton* (1897), *What Maisie Knew* (1897), *The Awkward Age* (1899), and *The Sacred Fount* (1901) (together with *The Other House*, 1896, and *The Turn of the Screw*, 1898). James's great problem as an artist from the time of the first novel he wrote (the very gauche *Watch and Ward*) was how to incarnate his sensibility: how to realize it firmly within the clear outer shapes of action and characters in such a way that his private disabilities could become artistic advantages, personal feelings could gain clarity from formal detachment, and contrived fictional structures could gain vitality from feelings. It was really a version of the problem which faced so many of his unfulfilled heroes and heroines, and which faces any writer. He sought to spend himself, to declare and articulate his inner conception in the outer forms of an action—the 'imitated action', in Aristotle's phrase, that constitutes plot. Of these novels of the period, *The Sacred Fount*, for all its appeal to our modern interest in ambivalence, parody, and aesthetic texture, is the one in which James's full imagination and feelings seem to be most dissociated from his craftsman's virtuosity and his intellectual sportiveness. There is something of a vacuum at the heart of the labyrinth. Other aspects, too, of the later James are disquieting: the note of morbidity and self-pity; the occasional simple failure of taste that makes *The Other House*, for example, so inhuman a work; the occasions when James seems to have lost contact with some of the facts of common feeling and common behaviour; the sense of sustained mental process beginning to erode the tangible world. Every reader, surely, has had his bad moments with James—and even before the full onset of the late style. Considered as a whole, his fiction is one of the most delicately balanced of all major achievements in our literature, and his great strengths as a writer are such that they are liable at times to appear precisely as his greatest weaknesses.

The Spoils of Poynton—though many readers have seen it as another example of the later James walking his tightrope, and even as a case-study in Jamesian neuroticism—appears to me on the whole to be a very different affair. It illustrates the way in which James can suddenly, even a little to his own surprise perhaps, come upon a fulfilling image—a character, a situation— that will absorb and precipitate, in full coherence, some of his best powers and most deeply felt interests. It is a book that is sometimes said to show James's obsessive concern with renuncia- tion—a motif which undoubtedly appears often enough in varying forms through his works to make us always alert to the danger of its taking on, at any point, the deadening aspect of an *idée fixe*. The frequency of its appearance is no doubt significant in itself for the biographer, but the initial concern of the critic is to consider each work in its own right, and only to turn to the concept of the personal *idée fixe* to explain a failure, or a peculiarity, that has first been diagnosed in literary terms.[1] And *The Spoils of Poynton*,

---

[1] The *idée fixe* sometimes seems to be that of the critic, rather than James. C. C. Walcutt's over-emphasis on 'renunciation', for example, makes James's characters sound like the crowded inmates of a Victorian lunatic asylum: 'His people are everywhere missing the boat, failing to speak or act, retreating into a hundred protective corners where the self huddles in a posture of refusal, refining its perceptions and sensibilities precisely because it is not strenuously living' (*Man's Changing Mask: Modes and Methods of Characterization in Fiction*, Minneapolis, Minn., 1966, p. 181).

while a novel of considerable difficulty, and one that will always provoke varying interpretations, does establish itself, I think, as a validly rounded and graspable work of art. It is too subtle and qualified in its attitudes to be obsessive, essentially too recognizable in terms of human value and traditional literary form—comic and tragic—to be merely subjective or impenetrably ambiguous. And if it values the moral power that genuinely difficult renunciation can purchase, it also (as so often in James) provides a critique of renunciation, by showing the value of things contrary to it: expansion, personal power, marriage, the possible fusion of aesthetic taste with will and feeling. It is a story about human passions rather than perversity: conflicting passions for a house, for precious objects, for a man, for common goodness and uncommon goodness, for imaginative contemplation, for simple action, and for moral discrimination. And when each of these passions appears in the life of one person—Fleda Vetch—the result is a central character as vivid, as racked, and as intimately known to us as any that James created.[2]

Though *The Spoils of Poynton* may not be perverse or wilfully obscure in content, its style offers certain problems which have clearly contributed to the unease many people have felt about the book. Yet the problems are only a developed version of those we have touched on in almost every work so far discussed. It is basically a case of stylization—of that peculiarly Jamesian stylization that makes the question of narrative 'point of view' in the novels rather more complex than is allowed for in the Prefaces or by the analyses of Percy Lubbock and his successors. The Jamesian narrative mode is never really one of a totally 'sunk' point of view—within Fleda's 'theatre of consciousness', say. It is an extraordinary mixture of meditative authorial monologue and

---

[2] So much has been written on *The Spoils of Poynton* from the most diametrically opposed standpoints—Fleda as angel, Fleda as egotist, Fleda romanticized, Fleda ironized, Mrs. Gereth good, Mrs. Gereth bad, James as pro-Spoils, James as anti-Spoils, James as out of his depth—that one wonders at times whether Swift's Grand Academy of Lagado may not have had its section devoted to James studies. The reader is referred to Oscar Cargill's résumé in *The Novels of Henry James*, New York, 1961, pp. 218–43, supplemented by the best-known of the 'ironic' readings of the novel, R. C. McLean, 'The Subjective Adventure of Fleda Vetch', *American Literature*, xxxvi, 1964–5, 12–30. An altercation on *The Spoils* was conducted between Alan Bellringer and John Lucas over three volumes of *Essays in Criticism*, 1966–8, in which many of the main issues and critics were touched on (and slightly trampled on).

dramatized action and dialogue, both of the latter being nevertheless essentially within the former, and never entirely detached
from that one presiding, intelligent voice—though detached
enough for variety and dramatic conviction. This unity of personal
tone, which is never egotistic and always maintains its own form
of negative capability, is one that can accommodate in this book
an almost innocent limpidity on the one hand and a highly wrought
theatricality on the other—a combination that produces by the
end a full dramatic poetry of complex human behaviour and
emotion. At the beginning, especially, we find a system of simple
and even farcical schematic contrasts and character-profiles,
expressed through allusions or images that have been wittily
refined and developed to the point of grotesqueness. The un-
redeemable ugliness of Waterbath (the House Ugly), set against
the natural and artistic perfection of Poynton (the House
Beautiful—as James originally and unhappily entitled the story),
is of such a kind that even in the garden 'The flowers would
probably go wrong in colour and the nightingales sing out
of tune.' The horror of the wallpaper has kept Mrs. Gereth awake
in her room, and both she and Fleda have 'given way to tears'
at the sight of 'comic water-colours and Centennial souvenirs'.
For the sensitive spirit it is a relief to see 'the great tranquil sky,
from which no blue saucers were suspended'. And perhaps most
grotesque of all: 'The worst horror was the acres of varnish,
something advertised and smelly, with which everything was
smeared: it was Fleda Vetch's conviction that the application of it,
by their own hands and hilariously shoving each other, was the
amusement of the Brigstocks on rainy days.'[3] Waterbath, in fact,
is presented as something of a small-scale Timon's Villa, a place of
representative falsity and aridity, with even its own comic equivalent of 'Nilus' dusty urn': 'She remembered at Waterbath a
conservatory where she had caught a bad cold in the company of a
stuffed cockatoo fastened to a tropical bough and a waterless
fountain composed of shells stuck into some hardened paste'
(p. 35). The Brigstocks' farewell to Poynton, at the end of their
first and last visit to Mrs. Gereth there (bearing her the unwanted
gift of a modish ladies' magazine), culminates in a complete cartoon,

    [3] *The Spoils of Poynton*, London, 1897, p. 6. Future page-references are to
this, the first English edition.

in which Owen's remark seems to be printed in a little balloon
above his head:

Mrs. Gereth, delivering herself from the doorstep, had tossed the
periodical higher in air than was absolutely needful—tossed it toward
the carriage the retreating party was about to enter. Mona, from the
force of habit, the reflex action of the custom of sport, had popped out,
with a little spring, a long arm and intercepted the missile as easily as
she would have caused a tennis-ball to rebound from a racket. 'Good
catch!' Owen had cried, so genuinely pleased that practically no
notice was taken of his mother's impressive remarks. It was to the
accompaniment of romping laughter, as Mrs. Gereth afterwards said,
that the carriage had rolled away. (pp. 37–8)

Characters, especially the secondary figures like Owen and
Mona, are identified by almost surreally isolated details of
appearance and attitude. Mona has a 'voice like the squeeze of
a doll's stomach' and 'eyes that might have been blue beads, the
only ones she had'. And, very memorably, she becomes associated
with the hard shining toes of her patent-leather shoes that she
likes to kick up to contemplate—the very image of Mona the self-
regarding, Mona the patient and the stubborn, Mona of the
unmitigated will, whose very ignorance is always 'obscurely
active'. Owen, similarly, if very much more sympathetically, is
'all nature in one pair of boots'; he is stature; he is flashing white
teeth; his impatience shines 'in his idle eyes as the dining-hour
shines in club-windows'; and in his room he displays fifteen rifles
and forty whips. For Mrs Brigstock there is this cruel ideogram:
'She had a face of which it was impossible to say anything but
that it was pink, and a mind that it would be possible to describe
only if one had been able to mark it in a similar fashion. As nature
had made this organ neither green nor blue nor yellow there was
nothing to know it by: it strayed and bleated like an unbranded
sheep' (p. 183). And as for Mrs. Gereth, she enters a room 'in a
dressing-gown and a high fever'; administers to Fleda 'a kiss
apparently intended to knock her into position'; and thrusts the
reluctant girl 'down the fine open mouth (it showed such perfect
teeth) with which poor Owen's slow cerebration gaped'. She
reacts to the replacement of Poynton by Ricks as to an amputation
—'Her leg had come off—she had now begun to stump along
with the lovely wooden substitute.' And the thought of her

living at Ricks without the Spoils around her is to Fleda like the 'idea of Marie Antionette in the Conciergerie, or perhaps the vision of some tropical bird, the creature of hot, dense forests, dropped on a frozen moor to pick up a living' (p. 155).

The development of Fleda's relationship with Mrs. Gereth—and it is Fleda's relations with everyone and everything that comprises the structure of the novel—is in accord with this style of witty and slightly eccentric refraction. Its movement is jerky and highly compressed, and is marked by exceptional intimacies and exceptional oppositions which alternate with some violence. Throughout the affair the two women are for ever embracing and weeping, or else flying apart in explosive derision (from Mrs. Gereth) and tremulous disapproval (from Fleda). Fleda from the very start has strong reservations towards her new friend and protectress. She can see with utmost clarity the deficiencies of Mrs. Gereth's sensibility, the more corrosive effects of her 'taste', and the peculiarly auxiliary, not to say servile, position which she, Fleda, is being forced to take up. Fleda's reserves and disapprovals—at one point she even comes to hate Mrs. Gereth 'for an hour'— are in fact one measure of her attachment to the older woman. Theirs is an intimacy that thrives on disagreement and failure to understand—and we feel it is a very real if very limited relationship. It even seems to thrive on the tension created by their financial and social differences—differences which have considerable importance in the book. It is Mrs. Gereth's social position that allows her her cutting edge and her high sardonic style (in which James so delights); and it is the threatened loss of that position, through the rule that the son inherits before the widow, that explains so much of her bitterness. And it is Fleda's much greater financial insecurity and utter loneliness on the merest fringe of society that help to draw her towards Mrs. Gereth in the first place—even Fleda's travelling-bag has to be a gift from her companion. But these same social factors also confirm her distance from Mrs. Gereth in moral terms, since they have obviously fostered her inwardness, her private spiritual ardour, her hesitancy and scrupulosity. Fleda has struck many readers as a disguised New England heroine, and one could perhaps interpret the detailed squalors of her life at 10 Raphael Road, or at Maggie's in the suburbs, as the equivalent of that American social penury which James associates elsewhere with the self-consuming spiritualities and intensities of New England. The social and monetary distance between Fleda and Mrs. Gereth is as marked as the distance between beautiful Poynton and philistine Waterbath, and it represents James's perpetual concern with the gap that so often opens up between intelligence and worldly power, scruple and financial mobility: one thinks of the aristocratic sensitivity of a Hyacinth Robinson, fatally trapped in the North London slums; one thinks of the social forces built up against the remaining scruples of Kate Croy and Charlotte Stant. No doubt Philip Rahv has a case when he regrets, mildly, that James valued personal relationships at the expense of a sense of history, and no one could seriously claim that *The Spoils of Poynton* is a diagnosis of class and wealth in nineteenth-century England.[4] But given the primacy of James's interest in the moral and psychological crisis within the individual, he can also suggest so well, in terms of all these different material pressures that come to bear on his individuals, facts and conflicts of the most general kind, economic and cultural as well as metaphysical. There is certainly a strong economic and social element in the story of Fleda Vetch, Mrs. Gereth, and the Brigstocks, and a clear implication—though it remains an implication—about the era (Mrs. Gereth calls it 'this awful age') that could precipitate such rabid contentions and such uncertainty as to values. And in any event, one might add, it would be a very inadequate sense of history, and a very mechanical analysis of society, that was not grounded in something of the Jamesian sensitivity to human relations and emotions.

What first brings Fleda and Mrs. Gereth together across the gap is their passionate awareness of the power of beauty. Mrs. Gereth's has been achieved through long experience in collecting, but Fleda's is unacquisitive and inborn ('The museums had done something for her, but nature had done more')—and in this distinction, already, lies the root of other differences. Many of the contrasts between the two women emerge like this from an initial and close similarity. Both display 'passion' and 'patience', and they both exercise 'cunning'—in the elder's case it is on behalf

---

[4] Philip Rahv, *Image and Idea*, Norfolk, Conn., 1949, p. 70. John Lucas, however, suggests that 'Probably the best way of approaching *The Spoils of Poynton* is via Veblen's *Theory of the Leisure Class*' (*Essays in Criticism*, xvi, 1966, 482).

of the beautiful things she wishes to protect and to possess, and in the younger's case it is on behalf of 'the right' (which has a beauty of its own). Both are established as being heroic, even Quixotic: the imagery of the battlefield, often comically, is applied to both, and at one point we hear Mrs. Gereth crying, in a voice that could be Fleda's, 'When I know I'm right, I go to the stake.' Fleda, again, is not simply passive in contrast with Mrs. Gereth's manipulative and self-aggrandizing strengths, for at her very first meeting with Owen we are told: 'She herself was prepared, if she should ever marry, to contribute all the cleverness, and she liked to think that her husband would be a force grateful for direction. She was in her small way a spirit of the same family as Mrs. Gereth' (p. 9). Throughout the story she is the most important potential agent of change: there are more reins in her hands, to pull or not to pull, than in anyone else's, even the distant Mona's. Yet it quickly becomes clear that Fleda imposes limits on her own power to direct others—and that in this self-limitation lies her greatest power of actual moral activity, and her greatest distinction from the undiscriminating 'cleverness' of Mrs. Gereth. Mrs. Gereth's pride is another of her most salient features; and Fleda, too, is perpetually alert to when she is being used or humiliated, and to her need to save something of her own identity when she is financially so beset and so forced into the role of a 'parasite'— 'She couldn't do anything at all, in short, unless she could do it with a kind of pride.' And in a similar way, if James explores the differences between Fleda's and Mrs. Gereth's perception of the beautiful, he also allows important likenesses to stand, and argues openly for the presence of 'an element of creation, of personality' in Mrs. Gereth's relation to the Spoils: 'It was not the crude love of possession; it was the need to be faithful to a trust and loyal to an idea.' Again, 'she cared nothing for mere possession. She thought solely and incorruptibly of what was best for the things'—to the extent of being prepared to forgo them for herself if only a married Fleda and Owen might cherish them in Poynton, their true home and setting. Mrs. Gereth is never the amasser of dead *objets* but the kind of appreciator who contributes to the expressiveness of their beauty by her sensitive response—a positive view of connoisseurship that James did not invoke in the case of George Dallow, in *The Tragic Muse*. She humanizes her collection of 'things' into 'the record of a life', and, more importantly, evokes their own living quality: 'There isn't one of them I don't know and love—yes, as one remembers and cherishes the happiest moments of one's life. Blindfold, in the dark, with the brush of a finger, I could tell one from another. They're living things to me; they know me, they return the touch of my hand. . . . There's a care they want, there's a sympathy that draws out their beauty' (p. 32). The trouble with Mrs. Gereth is not at all that she is a sterile aesthete but that her 'taste' is, like most of her attainments, so very much narrower than Fleda's. 'Almost as much as Mrs. Gereth's, [Fleda's] taste was her life, but her life was somehow the larger for it'—whereas, 'all Mrs. Gereth's scruples were on one side and . . . her ruling passion had in a manner despoiled her of her humanity.' Fleda's heroic ideal is to conflate, or at least reconcile, aesthetic and moral beauty, and to make 'taste' wide enough to include 'tact', a feeling for people and situations. For example, her sense of outrage at Mrs. Gereth's 'robbery' of Poynton is a mixture of straightforward moral disapproval of a larceny, purely personal sympathy for Owen's hurt, and, not least, a condemnation of what is aesthetically harmful to the 'things'. At times, even, Fleda is able temporarily to discard aesthetic taste, with a freedom of movement denied to the fixed Mrs. Gereth. Her 'fine instincts' can in certain cases make her 'stand off' from the source of beauty; and she has 'hours . . . of sombre wishing that she might never see anything good again'. And in contrast to that qualification of Fleda's 'taste', Mrs. Gereth's taste, though genuinely selfless in the ways we have seen, is nevertheless shadowed at times by the way she seems to get a very selfish pleasure out of the whole battle for the Spoils. The artistic end may be noble, but it is a little smirched by means that provide such satisfactions to egotism and the love of personal power. Another motive behind her battle, after all, is her protest against the way the English have discriminated against widowed mothers, legally and socially (Lady Agnes Dormer made a similar protest). Mrs. Gereth wishes to have influence and be adored; and envies her French friend, the widowed Madame de Jaume, for having 'to the end of her days the supreme word about everything'. And lastly, as another element in this growing tangle of similarities and differences, attractions and repulsions, we can see that if Mrs. Gereth is unscrupulous and guileful in the pursuit of her ends, the duplicity in her handling of Fleda is thoroughly reciprocated.

Fleda, with all her standards of honesty, always conceals, prevaricates, speaks in a double way to her hostess; and from the very outset, we are told, her love of Owen has produced a 'flaw in her frankness' with his mother to which she continually adds. The similarities and differences are not really a tangle, of course, but an emerging structure. It is by forcing us to discriminate, as between Fleda and Mrs. Gereth, and to recognize the mere hairline that at times divides values and creates disparities that James draws us into the book's essential process—and into the character of its endlessly and tragically discriminating heroine.

The beginning of the very different relationship between Fleda and Mrs. Gereth's son is another element in the book's highly stylized and simplified opening—part of the economy that James so consciously strove to adopt from the drama as he wrote it. Perhaps there is a minor flaw here—a suspicion of plot-mechanism in the way Fleda's 'inclination' is made to develop into a secret love almost immediately, instead of growing a little more slowly out of initial indifference, or even contempt. James at this stage underestimates the difficulty of persuading us that a girl of hyperacute perceptions like Fleda could so quickly devote herself to such a naïve figure as Owen. 'Difficulty' of persuading us, not 'impossibility': for one of the book's successes is that as it takes us further into Fleda's sensitivity we ourselves begin to see more clearly that there are considerable merits within Owen's fumbling, inarticulate decency. The trouble is, we have to know her better before we can respond to Owen. She falls in love with an apparent nonentity as soon as the story opens, and we have to take this love on trust for some chapters until James can fill it out and thereby 'justify' it. But the strain this may involve for the reader is really very slight, especially if one is able to make the initial imaginative response that any stylized drama requires.

Much of the eventual 'justification' of Fleda's love for Owen— much of its convincingness—comes from our response to the quality of freshness in it: a simplicity of tenderness that persists despite the complexity of her personality and situation. Fleda, throughout, shows a youthful urgency of feeling that complements her modesty and also the natural sophistication of her moral imagination. As we have been told, she is a product of nature (as well as of the museums), and into her composition goes much of the Jamesian tradition of vital innocence that goes back to Bessie Alden, Daisy Miller, and the unmarried Isabel Archer. And it is her own persistent quality of simplicity—simplicity of heart above all—that she finds in Owen, and that we ourselves, bound to Fleda, eventually prize in him too. This perception adds sufficiently to the apparent sketchiness of James's opening portrayal of Owen for us to begin to suspect that this character, whom readers have often found insufficient, is one important key to the book's nature. We discover through Fleda his shambling, boyish charm, his total dependence, his slowness of mind that is quite compatible with some instinctive regard for the feelings of others. He cannot articulate—'his quick speech, which shyness made obscure . . . was usually as desperate as a "rush" at some violent game'—and always needs Fleda to provide words for what he senses (their increasing closeness is emphasized, later on, when Fleda discovers that she cannot think of him in his absence, or of 'some other things' of value, without resort to *his* slangy vocabulary). He has his sophistications, and can move through society (almost as glamorously as Sir Claude in *What Maisie Knew*), 'delicately dressed, shining and splendid', with a high hat, 'light gloves with black seams, and a spear-like umbrella'. But he is also, and more importantly for how it affects Fleda, a healthy and physically handsome figure of the open air, all 'manly magnificence', with a voice that she hears 'ring out like a call to a terrier', and a costume that 'never failed of suggestions of the earth and the weather, the hedges and the ditches, the beasts and the birds'. He can deliberately put out of his mind memories that would be embarrassing to others—for example, the memory of Fleda having been virtually 'offered' to him as a suitable bride by a frantic Mrs. Gereth. He can write a supremely tactful, simple letter by 'a kind of divination', and with more sureness that 'the cleverest man in England'. He has little taste (despite a 'feeling' for the Spoils that *could* become aesthetic, with help), but he has a strong sense of justice, tempered by a desire not to press the claims of justice beyond those of general peace and compassion. He grows, he matures a little, he learns to suffer. He discovers what it is to know a woman like Fleda, and expresses his affection and confidence in the warm silence of his stare. He can be nervous, indecisive, and importunate, with a kind of 'friendly violence'; he perpetually needs help and advice. He has a sense of shame (like Fleda), as well as a sense of the importance of his own happiness—each sense being too wavering to allow him to choose any clear path of action. And to complicate it all, his will, unlike Mona's (unlike Mrs. Gereth's, unlike Fleda's in its own way), is notoriously and spectacularly weak—'a weakness somewhere in the core of his bloom, a blessed manly weakness of which, if she had only the valid right, it would be all a sweetness to take care'. Faced by such complications, and surrounded by such formidable women, the undirectedness of Owen's masculinity takes on quite a positive, and certainly a sympathetic value. Ultimately, his weakness makes him neither unconvincing as a character nor puzzlingly unlovable as the man Fleda would have married. Her love for him illuminates what is faint within him and stirs something there into new life. And while it is his feebleness that helps to betray them both, it was the same feebleness in the beginning that aroused her tenderness, drew her out of shyness and solitariness into the strength and responsibility of love, and made everything—the fuller happiness, the fuller bitterness—possible. This fuller happiness, which would be brought about by their marriage, comes to be associated with the symbolic power of the Spoils themselves. The relationship of Fleda and Owen is made adequately real in psychological terms, but their possible union also draws significance and imaginative appeal from the fact that it alone would save the Spoils, and all that comes to underlie the Spoils. Fleda dreams of how, as mistress of Poynton, she would fill its air with 'beautiful peace', and how 'the palace would unbar its shutters and the morning flash back from its halls.' The fulfilment of their love becomes another of the elements of richness and promise that the Spoils amass— just as Fleda's adoration of their beauty flows into her secret adoration (her 'hidden treasure' of feeling) for Owen. The Spoils of Poynton do not dominate this book as much as one might expect, but they are always present catalytically, and, like the Aspern Papers, they provide a single, ultimate image for so many sought-after qualities and powers—personal and impersonal, sexual and aesthetic, moral and social.

The struggle for the Spoils—James in the Preface compares them as a *casus belli* to Helen of Troy—becomes an intricate system of pressures with Fleda and Owen at the heart of it. The external situation, with an inevitability and almost a will of its own, is felt forcing them into intimacy. They can both only bow to the fact by the time they have realized what is happening to them. Fleda, as intermediary, is obliged to put all of Owen's feelings about Poynton into words for him, and to report them to Mrs. Gereth, just as she will soon have to help him to interpret the nature of his love and of her love, and of what threatens it. And as they discuss the affair, in their apparently impersonal chats and strolls of negotiation, we share in the sense—a sense that is delicate and quite unmawkish—of two people finding each other, and finding themselves. The scene between them in Oxford Street and Kensington Gardens in Chapter 6 is the most perfect expression of this stage in their relationship, where everything is merely nascent and embarrassed, instead of tortuous and tormented, as it becomes. Fleda's modest bewilderment, confronted by an affianced Owen who seems to be stumbling towards an affection for his mother's impecunious companion, is very natural in origin and in expression. Her frightened retreat—that vivid and pathetic 'ugly gallop down the Broad Walk'—then her 'red disgust' at having snubbed Owen so gracelessly; her consequent tears within the refuge of a hansom cab; and, seen distantly through it all, the 'confused, handsome face' of a troubled Owen, troubled for the first time in his life, comprise one of the most simply affecting incidents in the book. We feel with Fleda— having made the slight effort of adjustment that is required to accept the greater social and contractual importance of an engagement to be married. It is far more than a social convention, of course: it is also a question of the engagement of personal trusts, expectations, and intimacies. There has been a giving, as well as a promising, between Owen and Mona, that cannot be easily annulled. Fleda's predicament is a desperately awkward one on every ground—we must never lose sight of the simple and straightforward invidiousness of her position. And it is particularly invidious when she is being compromised by a man who is so clumsily uncertain about what his intentions and obligations are that she can never have total confidence in the lasting quality of his feelings for her. Owen always looks first to Fleda rather than to himself. This comes out most clearly amid the extraordinary tensions and undertones of Chapters 8 and 9, where Owen finds Fleda at Ricks, amid the purloined Spoils, and proceeds to fumble out an 'official' communication of his and Mona's wish that the Spoils be returned forthwith. Beneath his words—expressed in hesitations and fidgets, and in his assumption of familiarity—he is comunicating precisely the opposite, only half-understood by himself: that Mona is forcing him to do violence to his nature, and that if Fleda could find a way of keeping the Spoils at Ricks then Mona, cheated of her 'rights', might perhaps break the engagement, and Fleda thereupon might perhaps care to. . . . At that point even his unconscious inclinations tail off into a mere pleading silence: he wishes to be helped, to be taken over, to be told how to feel. This is his unfairness to Fleda, that he inevitably asks too much of her, having already asked so much that is still unretracted of another woman. Fleda's conversation, too, is thoroughly at odds with the direction of her thoughts. She can think only of the fact that Owen is apparently revealing a personal interest in her, whereas all along (except in Kensington Gardens) she had considered that her own feelings for him were necessarily unreturned. And meanwhile, where all is so unclear, and where Owen's silent hints are placing her in so impossible a situation, her talk can only be about the Spoils and her duty to ensure their return. This duty is strongly enforced by her place in the household as a disinterested outsider with a natural sense of justice. And to perform it now will ensure that the man she loves, and who seemingly loves her, will marry another woman for whom he possibly no longer feels anything.

The difficulty which for the first time begins to appear at this point—brought out by this new pitch of tension between them— is the major difficulty which readers have experienced in the book. Is Fleda being simply perverse in her refusal to lift a hand to help Owen to 'free' himself in order to marry her? Is she intended by James to be a study in pride, or in a life-denying idealism, and is the picture of her intended to be ironical? Do her rigours have the same chill as those of Euphemia de Mauves? Is she so self-deluding, some have even speculated, as merely to have imagined, neurotically, that Owen is in love with her, and to be a prime example of subjective and unreliable point of view in narrative? Alternatively, if we accept that James wished her to be a heroine and not a monster (and the Notebook entries clearly bear this out, apart from the novel itself), does Fleda strike us as being unintentionally perverse? Does she signify some fundamental breakdown in James's capacity for objectifying and understanding his fictional material, and even in James's own grasp of life, the whole thing dissolving into the ambiguities of an inadvertent autobiography?[5] Or—very far from that—should we approach her extreme moral scrupulousness not at all in terms of realistic characterization but as being purely symbolic, and the whole book, then, as moving towards the high conventions of French classical drama, or of a courtly romance, or of a *Princesse de Clèves*?[6] There are attractive possibilities contained in the idea of poetic conventions, but as a complete account of *The Spoils of Poynton*, or as the best way to consider the problem of Fleda Vetch, it is not really tenable. The book as a whole, for all its elements of non-naturalism and poetry and theatre, for all its later moments of mysterious elevation, simply does not read in that way. It is too firmly tethered to precise, local details of scene and place and thought and feeling, and above all to the natural reality of so much of its heroine's experience. As so often in James, it is a complex amalgam, and one that changes the balance of its elements very subtly from place to place in the novel—hence the acute difficulty of pinning it down as to tone or genre. There is never one satisfactory analogy for James's blend, especially in his later work, and it is as true and as false, as helpful and as misleading, to cite late Ibsen or Maeterlinck or Debussy or (if he can be put in such a *galère*) Racine, as it is to cite George Eliot, Balzac, and Turgenev.

When Fleda restrains her own feelings and ejects the importunate Owen from the cottage at Ricks before he can declare himself (in Chapter 8), it is neither a psychiatric matter nor is it necessarily a symbolic matter. We have, instead, a sense of a human truth and inevitability about what she does and thinks— a little modelled and heightened, as always, by dramatic device and selected epithet. The daunting intensity of her inner life is there in front of us; there is little escape from it for the reader of this book. The continual alternation between scrupulously

[5] Let one example suffice at this point. Yvor Winters writes: 'Fleda's attitude is never resolved; nor is ours; but the experience has been intense, and as we have not understood it, we cannot but feel it to be essentially neurotic and somewhere beyond the margin of the intelligible' (*In Defense of Reason*, London, 1960, p. 320).

[6] See, for example, J. K. Simon, 'A Study of Classical Gesture: Henry James and Madame de Lafayette', *Comparative Literature Studies*, iii, no. 3, 1966, 273–83. The essay deals more with *Madame de Mauves* than with *The Spoils of Poynton*, but the resemblances to Madame de Lafayette it suggests— of theme as well as manner—are of general application to James.

withheld feeling and passionately released feeling determines the shape of the narrative itself, and is the source of its energy. In this, *The Spoils of Poynton* is a little reminiscent of Jane Austen's *Persuasion*. The differences are enormous, of course, but it is perfectly possible to see Anne Elliot as the subject of similar claustrophobic pressures, from inside and outside, and as attempting to find for herself the critical point of balance (which becomes a point of marriage) between insistent emotion and the moral intelligence. At any rate, it is of Anne Elliot one thinks when Fleda at last gets Owen out of the door of the cottage and dashes upstairs to the seclusion of her room to unravel her inner confusions. There, having discovered the 'secret' that Owen sees her as an 'object of desire', she allows herself for half an hour to submit to her feelings: 'the rush of a flood into her own accumulations', and the overflowing of fathomless 'stored depths'. And at the same time Fleda faces up to her 'temptation', and to a case of such moral complexity that the Spoils themselves, all around her, seem to fade into irrelevance. Her temptation is to try to gain a personal fulfilment and happiness—to allow the 'stored depths' to flow permanently—at the expense of certain other values on which happiness is equally dependent. The easy thing, the everyday 'human' thing, would be to act in the dispute in such a way as to bind Owen to her while he is still pledged to Mona: 'Owen had put it before her with an art beyond his own dream. Mona would cast him off if he didn't proceed to extremities; if his negotiation with his mother should fail he would be completely free. That negotiation depended on a young lady to whom he had pressingly suggested the condition of his freedom' (p. 111). But Fleda's idea of love is incompatible with the idea of manipulation or hegemony: 'There was something in her that would make it a shame to her for ever to have owed her happiness to an interference.' At the very outset of Fleda's apparently hopeless love for Owen she was prepared to consider providing 'direction' for his own 'force', as we have seen. But it is now clearer to her than before that this must not involve abrogating Owen's responsibilities to 'his good nature and his good name', and his own will as an individual. Mrs. Gereth is a manipulating person with little sensitivity to the needs and rights of others; and Mona is a woman with a patent-leather foot, who wishes only to make use of her lover. But Fleda, with her sympathetic imagination, which is the tap-root of morality, loves Owen too much to do violence to his individuality. (Her love is different from Julia Dallow's, in *The Tragic Muse*—that narrow passion which, as Nick Dormer sensed, seeks to isolate and convert the object of love into its own image.) The most Fleda can do is to urge on Owen a very general course of action. The details of how he must break with Mona, without brutality and with respect for her rights as a once-loved and still-contracted fiancée, must be left to him. He already has a half-perception of this responsibility, revealed to Fleda in the shamefacedness of his attitude—a shame at his own lack of courage and at his 'disloyalty' to Mona. This shame and the cause of it must be overcome by himself before his new love can be built. Fleda's gamble (which is the proof of her love) is that Owen will be moved by her to discover in himself sufficient manliness, subtlety, and sense of honour to get free of the entanglement and to make himself, for the first time, accessible to her love for him, and deserving of it. This is the measure of her very real activity in the affair, for all that she apparently does no more than stand and wait. For she is never negative even in her stillness, and her painfully difficult refusal is a creative one in its motive: the man she loves must be helped to forge his own moral will and his own identity.

Fleda recognizes Owen's unfairness to her, and though she forgives it she very firmly declines to be put upon by it. As a morally sensitive person, she can very properly appreciate her own rights as well as Owen's and Mona's—her rights of self-respect with which her love of him must be reconciled, and on which that love partly depends. Just as her love of Owen creates in her a vision of how he might become—'sublime' in new strength —so it awakens her to a vision of herself. Love must try to include a clear vision of the self, and of the self's integrity, as well as of union with another.[7] Hence Fleda's 'pride': not the damning pride of the isolated self-seeker but the justified pride of a woman who wishes to make herself and her lover worthy of their mutual love. She has too great a respect for the privileges and the demands of genuine intimacy between people to risk entering into one that

[7] This clinging to personal wholeness comes out later even in such a small touch as Fleda's insistence that she, and not Mrs. Gereth, must pay the shilling for her last despairing telegram to Owen—'To succeed, it must be all me!' (p. 243).

has not been properly founded and attested. Fleda's idealism is never solipsistic or without application to the living world of people and events; James knows too much about the harmful divagations of idealism not to be clear on this point. Fleda is prepared to risk losing her lover for the sake of love, but this love is more than a purely private or a purely abstract ideal. It reflects general and traditional human values, and it is an influencing and informing ideal—a source of specific acts and relationships. That is, Fleda's hyperactive imagination, 'a faculty that easily embraced all the heights and depths and extremities of things', takes her towards certain perceptions that transcend herself but do not transcend the life around her—one of these perceptions being of the part played in her affair by love as a general principle in human experience: 'Nobody had a right to get off easily from pledges so deep and sacred. How could Fleda doubt they had been tremendous when she knew so well what any pledge of her own would be?' (p. 114). Here is something to add to our acceptance of the comparatively trivial point that engagement meant more in the 1890s than today. Fleda has the capacity to refurbish the importance of fidelity and engagement—even that of her lover to another woman—by the way she values love itself. She thinks of a hypothetical 'pledge of her own', and will always do so, to an important extent: the general concept must also be made specific. But the personal case is not the only criterion for her. She is aware, and the whole tenor of the book suggests, that love is also 'sacred'; something that is beyond individuals as well as within them.

Not that Fleda can ever spend very long in the realm of the self-transcending. Anne Elliot she may be, to some degree, but not quite Lionel Trilling's Fanny Price—not quite the supposedly sacrificial and self-denying Christian heroine.[8] She is always full of doubts that come from the much less idealizing side of herself, and they are expressed not just by the current of her restrained feelings but even in her cooler self-analyses: 'Even in the ardour of her meditation Fleda remained in sight of the truth that it would be an odd result of her magnanimity to prevent her friend's shaking off a woman he disliked. If he didn't dislike Mona what was the matter with him? And if he did, Fleda asked, what was the matter with her own silly self?' (pp. 114–15).

[8] In Trilling's famous essay on *Mansfield Park* in *The Opposing Self*, 1955.

James's irony at the expense of Fleda's contradictions is very benign, but it is very important for that whole aspect of her personality it keeps before us: 'She was meanwhile so remarkably constituted that while she refused to profit by Owen's mistake, even while she judged it and hastened to cover it up, she could drink a sweetness from it that consorted little with her wishing it mightn't have been made' (p. 116). When she receives a letter from Owen, and, very astringently, hesitates to open it lest it contain some outpouring that will force her to end communication with him, she is then 'just a trifle disappointed' to find there is not a syllable out of order. Again, we are asked to smile at the fact that she can afford to be generous towards Mona's rights partly because she has a certain sense of personal triumph over Mona at having secured Owen's affection without the advantage of Mona's beauty or Mona's 'permissions'—the normal sexual 'permissions' of the betrothed woman. And above all, in the early stages, our attention is drawn to the fact that Fleda also has a strong and down-to-earth hope of success that offsets the high flight of her heroism: the hope that Mona will herself cut the Gordian knot for them by choosing to break with Owen. Her renunciation of interference is a quite practical, as well as an idealistic, method, since to interfere where Mona is concerned (as Mrs. Gereth discovers later) would make Mona march Owen off at once to the Registry Office; and though Fleda tells herself she had no right to speculate on the possibility of success for herself, the thought of it is always shown to have 'affected the total of her sentiments.'

The rich mixture of so many elements in Fleda is suggested by one striking image (it comes at the end of her half-hour of introspection after Owen's visit to Ricks):

Their protected error (for she indulged a fancy that it was hers too) was like some dangerous, lovely, living thing that she had caught and could keep—keep vivid and helpless in the cage of her own passion and look at and talk to all day long. She had got it well locked up there by the time that from an upper window she saw Mrs. Gereth again in the garden. At this she went down to meet her. (p. 116)

The image is one that combines power and imprisonment, menace and tenderness, authority and submission. The idea of love between Owen and herself is properly seen as an error and must still be restrained, even punished. But the restraint is also a kind of

F

cherishing and a fostering: the cage will become one of reciprocated feeling. The creature in it is a dual creature, and as she
talks to it in gentleness 'all day long' she is herself as much in the
cage as outside. The force of her own controlled passion fills her
life as the force of a dangerous creature fills its cage. Yet her passion,
so bounded by the cage of her consciousness and her conscience,
has all the pathos of the unfulfilled—and therefore all the beauty
of the unexhausted. And her passion is itself a cage, as much as
her restraint is a cage; for to drive her passion into herself, as
she does, is to increase its demands and its contradictions until it
grows and imprisons her whole life.

Fleda's cage is created by her own equivocations as well as by
her lucid knowledge. Forced deeper and deeper into lying by her
'gagged and blinded desire' for Owen, she comes to feel 'an odd,
unwonted sense of age and cunning'. Fleda's duplicity—towards
Mrs. Gereth especially, in concealing her love for Owen, mis-
representing the state of Owen's mind, and concealing Mona's
ultimatum to him—has little to do with that life-enhancing function of role-playing that James celebrates, with irony, in so many
other books.[9] It simply adds to the pathos of the girl's position
that she has to be untruthful in order to carry out her complicated
and highly moral plan of not making things too easy for Owen.
She does not enjoy her evasions, but on the other hand she carries
them out with a certain aplomb, and seems to suffer no agonies
of conscience over them. And this is another factor to correct any
tendency in the reader to idealize Fleda too much, and to see her
as some kind of uncompromising Jamesian angel. For all the
extremeness of the case, and the manner of the telling, Fleda is to be
seen picking a very careful and painstaking way, with recognizably
human steps. She is thoroughly within Mrs. Gereth's worldly
jungle, and one word wrong—one glimpse of the true facts—might
precipitate all of that wonderful woman's destructive impulsive-
ness. And if she were to make too strong and too pure-minded a
plea to Mrs. Gereth to do the honest thing and replenish Poynton
—which was Fleda's 'definite vow' to Owen—that would make
things just too easy for Mona. It is interesting to see that James
in his Notebooks originally intended Mrs. Gereth to deduce
Fleda's secret love for Owen from the vehemence with which

---

[9] See, for example, my account of Christina Light (above, pp. 37–38),
Miriam Rooth (above, pp. 103–8), and of *The Wings of the Dove, passim.*

Fleda urges her to surrender the Spoils 'in the light of honour, duty, etc.'[10] In fact, though Mrs. Gereth makes her discovery, Fleda does nothing more direct or more idealistic than refuse to 'dissociate herself' from an 'implied view of the propriety of surrender'—and at one point even denies, with a blush, that she has any direct interest at all in what Mrs. Gereth decides to do with the things.

An extraordinary psychic battle is being fought out between a more and more suspicious Mrs. Gereth and a more and more desperate and defensive Fleda—Fleda's desperation being the keener in that something in her longs for expression and exposure. It is a relief as well as a pain to her when Mrs. Gereth suddenly cuts through the tangle of their double-talk with a loud cry of affectionate triumph at having guessed the fact of the girl's love. The confession means 'shame' for Fleda: the shame of a cherished element of privacy being dragged into the open, where it has apparently as yet no public right to be, and where there is no Owen to help to bear the exposed burden of love, only—as always —herself. If it is a relief to Fleda, as well as a shame, it is also a relief to the reader. It is an important feature of the book that James at certain points should allow us to identify temporarily with Mrs. Gereth. Her vigour and her loud and brisk practicality take some of the strain off us as we try to keep up with Fleda and her demands on life—demands that Fleda herself, of course, sustains with difficulty and oppression.[11] And yet, that said, we very quickly veer back to Fleda when Mrs. Gereth's delight assumes a bullying note, and when Fleda's tearful relief is forced to turn into subtlety and defensiveness again, as she protects Owen (and their fragile chances of success) by denying to his mother that he reciprocates any feeling for her. Because no matter how we are at first stirred by the forthright naturalness of Mrs. Gereth when she urges Fleda to 'Get him away from her!' by 'letting yourself go', we know Fleda too well not to resent the jarring crudity of

---

[10] *The Notebooks of Henry James*, ed. F. O. Matthiessen and K. B. Murdock, New York, 1947, pp. 217–18.

[11] Another slight analogy to Jane Austen comes to mind here—the relief felt by the reader in the earlier part of *Emma* when the curt John Knightley briefly refuses to play the delicate Hartfield game of putting up with the foibles of Mr. Woodhouse. We can accept the greater moral sensitivity of Emma and his brother George, in this matter, all the better for our being able to let off a little steam with John Knightley, when he threatens to bring it all toppling down with his impatience.

such commands (the crudity only made more painful by our realizing, through the girl's inner tensions, the amount there is in her to 'let go', the heavy 'accumulations of passion'). The pressure on Fleda grows, with this intrusion into 'the chamber of her soul'. Mrs. Gereth has got hold of 'her young friend's soft secret', and intends to put it to immediate and somewhat callous use: 'Pressed upon her, goodness knew, the crisis had been, but it now seemed to put forth big, encircling arms—arms that squeezed till they hurt and she must cry out.' The pressure grows outwards from within, too. And the irony is that Fleda, in fleeing from Ricks to London to escape these pressures and to be superlatively quiet and detached and watchful, falls straight into the 'trap' of direct encounter with Owen—the trap towards which Mrs. Gereth's 'brutality of good intentions' had all the time been forcing her, like a driven animal.

Fleda in London is really a preparation for Fleda down at her sister Maggie's, in that 'mean little house' in a 'stupid little town'— the pivotal scene of the whole book, in Chapter 16. That chapter is the book's one *scène de passion* (as James himself describes it), and it comes as the climax to all the pressures which we have seen build up from the beginning, and which London has only intensified. There is, for example, the isolation and friendlessness of Fleda's life in the city: 'when she failed in the attempt to lose herself in the flat suburb she felt like a lonely fly crawling over a dusty chart.' Her father's rooms in West Kensington offer only a mechanical ugliness that causes her to be 'swept . . . by short wild gusts of despair'. And her father himself, like Lionel Croy in *The Wings of the Dove*, is one of James's parodies of a parent, with Fleda, in consequence, as another of James's virtual orphans, another of his 'free spirits' whose freedom of mind is equally a form of homelessness. Mr. Vetch is also a parody of the true collector like Mrs. Gereth. His Spoils, excruciating to Fleda, are 'old brandy-flasks and matchboxes, old calendars and hand-books, intermixed with an assortment of pen-wipers and ashtrays, a harvest he had gathered in from penny bazaars'.[12] And it is in the very moment of staring into the bleak truth proffered to her by a local shop-window, that as a single woman she can hardly earn a living to let her escape from this milieu, that Fleda turns to find

[12] Even the phrase, 'gathered in', occurs for the *real* Spoils later on, in Chapter 20.

the figure of Owen beside her, shining with purpose and male handsomeness in his city finery: 'his pull was tremendous.' Acted out in the presence of such facts and such knowledge, their long *tête-à-tête* in her father's parlour brings things between them to the verge of crisis. Fleda's resistance and her ability to prevaricate with him are further weakened by Owen's new clarity about his feelings, and by his information that Mona is now bitterly resentful of Fleda: 'It was a sudden drop in [Fleda's] great flight, a shock to her attempt to watch over what Mona was entitled to. While she had been straining her very soul in this attempt the object of her magnanimity had been practically pronouncing her vile' (p. 175). The interruption of an offended Mrs. Brigstock, at the moment when Owen grasps Fleda's arm and talks of love, is the most blatant piece of 'theatre' in the book. But not only is it perfectly effective in its stylized comedy—in the way Mrs. Brigstock's shrewd eyes single out the nibbled biscuit that lies on the floor as evidence of an intimate 'scene'—it is perfectly functional in creating yet another pressure on Fleda, another sharp turn of the screw.

Out of these sudden embarrassments and intensifications, climaxes and anticlimaxes, comes the episode at Maggie's. Fleda, having gained a breathing-space, receives Owen there, and in a superbly handled scene of great feeling, the complexity of the whole Poynton situation suddenly yields to the inner pressures of their love. Owen asks her to marry him; Fleda confesses that she has loved him all along; and a tide is released. It is a brief crisis, but a particularly moving one:

The words had broken from her in a sudden loud cry, and what next happened was that the very sound of her pain upset her. She heard her own true note; she turned short away from him; in a moment she had burst into sobs; in another his arms were round her; the next she had let herself go so far that even Mrs. Gereth might have seen it. He clasped her, and she gave herself—she poured out her tears on his breast. Something prisoned and pent throbbed and gushed; something deep and sweet surged up—something that came from far within and far off, that had begun with the sight of him in his indifference and had never had rest since then. The surrender was short, but the relief was long: she felt his warm lips on her face and his arms tighten with his full divination. What she did, what she *had* done, she scarcely knew: she only was aware, as she broke from him again, of what had taken place in his panting soul. What had taken place was that, with the click of a spring, he saw. He had cleared the high wall at a bound; they were together without a veil. She had not a shred of a secret left; it was as if a whirlwind had come and gone, laying low the great false front that she had built up stone by stone. The strangest thing of all was the momentary sense of desolation. (pp. 200–1)

The sympathetic power of the passage comes from the felt release of accumulated tension. The somewhat mannered gestures and language—'prisoned and pent', 'throbbed and gushed', 'deep and sweet', 'together without a veil'—are not false or precious, but in their context are as expressive as any other dramatic conventions. But the power comes also from the startling reversal of that last sentence: 'The strangest thing of all was the momentary sense of desolation.' This 'desolation' is primarily Fleda's instinct for the fatedness of their relationship. When she later describes the event to Mrs. Gereth she uses similar terms: 'the strangest part of all is that it isn't even happiness. It's anguish—it was from the first; from the first there was a bitterness and a kind of dread' (p. 233). Her 'dread'—Owen himself sees it as 'some darksome process of her mind'—is clearly justified by the facts of the situation. She knows Mona's obstinacy, and even in Owen's joy and confidence now, at the moment of revelation, Fleda detects his perpetual note of weakness and 'the tone he so often had of a great boy at a great game'. Fleda's 'dread', that is, is a natural and rational one, and should not be seen as some innate and paralysing terror of all sexual experience, or of 'life' itself. Nevertheless, there seems to be a deeper resonance to this 'strangest thing of all' than can be quite summed up in such pragmatic terms. It has to do with Fleda's emotional drives, with her imaginative idealism, and with the actual strength of her capacity to envisage real and lasting happiness—the inevitable corollary of these strengths being the more inhibiting perception of how rarely reality can match such possibilities. That is, Fleda's 'dread', in its deeper implications, is not pure inhibition but part of a more complex and in its way more positive thing. It is as positive as a tragic insight—though the energy that traditionally accompanies tragedy appears now in the form of those incandescent states of thinking and waiting that characterize much of Fleda's action in this book.[13] We have long since been prepared for the

---

[13] Often there is almost as much significant *waiting* in a James novel as in a

way in which Fleda's response to a particular situation can quickly become an intuition of larger issues, including, it now seems, the tragic issue of human fate: 'This imagination of Fleda's was a faculty that easily embraced all the heights and depths and extremities of things; that made a single mouthful in particular of any tragic or desperate necessity' (p. 144). And for her 'sense of desolation' to occur at the moment of her greatest ardour affects us with some of the force of romantic tragedy itself—James being so poised between romanticism and modernity, and being himself so stirred always by discovering a melancholy in the very temple of his characters' delight. 'Fleda's *aveux* are all qualified', he writes of this scene in the Notebooks, '—saddened and refined, and made *beautiful*, by the sense of the IMPOSSIBLE.'[14] Fleda's own sense of the universally impossible, which springs up out of her knowledge of the immediately improbable, even affects Owen, very briefly—Owen, whose easy life up till now has been one dominated by 'the personally possible': ' "Ah, all the while you *cared*?" Owen read the truth with a wonder so great that it was visibly almost a sadness, a terror caused by his sudden perception of where the impossibility was not. That made it all perhaps elsewhere' (p. 201). The phrasing is ungainly, but not haphazard. 'Impossibility' takes on a vastness by its being recognized negatively in the sentence—a darkness that looms up and is defined by contrast with the one point of light in it, the fact that Fleda, after all, does love him. And the natural speech-stresses of the last sentence, falling on 'all' and 'elsewhere', make even wider the vista of tragic 'desolation' for the two of them.

Fleda's pain, that accompanies her one moment of 'letting go' with Owen, has for its more immediate cause, as we have seen, her knowledge that the 'letting go' is still unjustified and impermanent, since Owen has not yet freed himself. And the almost religious intensity of that moment—'He clasped his hands before her as he might have clasped them at an altar, . . . as if she had

---

Chekhov play. And as with Chekhov, the waiting is not always that of inanition or the failure of will and desire, but of glowing frustration. 'If only we knew, if only we knew!', is Olga's cry at the end of *The Three Sisters*. There is so much in these characters to give and to do, if only they could find a way: if only they could find an occupation, or plant a new cherry orchard, or get to Moscow; if only an Owen Gereth, 'sublime' in new strength, would lead Fleda into the House of a new life.

[14] *The Notebooks of Henry James*, p. 254.

really been something sacred . . . till she laid consenting hands on him, touched his head and stroked it, held it in her tenderness . . .' —quickly dissolves into the old protestations and arguments that their situation prescribes. 'Everything must come from Mona', Fleda reiterates. 'There are things too utterly for yourselves alone. How can I tell? What do I know?' Fleda's moment of surrender has been a profound one and a disturbing one for a girl so schooled in isolation and in self-scrutiny. One small particle of the 'desolation' she felt when the 'false front' came down was certainly at the loss of privacy involved—a natural element in any instance of sexual giving, and particularly in an instance where giving has had to be withheld for so long. Fleda cannot give any more of herself to Owen—to the extent of acting as though he had already taken a decisive step, or of deciding *for* him that his own feelings for Mona and Mona's for him are now truly defunct. But her old style of argument—that a heart once engaged is never free from obligation of a kind, that the offering of marriage to a woman changes her life in a way that even the death of love cannot eradicate—is fraught with a new and significant confusion, after a scene that has marked a turning-point in her own life. Fleda has lost her old lucidity, along with her privacy. 'The great thing is to keep faith', she urges Owen; but when he asks if he must keep faith by marrying a woman he hates, she confesses, 'Anything is better than that.' Fleda at the end has been driven into the centre of her own unbearable contradictions: the narrow place that shapes her suffering. The new confusion, the dis-connected phrases, the kiss she gives Owen as blindly as Julia Dallow kissed Nick Dormer on the lake, all convey a sense of desperate and reluctant change of ground—a liberation that promises no freedom. And the scene between them, the scene in which the cage was opened and the 'whirlwind' tore down the stones, ends in darkness and dispersal—Fleda fleeing helplessly to her room, and Owen, with his burden of responsibility, to the doubtful mercies of Waterbath.

Fleda's rigorousness towards Owen, which we once saw as being inevitable and as a schooling of him, we now begin to see rather more as a gamble. And the gamble is lost through someone else's gamble—that of Mrs. Gereth, who, having learned from Mrs. Brigstock that Owen loves Fleda, dramatically returns the Spoils to Poynton. She does so as a colossal bribe, a challenge to obligation, and at the same time as a genuine token of her affection for Fleda. It is all done for Fleda, and she must marry Owen quickly now to save the Spoils and to justify Mrs. Gereth. It is an ironic counterpart to what Fleda has all along been imposing on Owen: it is an appeal to her sense of 'honour', and the gesture of a 'noble trust' in her. The pressure on Fleda from both gambles is intolerable. Mrs. Gereth's passionate feeling for Poynton bears down on her as strenuously as her own simple longing for Owen, each of them forcing her in the one direction, that of the ultimate breakdown of scruples: 'Fleda had listened in unbearable pain and growing terror, as if her interlocutress, stone by stone, were piling some fatal mass upon her breast. She had the sense of being buried alive, smothered in the mere expansion of another will' (p. 223). The sense of claustrophobia is marvellously conveyed throughout this book: the feeling of being *driven*, choked by passion and by the will of others, and trapped by circumstances, while the conscious mind struggles to achieve equilibrium. Fleda's abasement now, at the hands of Mrs. Gereth, is entirely pathetic: 'I haven't a rag of pride; I used to have, but it's gone. I used to have a secret, but everyone knows it now.' We have no easy sense of triumph over the fall of an excessive idealist. Certainly, Mrs. Gereth's tirades against Fleda's 'idiotic perversity' and 'sweet little scruples', which she at once sees have lost her the game by allowing Owen to return to Mona, release the Mrs. Gereth that exists in all of us. There is a liberating fury in her denunciations. But essentially we can think none the less of Fleda, and of what she has attempted, even when we know that Mrs. Gereth's point of view has its enormous strength, too—the strength of the embattled usualness of human behaviour (it comes as a 'blind profanity' after Fleda's 'sacredness'). Fleda's collapse into weakness—'I'll go to the Registrar now'—is partly because she suddenly realizes the irrelevance of collapsing or not collapsing, after such a delay. Mona, knowing her malleable human material well, will have finally 'let herself go', and secured Owen. The opposition of the two attitudes to life, the morally refined and the morally coarse, the ideal and the practical, is nowhere in the book more dramatically or more rhetorically stated than in this confrontation between Fleda and Mrs. Gereth (in Chapters 17 and 18). We respond fully to the cogency of Mrs. Gereth's outrage at 'the insanity of a passion that bewilders a young blockhead with bugaboo barriers, with hideous and monstrous sacrifices'. And we respond fully to the cogency of Fleda suffering for the sake of her sensitive mind, as when she protests, 'You simplify far too much. You always did and you always will. The tangle of life is much more intricate than you've ever, I think, felt it to be. You slash into it . . . with a great pair of shears.' These are endemic contradictions, present within individuals as well as between them, and the kiss on which the two women character-istically close the scene offers no solution but only a touching note of emphasis and hopeless confirmation.

Fleda cannot exist outside these contradictions, either in her 'high flights' or in her humiliations. Her ability to appeal to us, as a character, comes from her life within them; and if she is exemplary at all it is only by the intensity and passion with which she suffers them. Her mental state throughout the concluding chapters is 'composed of pulses as swift and fine as the revolutions of a spinning top'—a movement which becomes that of the action itself. There is an effect of great speed and complexity, on a very compressed scale: an almost overwhelming rhythm of ups and downs, recoveries and defeats, and underlying it all, like an inescapable current, the sense of a steady progression towards disaster. As Mrs. Gereth and Fleda wander through London in search of Owen, they see in their mind's eye the vision of a Babylon-like Poynton with its Spoils and its pride now restored, 'a shining, steady light', 'the old splendour', reflecting greatness and 'arrogance of energy' back at the Mrs. Gereth who has replenished it. And against this vision—so the rhythm goes, in alternation—is the threatening vision of Mona and Owen together somewhere, and the whole encroachment of an unreal actuality. There is the 'great grey platform' of Euston; the 'fat woman with a basket' and the 'two men with bags and boxes' who seem to imprison Fleda in her railway compartment. And most movingly of all, as Fleda sits immobile in her cab outside Owen's abandoned club, there is the 'great hard street' with its 'passing figures that struck her as puppets pulled by strings'. These are deadening images of Fleda's 'desolation'—like the stage-property Venice that haunted the editor in the climax of *The Aspern Papers*, and like the 'thick prospect' of a 'fifth-rate world' that settled blackly over a rejected Peter Sherringham in Miriam Rooth's London garden.

The vision of the 'old splendour' allows Fleda one extraordinary and brief moment of equanimity. As she waits in vain for an answer to her final unqualified and desperate appeal by telegram to Owen—'come to me'—she passes beyond the oscillations of her unhappiness and her hopes into a 'cold, still chamber'. It is a state of mind for which even the words 'indifference, resignation, despair' are irrelevant, 'the terms of a forgotten tongue'; and she arrives at it by meditating, one by one, on the items of the re-constituted Spoils:

It was the beauty she was most touched by that, in tons, she had lost—the beauty that, charged upon big wagons, had safely crept back to its home. But the loss was a gain to memory and love; it was to her too at last that, in condonation of her treachery, the old things had crept back. She greeted them with open arms; she thought of them hour after hour; they made a company with which solitude was warm and a picture that, at this crisis, overlaid poor Maggie's scant mahogany. It was really her obliterated passion that had revived, and with it an immense assent to Mrs. Gereth's early judgement of her. She equally, she felt, was of the religion, and like any other of the passionately pious she could worship now even in the desert. Yes, it was all for her; far round as she had gone she had been strong enough: her love had gathered in the spoils. She wanted indeed no catalogue to count them over; the array of them, miles away, was complete; each piece, in its turn, was perfect to her; she could have drawn up a catalogue from memory. Thus again she lived with them, and she thought of them without a question of any personal right. That they might have been, that they might still be hers, that they were perhaps already another's, were ideas that had too little to say to her. They were nobody's at all—too proud, unlike base animals and humans, to be reducible to anything so narrow. It was Poynton that was theirs; they had simply recovered their own. The joy of that for them was the source of the strange peace in which the girl found herself floating. (pp. 252–3)

Fleda's 'strange peace' is contemplative, aesthetic, and impersonal. The everyday world and her own individual troubles fall away beside the intensity of her imaginative grasp of the beautiful. Clearly this is a capacity in Fleda that is intimately related to her capacity for moral idealism and for tragic perception. And no more than in the case of the latter two do we judge it as escapism or as a self-induced ecstasy that amounts to a rejection of the real. James has some knowledge of this 'cold, still chamber', and there are places in his fiction where the attractions of 'loss', as 'a gain to memory and love', are allowed to go beyond what most readers are prepared to accept as normal or natural—as witness the rather garish and morbid qualities of *Maud-Evelyn* and *The Altar of the Dead*, for example. But in Fleda's case it is all eminently controlled by James. She is allowed her spiritual consolation without quibble, for it is never shown as more than a consolation—and all the other things in her life surround it, qualify it, gain from it, and in the end go far towards extinguishing it. Her visionary aestheticism, both at this point and before her last trip to Poynton, is a real part of her life, as it might be of any life; but it is not the root of it. For all the peace it gives her now, it is only another of the opposed poles that are turning her in her passion like 'a spinning top'.

For there are losses now, for Fleda, that quickly break her 'strange peace', and afford a pain too immediate for any thought of what memory might gain by them. Mrs. Gereth comes down to announce to her that Owen and Mona are married. And after an initial calmness—the fruit of her contemplation of the Spoils— Fleda breaks; and now her grief flows with the same violence as her love had flowed when she last saw Owen, and with the same resultant loss of lucidity—'I don't understand—I don't understand!' And as for Mrs. Gereth, placed beside her in a formal and almost symbolic tableau, she is 'a tired old woman . . . with empty hands in her lap', her face a 'dead grey mask' as she stares at 'the face of the stopped Dutch clock': 'she represented the final vanity of everything.'

Yet, as part of the book's closing fluctuations, there is at once an unexpected recovery and a partial reconciliation. Mrs. Gereth, with her flair for 'composition' and 'arrangement', transforms the cottage at Ricks, using only the original furnishings of the place. And Fleda completes the miracle by her conscious interpretation and appreciation of what Mrs. Gereth has done. That is, the two women collaborate in a minor act of unification that implies, very subtly, the greater unity that has failed to come about. Mrs. Gereth has skill in the more practical fostering of beauty, Fleda in the more imaginative. The active hand and the appreciative mind, at least in this little way, discover a harmony. One woman brings out, in a genuinely creative manner, the hidden possibilities of the cottage's own 'little worn, bleached stuffs and the sweet spindle- legs'. The other ('For action', Mrs. Gereth tells her, 'You're no good at all'), by her sympathetic mind, invests these things with a

human symbolism: the imagined story and grief of the dead
maiden aunt who once owned them:

'half the beauty resides [says Fleda] [in] the impression, somehow, of
something dreamed and missed, something reduced, relinquished,
resigned: the poetry, as it were, of something sensibly *gone* . . .
    . . . It's a kind of fourth dimension. It's a presence, a perfume, a
touch. It's a soul, a story, a life. There's ever so much more here than
you and I . . .
    . . . It seems to me ghosts count double—for what they were and for
what they are. Somehow there were no ghosts at Poynton,' Fleda went
on. 'That was the only fault.' (pp. 266–7)

Fleda's imagination here is trying to recover something like that
'strange peace' she enjoyed at Maggie's—by seeking to recover,
through an image, and for 'memory and love', a life that is lost, a
life she imagines to have been one of 'a great accepted pain', and
that is therefore to be a metaphor of her own. And James is
perfectly able to show up, by gentle irony, the element of strain in
Fleda's 'feverishly jubilant' mental exercise—'Fleda ingeniously
and triumphantly worked it out.' The imagination can preserve
a great deal out of what life wastes and destroys; but it is powerless
against the holocaust itself.

Because of course the final holocaust is expected and essential.
It is so wrong to complain that the ending of *The Spoils of Poynton*
is melodramatic when the whole closing implication of the book
has been one of division and disaster. The Spoils are as doomed as
the full harmonious life they have come to represent: as doomed
to impossibility as Fleda's imagination of love, and as impermanent as any human conception or man-made image of a supreme
beauty. The burning of Poynton is like the withdrawal from the
human scene of some venerated but dangerous god. Life itself is
the incendiarist, as usual, and tricks Fleda into her last illusion of
happiness by holding out to her the promise of the Maltese Cross,
offered to her 'as a remembrance' by a distant Owen, honey-
mooning (unimaginably!) with Mona. A great deal has been made,
and might be made, of the symbolism of the Cross;[15] and also of
the enigmatic ending to Owen's letter—'You won't refuse if you

[15] See A. Goldsmith, 'The Maltese Cross as Sign in *The Spoils of Poynton*',
Renascence, xvi, 1964, 73–7.

will think a little what it must be that makes me ask.' Owen's appeal, though it puzzles Fleda, is presumably only to the memory of their relationship: a not insensitive desire on his part that there should be some kind of appropriate and unembarrassing link between them (though it has its possible hurtfulness). Fleda is puzzled largely because she dare not consider the other possible implication of the phrase, that Owen is not happy and still longs for her. And as for the Cross, if there are suggestions in it of a religious conclusion to Fleda's story, they are too faint to have much effect on the reader compared with the much more arresting picture of Fleda once again turning to her imagination and then being betrayed by the facts. Owen's letter is a temptation for her to relive in her mind all that happened between them—she must keep that at bay at all costs. So her bruised imagination—that faculty that could 'embrace all the heights and depths and extremities of things'—turns once again to the contemplation of beauty. But this time beauty, in the imagined richness of the Spoils, is not impersonal and peaceful, but for a little while anyway appeals to the same passion, personal and sexual, that she felt for Owen. That thwarted passion finds expression now in the idea of her going to Poynton to take away the Cross that is 'the gem of the collection': 'the passion . . . found here an issue that there was nothing whatever to choke.' Only through the imagination can she 'let herself go' for the last time, allowing her mind luxuriously to 'possess' the great crammed house to the full, in the way that she might have possessed other things in reality. 'She would act with secret rapture', and at last 'her choice should know no scruple.' It would be 'an hour to dream of and watch for; to be patient was to draw out the sweetness.' And as she travels down, the thought of the Spoils swells up before her, giving her a sense of personal pride and possession. They are a mirage, with a tell-tale excess of opulence in them, like a glimpse into one of Turner's paintings of the rooms at Petworth—'off in that quarter was an air of wild rain, but there shimmered straight across it a brightness that was the colour of the great interior she had been haunting.' The excess is irresistible, and it is difficult to grudge Fleda her vision of a satisfaction that is very real—if also somewhat surrogate. But James can perceive the element of self-destructiveness inside it—there is always a spark, at least, of the final fire within the very nature of Fleda's formidable imagination, since the imagination itself, as *The Tragic Muse* assured us, is always a double-edged weapon.

The ending of *The Tragic Muse* reconciled us to such imperfections: it celebrated the transforming power of art but it equally celebrated the sanity of compromise and realism—our need to accept what life gives. But what it gives at the very end of *The Spoils of Poynton* is too bitter for that. What it gives is smoke. The Poynton vision is lost in it. Fleda journeys from London through a storm in which green fields turn black and the sky is swept by a high premonitory wind to find—smoke everywhere. 'A great acrid gust' of it envelops her life in darkness till she covers her face with her hands and speaks the three monosyllables that end the book, so movingly, like a knell: 'I'll go back.' It is, marvellously and painfully, an image of turning away, of Fleda finally retreating into herself. And yet, paradoxically, beneath that it is equally an image of returning to the world and to 'the London labyrinth' that is waiting for her. Fleda, being a 'stiff little beggar', is not done with life yet, or with her soul's attempt to steer a way, with understanding and discrimination and freely-accepted responsibility, through all the contradictions of the labyrinth. She has been defeated, but she has made most of the choices for herself. Nevertheless, here in the quick of the catastrophe, the cost strikes us as tragically high. In such a waste of smoke, baffled passion, and lost beauty—in such a waste of shame—it is the terrible expense of spirit that seems to matter most.

6

The Sense of Life in
The Wings of the Dove: I

I

AFTER the spareness and speed of *The Spoils of Poynton, The Wings of the Dove* comes as a shock to the unprepared reader. Like *The Ambassadors* and *The Golden Bowl*, it is a colossus: highly wrought, slow-moving, and stringently demanding. Its scenes of actual physical activity are not frequent; its characters feel, think, and speak with a complexity or with an undifferentiated elegance far beyond what we agree to call the normal; the language often moves elliptically and exasperatingly; and on a first or even a second reading its proliferating analyses of situations and states of mind seem to come dangerously close to dissolving, instead of interpreting, the life we know. Here is intelligence, sensibility, and a responsiveness to the nuances of human behaviour developed to the point of profligacy: perhaps (with *The Golden Bowl*) a *ne plus ultra* of elaboration in the novel-form. And yet—despite everything—the book is an undoubted masterpiece, full of weight and distinctness and variety, and one comes to the end of it, on subsequent readings at any rate, with the clear sense that distinguishes the masterpiece: the sense of its having after all, within so intellectual and so unphotographic a medium, a strong grasp of the actual felt processes of living. This is one aspect of the 'sense of life' in *The Wings of the Dove*: that it represents perhaps James's most profound, if certainly not his most direct, entry into a recognizable section of complicated human experience. In the end it does not deny our sense of normality, but extends it. And the labour it imposes on the reader is the labour of discovering just how dense and intricate the human scene really is, beyond the reach of our everyday myopia and the elisions that our practical convenience demands. All of this novel's exhaustive and cunning methods—so analysable and so admirable for their own sake—have as their end not self-display or a purely formal beauty but dramàtic exploration; and it is not at all so virtuoso or shapely a work as to ignore those 'local' effects, loose ends, and tentative suggestions, on which the illusion of 'life' in art partly depends. For all its economical use of scene and for all the typical presence of a discriminating narrator around and above its supposedly 'sunk' points of view, *The Wings of the Dove* is ultimately and essentially a drama. It is a representation of the actual process of certain human relationships and individual fates into which we enter via analysis and via the author's intelligence and feelings. Within the apparently verbose textures of the book we are made to encounter specific events, psychological and moral, of the most intense and real kind. And the movement of this Jamesian drama into which we are drawn is, as always, not one of syllogism but of the extensive interplay of opposites. What is primarily insisted on, for example, is not that Milly Theale is to be our guiding light and Kate Croy our devil, but that we are present in each of them and each of them in us. The moral life is importantly upheld in this book by the way James shows it to be a vitalizing constituent of the human action he is investigating, rather than by himself exercising any final moral judgement on those who take part. For James, the moral imagination, which has in it something akin to dramatic illusion, is always anterior to moral judgement, and is of greater relevance to the aims of the novelist and to the nature of novel-reading. The characters of his fiction are inevitably more closely engaged than is the novelist in moral combat and in the struggle to define and delimit and judge for themselves. This is what helps to ratify their humanity for us as we watch them. And the greater freedom, generosity, and moral tentativeness of the artist who creates them—art always being morally larger than our normal lives—are the qualities that specifically allow for drama, as well as for morality. Such qualities create a wide stage of moral and psychological possibility: a field of choice, exactly as wide as the author's own moral sensitivity, within which these diverse characters are to be defined through their actions. James may well be a moralist—and that is how he is usually described—but only in this very basic sense. Moralism, of course, is a thing he abhors, and a thing that any child of Henry James Senior was taught to abhor. He is concerned for moral value only in so far as he is concerned for people, and he uses the language of morality in order to understand and to release his imagined world of people, rather than to fix them or to exhort them. Judgement becomes an aid to representation—not the other way round. To judge his characters by 'value' is for James virtually the same as 'faire valoir' (in the phrase he uses of Balzac's characterization in 'The Lesson of Balzac'): a way of making them 'count', a way of perceiving and creating them in the full 'value' of their independent existence. It is the old question of Jamesian ambiguity as we found it at the very beginning of this study: ambiguity of judgement will be possible in *The Wings of the Dove* without moral chaos or total open-endedness of meaning. It is part of the drama that is the 'life' of the book, and that 'life' is essentially and unambiguously our life.

If the sense of life is too strong in this novel for it to be read as a moral fable of good and evil, it would be similarly misguided to see it as a stark collision between two extreme modes of being, the profane world of Lancaster Gate and the divine world of a Beatrice-like Milly. There are certain moments, to be acknowledged later, where an element of mystery and of the 'transcendental' undoubtedly appears, but not strongly enough to change the underlying realism of James's view. As in *The Spoils of Poynton*, and as always when at his best, James is able to 'naturalize' the transcendental, and to make the world of the spirit a part, even if a tragic part, of our natural living. There is poetry in *The Wings of the Dove*, but it is not, as some readings of it come close to suggesting, a mystic meditation on the nature of the eternal.[1] Milly is thoroughly endowed with flesh and blood and knowledge: there would be no tragedy if she were not. And James is far from succumbing to some other-worldly tendency of his own mind near the end of his career, seeking to follow Milly, on the wings of Style, into the modern Valhalla of 'pure' Proustian consciousness. Milly Theale's qualities, including her supreme quality of mercy, are not angelic but personal, and they are always shown to us within the context of her relationships with other characters: that is, a dramatic situation again, rather than an exemplary one. Just as in *The Tragic Muse*, James does not pin his faith to the transformative powers of Mind or Spirit (or Art) at the complete expense of the recalcitrant world. He simply portrays the ebb and flow that exists between them, and

---

[1] See below, p. 182, n. 10.

the endless ways in which each penetrates the other. This flow is enacted, with differing degrees of violence and clarity, within each of the main figures of the novel, and it is in these figures that the interest lies. James's subject, while it involves good and evil, and even the occasional brief intimation of divinity, is primarily the intensity and pressure created in life through strengths, weaknesses, and desires in certain individuals and in a society. For all that it belongs to James's apparently most abstract and modernist phase, we have here a remarkably concrete and worldly book.

The sense of life that affects us in reading *The Wings of the Dove* does not only come from its very basic correspondence with experience, but from the fact that its characters are themselves driven by their own particular sense of life. What they all wish is specifically to confront 'life', in some of its most complicated and implicating forms. The word 'life' could be vague in itself, but when it appears it usually takes on substance by the way it conflates so many things, already portrayed and experienced by us in the story, that are themselves precise and detailed. And while there is, in fact, one clearly recognizable general goal represented by the word—the urge of any personality to expand itself, to experience fully, to intensify its awareness and all its contacts with the world—the actual details of the experience vary from character to character, and in different scenes and moods. And in this fact, too, is another answer to the common objection that this Jamesian goal of 'life' is too private a distillation of experience, too selective and exclusive, and too empty of empirical reference. The reference is as empirical and as varied as the characters, events, and situations that embody the idea of it and give it meaning. And if there is a 'distillation' it is with the same end for which all art distils and selects: in order to make experience accessible and tangible to the imagination.

Partly because of this imaginative tangibility and particularity, one is reluctant to say that the desire to 'live', in *The Wings of the Dove*, has the abstract status of a *theme*—though it is difficult for the necessarily abstracting critic not to say it. In the same way, it is not quite adequate to say that the book is 'about' manners in the sense of offering a discursive account of them, though the nature of manners is undoubtedly of prime importance within the book. That is, *The Wings of the Dove* resists any blatantly thematic interpretation—and this by virtue once again of its own specifically dramatic nature, and of those qualities of James's mind, so receptive and adaptable yet so unseizable, that gave rise to T. S. Eliot's famous praise, 'He had a mind so fine that no idea could violate it.'[2] Any suggested interpretation, like the meaning of the Jamesian word 'life', requires immediately to be, as it were, dropped back into the pot again—to 'prove' itself locally by its ability to be absorbed into the texture of the scene in question. Even more than in the earlier books the critic (by whom I mean the articulate and alert reader) has to work in terms of detailed analysis and of painfully scrupulous qualification. It is for this reason that what is offered here is two long chapters of close commentary on a book that is already minutely analytical in itself—a taxing procedure that might seem to be a piling of Pelion upon Ossa. But it seems to me the most straightforward and useful thing to do, if possibly the least elegant. For my own experience is that criticism of such a novel tends to present a brilliant and shapely pattern of ideas and symbols that becomes strangely unhelpful and even incongruous when one turns back to the book itself, to its puzzling details, its difficult bulk, and its important rhythms. It is perhaps better to run the risk of being pedestrian than fail to do justice to its narrative density. Sprightliness and speed are not prominent among its own qualities, and the critic ought to feel at least some pressure to subdue himself to the temper of the work itself. To keep close to its plot-movement and to its changing moods, to be as true as possible to James's own principles of immersion and patient accumulation, and at the same time to allow general ideas to emerge freely from their context in the story appears to me no worse a critical method than any other of dealing with *The Wings of the Dove.* I say 'general ideas' even after so strong a caveat against thematic generalization because of course the book's essential dramatic nature, its drawing of the reader into each scene in its own terms, does not in the end preclude qualities of representativeness or of intellectual coherence—which are very different things from dogmatic fable or theorem. The lives of its characters are multifarious, and the body of the book is composed of their swarming variations and contradictions. But as in all great fiction, character combines with action to create something greater and more general than either alone.

[2] 'On Henry James', *The Question of Henry James*, ed. F. W. Dupee, London, 1947, p. 125.

When such characters are shown to us trying to 'live', with all the intensity and energy of their individual beings, the plot they forge in the heat of that endeavour begins to take on the shape of a collective destiny.

Confronting 'life', then, in her unique and yet representative way, we find Kate Croy on the brink of two opposed prospects. From one window she looks down on the squalor of Chirk Street, and from the other she looks over Hyde Park. It is the quintessential James beginning, and takes us right back to the excitements and fears of Longmore, in *Madame de Mauves*, staring at the glittering promise of the Parisian Babylon. But what a distance, of course, James has come since then—and what a packed density of meaning is presented to the reader in these superb opening chapters of *The Wings of the Dove*. The density, as so often in this book, carries with it an experiential quality. It is vital that we should feel the full personal presence and temperament of a woman like Kate Croy, since much of the dynamism of the whole plot will flow from her desire to fulfil this personal potential within a complex and challenging social milieu. And this is what James achieves from the book's first phrase: 'She waited, Kate Croy, for her father to come in. . . . ' We are at once drawn into Kate's posture— helped a little, even, by the fine sonority of her name (one of James's happiest choices) and by the commanding manner in which it makes its delayed entrance into that sentence.[3] And what we see is Kate looking at the reflection of herself, and in a specific setting. We are introduced to the burden and tension of her self-consciousness, and also to the onerousness of her surroundings:

She waited, Kate Croy, for her father to come in, but he kept her unconscionably, and there were moments at which she showed herself, in the glass over the mantel, a face positively pale with the irritation that had brought her to the point of going away without sight of him. It was at this point, however, that she remained; changing her place, moving from the shabby sofa to the armchair upholstered in a glazed cloth that gave at once—she had tried it—the sense of the slippery and of the sticky. She had looked at the sallow prints on the walls and at the

[3] Ian Watt has suggested on the contrary that the 'odd parenthetic apposition' of Kate's name in this sentence prefigures not her dominance but her enforced role of *waiting* throughout the novel ('The First Paragraph of *The Ambassadors*: An Explication', *Essays in Criticism*, x, 1960, 269–70).

lonely magazine, a year old, that combined, with a small lamp in coloured glass and a knitted white centre-piece wanting in freshness, to enhance the effect of the purplish cloth on the principal table; she had above all, from time to time, taken a brief stand on the small balcony to which the pair of long windows gave access. The vulgar little street, in this view, offered scant relief from the vulgar little room; its main office was to suggest to her that the narrow black house-fronts, adjusted to a standard that would have been low even for backs, constituted quite the publicity implied by such privacies. One felt them in the room exactly as one felt the room—the hundred like it, or worse—in the street. Each time she turned in again, each time, in her impatience, she gave him up, it was to sound to a deeper depth, while she tasted the faint, flat emanation of things, the failure of fortune and of honour. If she continued to wait it was really, in a manner, that she might not add the shame of fear, of individual, personal collapse, to all the other shames. To feel the street, to feel the room, to feel the table-cloth and the centre-piece and the lamp, gave her a small, salutary sense, at least, of neither shirking nor lying. This whole vision was the worst thing yet—as including, in particular, the interview for which she had prepared herself; and for what had she come but for the worst?[4]

This quality of being so rooted and so weighty is to be a sustained feature of the novel. Each of the main characters is seen for the first time in meaningful relation to a realistic environment: Kate in Chirk Street, Mrs. Lowder among her ostentatious possessions, Densher wandering aimlessly in Kensington Gardens, Milly Theale in the Alps. The 'life' that each of them quests for (including Mrs. Lowder) will always be one involving entanglement with things and places and people. And one of the most essential aspects of their story will be the fact that a setting to one's individual life, defined by 'manners' and 'relationships' as much as by physical details, can never be dispensed with.

Kate in these opening two chapters is testing her milieu and herself. How can she get the most out of each, and avoid the 'individual, personal collapse' that is represented by her father's house in Chirk Street? We very quickly feel the impossibility of her being reconciled to her father and to his dishonoured life, but not in a way that totally questions the sincerity of her offer now to throw up the social promise of Lancaster Gate if he will take her in. There is a tiredness and a resignation at first in her offer,

[4] *The Wings of the Dove*, Harmondsworth, 1965, p. 5. Future page-references are to this, the Penguin edition, which reprints the first edition of 1902.

a knowledge of the impossibility of its being accepted; but this is because it seems to come at the end of a series and of a real battle, and not because it is spurious, coming from a woman who is already a cold, hypocritical plotter. Kate's burden of self-knowledge—and to the very end of the book she knows herself, her powers, her ambitiousness, her danger of coldness, better than any of the other characters know themselves, including Milly—is added to by a more or less active conscience. She will always strike us as a figure of pain and constraint, whose inner divisions are being held together with great effort. And her last visit to her father, here, should be seen as a genuine though consciously futile testimony to her own vestigial sense of piety, abnegation, and 'decency'. Hereafter, she will risk everything in the hope of winning 'everything'.

If the limiting life of Chirk Street is impossible for Kate Croy, in what direction does her fulfilment lie? It lies, to begin with, in her sense of her own energies and her own identity: the confidence that she has a self to fulfil. Hence the importance of Kate's first action of looking at herself in the mirror, and finding the hint of a 'meaning' for her life in the fact that she can make out her own charm and presence:

If she saw more things than her fine face in the dull glass of her father's lodgings, she might have seen that, after all, she was not herself a fact in the collapse. She didn't judge herself cheap, she didn't make for misery. Personally, at least, she was not chalk-marked for the auction. She hadn't given up yet, and the broken sentence, if she was the last word, *would* end with a sort of meaning. (pp. 6-7)

Kate's perception of her independent powers and ambitions also frightens her a little: this comes out in the slight note of desperation that develops in her appeal to her father. And her fear is increased by understanding what it would mean to accept the alternative challenge of Lancaster Gate, since she is perfectly able to judge the dubiousness of that glittering society towards which her own desires and force of circumstances are combining to drive her (she tells Densher later that she went to her father 'to save myself—to escape', and 'to escape Aunt Maud'). Nevertheless, it is the poverty of Chirk Street, and the impossibility of escaping to such a quarter, that helps to define Kate's potentiality, even to herself, and eventually to define her personal destiny. The thought of poverty acts in her life as the thought of death in

Milly Theale's. For both young women there is a great gnawing
enemy whose presence highlights and gives significance to its
opposite: that is, the life of fullness, power, and health. Thus,
Kate's hatred of 'the faint, flat emanation of things, the failure of
fortune and of honour' in Chirk Street is not only like her
fastidious detestation of the smells of low living on the landing
and the hall at her sister's; it is also like her horror of the smells
of medicine and ill health which she mentions to Densher (and
which links her again with Milly, who in her own pride and
independence shares exactly the same horror).[5]

It is important that the blight which menaces the life-hungry
imagination of Kate should appear at this stage in the form of a
disgraced and untrustworthy father. The breakdown of proper
family ties and responsibilities is almost as important a motif in
James's writings as in Dickens's, and we have already seen him
use such false parents as Mr. Vetch, Mrs. Rooth, the Cavaliere
and Mrs. Light, and Mrs. Miller, in order to bring out the
predicaments of their children, who are forced into the dangerous
freedom and necessity of shaping their own lives. There are moments of very real pathos, as well as of splendid sarcasm, in the
encounter between Kate and Lionel Croy, where Kate's reiterated
appeal to be allowed to return to him collapses into a mutual
recognition of the utter failure of love and understanding between
father and daughter:

> She turned her handsome, quiet face upon him at such length that it
> might well have been for the last time. 'I don't know what you're like'.
> 'No more do I, my dear. I've spent my life in trying, in vain, to dis-
> cover. Like nothing—more's the pity. If there had been many of us,
> and we could have found each other out, there's no knowing what we
> mightn't have done. But it doesn't matter now'. (pp. 16–17)

The parent Kate turns to in her momentary flight from the
perils of 'Society' not only sends her back but proves to be a
warning caricature of that society. Kate is trapped by finding the
worst of Lancaster Gate firmly ensconced in Chirk Street. Lionel

---

[5] I do not think in the case either of Kate or Milly this kind of 'pride' has
quite the damning associations that Dorothea Krook apportions it (Miss Krook
is something of a Savonarola in her pursuit of pride through James's novels).
In each case, the alternative to 'pride' would seem to be a kind of annihilation—
and the effects of lack of pride are gruesomely evident in the character of Kate's
sister (*The Ordeal of Consciousness in Henry James*, 1962, p. 214).

Croy, and the Lionel Croys of the world, are partly created by the powerful society which his daughter admires and fears. He is the drifter and sponger: the empty man with a perfect delusive exterior provided by imitating society's conventions:

He looked exactly as much as usual—all pink and silver as to skin and hair, all straightness and starch as to figure and dress—the man in the world least connected with anything unpleasant. He was so particularly the English gentleman and the fortunate, settled, normal person. Seen at a foreign *table d'hôte*, he suggested but one thing: 'In what perfection England produces them!' (p. 8)

Croy's existence is something of a comment against Lancaster Gate, through his capacity and through his deep need to imitate its way of life. In that way of life, as we shall see, roles and conventions can play an enriching part—but Croy's hollow life of perpetual attitudinizing and play-acting prepares us only for the invidious aspect of manners, which is only half of the truth.[6] Similarly, when he denounces Kate's request to live with him, and angrily urges her to 'use' him as an object for her own profit as much as she can, he is revealing what happens when an upper-class system of give-and-take percolates this far downwards, and is stripped of those subtle, civilized qualities that balance, but never quite outweigh, its predatoriness. His perverse plea is ushered in by the almost Dickensian extravagance of his 'attack' on the morality of society, surely one of James's most effective moments of grotesque parody:

'Then, my dear girl, you ought simply to be ashamed of yourself. Do you know what you're a proof of, all you hard, hollow people together?' He put the question with a charming air of sudden spiritual heat. 'Of the deplorably superficial morality of the age. The family sentiment, in our vulgarized, brutalized life, has gone utterly to pot. There was a day when a man like me—by which I mean a parent like me—would have been for a daughter like you a quite distinct value; what's called in the business world, I believe, an "asset" '. He continued sociably to make it out. 'I'm not talking only of what you might, with the right

6 It is this one half of the truth that Millicent Bell (like many others) empha-sizes as the book's main theme—'the replacement of love by a commercialism of the emotions'—and quite rightly finds in this present scene: 'Croy's language of business is more than jocular; it makes explicit the market psychology that will dominate Kate's own thinking' ('The Dream of Being Possessed and Possessing', *Massachusetts Review*, x, 1969, 97–114). James will have more than this to say about the market, however.

feeling, do *for* me, but of what you might—it's what I call your opportunity—do *with* me. Unless indeed', he the next moment imperturbably
threw off, 'they come a good deal to the same thing. Your duty as well
as your chance, if you're capable of seeing it, is to use me. Show family
feeling by seeing what I'm good for. If you had it as *I* have it you'd
see I'm still good—well, for a lot of things. There's in fact, my dear',
Mr. Croy wound up, 'a coach-and-four to be got out of me'. (pp. 14–15)

In this, Croy shows a hideously firm grasp of certain social realities.
Like Mrs. Lowder and the others, he can 'appreciate' and estimate
his daughter's attractions only too well. His cynical analysis is
very lucid, and is delivered in a grand manner and even with a
kind of wit that apes the high style of Lancaster Gate and
Matcham. He even recognizes his spiritual kinship with Mrs.
Lowder (who would have apoplexy at the suggestion), accepts her
judgements and her values as better than his daughter's, and is
capable of one of those Jamesian pieces of occult inference (so
characteristic of the 'style' of that other social stratum) when he
senses quickly that Kate is reprehensibly in love with someone
not approved of by her aunt.

The casting-off of Kate by her father—and then by her sister
Marian, who so resembles the father in her distortion of family
feeling and her desire to 'work' Kate for the family's profit—
prepares us for another of the book's most important general
insights: that here is a whole society, marvellously and intricately
constructed in some ways, but sadly formless and shattered in
others. This society has its sustaining orders and hierarchies, and
has considerable composure, too—the Croy family is far from
being its precise analogue. But equally, it is riddled with gaps and
chasms—I stress the 'equally' since James in the end, I believe,
brings out the parity of its strengths and weaknesses. Thus, if
Kate is in her way a fatherless child without a true home, then
what of Densher, the man cut off from the world of action and
condemned by his education and lack of means to be a 'social
anomaly'?[7] What, too, of Mrs. Lowder, despised for her lack of

---

[7] The point made much later that Densher, unlike Kate, 'could have lived
in such a place' as Mrs. Condrip's (Kate's sister), and that 'it was not given to
those of his complexion . . . to be exiles anywhere' is only in appearance contradictory (p. 430). I think the ulterior point is that someone of Densher's 'complexion' is so essentially an exile *everywhere* that he can have a makeshift 'home'
in any spot. There is no doubt that the general impression of Densher is of a
man with no natural place or home in society.

real social status by those at Matcham, used by them for their own purposes, seen through by Kate, and herself desperately playing Kate and Milly as different cards in the game of *arrivisme*? Further, Milly Theale comes on to the scene as an orphan and wanderer, an exotic among the English and a merely amused spectator (in the National Gallery) when among Americans—she is the American *ingénue* turned discriminating and self-conscious. Susan Stringham, tragically bereft of family ties, belongs to New England and yet does not belong to New England (she worships Maupassant), and will be even more rootless after her experience of the life and death of Milly (she is much less American than Henrietta Stackpole, say, in *Portrait of a Lady*, who is essentially no wanderer and carries her America about with her). Even Lord Mark, for all his 'position', seems to be affected by the general social instability he himself describes for Milly as 'the senseless shifting tumble, like that of some great greasy sea in mid-Channel, of an overwhelming melted mixture'. He may be 'landed', and contemptuous of Mrs. Lowder, but there is clearly something parasitic and itinerant about him, too, in his half-hearted pursuit of both Kate's and Milly's fortune, drifting from Carlsbad to Venice, letting out his London rooms for a quick profit at Christmastime (and moving in with Mrs. Lowder!), and—the perfect, unforgettable vignette—sitting solitary and vengeful in Florian's restaurant in Venice, staring glassily at a rococo wall.

This may seem a far cry from Lionel Croy, performing like a pernicious marionette before the purple table-cloth in Chirk Street. But the point must be made that Kate's family situation is a social fact in the book as well as a personal one, and that Kate, Densher, Milly, and the others, including Lionel Croy, are all very much the children of such a society and such an age. From one point of view, this society is an admirable and inevitable structure, and its complicated manners reflect the important need of human beings to live publicly, through a code of intercourse, and aesthetically, through style and delicacy. But from another point of view—and just as inevitably—this society is inadequate, and prone to degeneration. And this is partly because no society can ever be a family, held together by the quality of feeling that animates a family. The relation between manners and family feeling is a crucial one. When it is sustained to any degree, we have the kind of civilization that Jane Austen described—or imagined. When it is not sustained, we have Lord Mark's civilization: a beautiful group of people, without a permanent centre, wandering blandly on the lawns at Matcham, waiting and longing to be interested or excited or, even better, further enriched. And this clarifies for us the nature even of the main characters of the novel who are not bland—their own lack of centre and security, their expectations and unease and ambitions, their prospects of something new, always something new, to be beheld from a balcony or a ledge in the Alps. A part of what they see there—a part of their vision of a life of fullness—will always take on the shapes that only a society can provide. And a part of their failure as people to achieve all that they see will be their society's failure, too.[8]

Consider Kate's vision of the world of 'things' and manners— and of a personal love set within it—that is her alternative to the vision of Chirk Street and to the quagmire of the Condrip household in Chelsea. All of her 'presence' and temperament is magnificently involved in the prospect. For all its dangers, this is for her the world of the richest possibilities of self-fulfilment, expression, and happiness; and the sense of her energies, piling to the moment of release, and coming against obstacles and counter-pressures, vibrates through James's account. One of the counter-pressures is Aunt Maud herself, and Kate's movement outwards into the world she sees 'from the high south window that hung over the Park' is momentarily restrained by fear of the woman who owns the window in question. As Kate's patroness and financier, she is the keeper of the gates of society and success— the keeper of Lancaster Gate. And Kate, on the verge of discovering her full selfhood, feels menaced and besieged in her own 'citadel' by Aunt Maud's powerful, manipulative will. It is only a pause, during which Kate experiences the same fear as before at feeling such a will to power in herself—fear, even, at recognizing how she will be able to beat Aunt Maud at her own game of influence and assertion. This is not a case of a Fleda Vetch

[8] The point made about Kate could apply to so many of them—and to so many characters in James's other writings—that consciousness itself, the capacity to 'see', is as much a curse as a gift: 'There was no such misfortune, or at any rate no such discomfort, she further reasoned, as to be formed at once for being and for seeing. You always saw, in this case, something else than what you were, and you got, in consequence, none of the peace of your condition' (pp. 25–6).

smothered by the will of a Mrs. Gereth. Aunt Maud is a challenge to Kate—the same challenge as that posed by the view over the Park—and Kate, in taking it up, soon goes beyond her aunt: 'what were the dangers, after all, but just the dangers of life and of London? Mrs. Lowder *was* London, *was* life—the roar of the siege and the thick of the fray.' The extravagance of Mrs. Lowder, and of James's early descriptions of her—'Britannia of the Market Place', 'a lioness', a 'prodigious' personality whose 'mass' looms 'in the thick, the foglike air of her arranged existence'—is to make her into a more potent version of 'the real' than Lionel Croy, for all her philistinism and 'false notes'. She is a figure of complex worldly power, with a strong commercial bias, 'as passionate as she was practical'. And in one of the perfect little systems of exchange that help to define the social life, Aunt Maud will use her funds and contacts to make Kate's social success if Kate will use her attractiveness to make Aunt Maud's.

Kate 'comes down' from her 'citadel'—and fully enters her story, her fate—through recognizing that the great world of Aunt Maud's London must be approached through conventions, and that conventions are simply the tactics and the forms that make 'experience' accessible. Manners, that is, are an essential instrument of living, and are as much a part of the self's adventure as spontaneity and privacy. It is all an adventure—the whole book a story of adventurers. And Kate already knows one of the main tricks and rules—that she must not just play a role but accept the roles that others have created for her, when it is helpful to everyone and compatible with 'decency': 'It wouldn't be the first time she had seen herself obliged to accept with smothered irony other people's interpretation of her conduct. She often ended by giving up to them—it seemed really the way to live—the version that met their convenience' (p. 20). Her 'irony' is the proper medium for such a complicated mode of existence. Irony is the little zone of freedom and reserve that always surrounds James's more developed social adventurers as they tack to and fro through a modern civilized life. By adopting irony, they can be themselves in privacy and at the same time make others easy; and in theory, therefore, through its adoption the whole system of manners can move on oiled wheels (until irony fails). Kate's theory of presenting a version of conduct that meets the convenience of others suggests an omen. Within it, in miniature, we can see the outright duplicity of her later plot against Milly and the charity that is also in that plot—since Kate, like everyone, will want to make things easy for Milly and indeed to give Milly the 'version' (of Densher's feelings) that will meet with Milly's 'convenience'. It *is* charity, in its strange two-faced way, and the 'plot' does proceed, by a perfectly seamless weave, out of society's viable and cultivated 'way to live'. No judgement of Kate must later fail to take this into account, or to pay respect to the completely organic way in which her plot grows out of her own life, out of the principles of her society, and out of what James sees as the absolute duality of all civilized living.

The duality is there to see—though at times a little indeterminately—in the very earliest stages of Kate's relation with Merton Densher. Each of them finds in the other a vital addition to his or her own 'reality' and possession of 'life'—but there are accompanying hints of a rift within the lute. The effect of discovery and of personal expansion is conveyed by James in the most sympathetic way. His detailed and realistic account of Kate and Densher's first meeting—at a boring and affected London party, and then on the Underground, where each named station (on the Circle and District Line, apparently!) adds a link to their relationship—comes closest to justifying such a description as Dorothea Krook's, that these are the 'most magnificent of James's lovers', whose passion gives the book 'the irrecoverable vibration of youth'.[9] The sense of a critical encounter comes sharply to Kate, and is given in a typical and effective late-James conceit:

It wasn't, in a word, simply that their eyes had met; other conscious organs, faculties, feelers had met as well, and when Kate afterwards imaged to herself the sharp, deep fact she saw it, in the oddest way, as a particular performance. She had observed a ladder against a garden wall, and had trusted herself so to climb it as to be able to see over into the probable garden on the other side. On reaching the top she had found herself face to face with a gentleman engaged in a like calculation at the same moment, and the two inquirers had remained confronted on their ladders. The great point was that for the rest of that evening they had

---

[9] *The Ordeal of Consciousness*, pp. 215, 287–8. The sense of real youthfulness hardly lasts, however, I think. Certainly, Kate regards herself as rather 'battered' at twenty-five, and her relation with Densher after this strikes me as no more pristine, in its bitter passionateness, than any in *The Golden Bowl*, in which the lovers appear to Miss Krook as 'curiously middle-aged' in comparison.

been perched—they had not climbed down; and indeed, during the time that followed, Kate at least had had the perched feeling—it was as if she were there aloft without a retreat. (p. 38)

But Densher from the beginning seems to have a rather more impassioned view of Kate's 'reality' than she has of his—a distinction that already suggests, just a little, what will later more clearly develop into an instability in their relationship. Densher is established, *par excellence*, as a character on the brink of his life: an adventurer who finds his adventuress. As yet he is uneasy with himself, and unfocused—'absent-minded, irregularly clever, liable to drop what was near and to take up what was far'. He has only one clear ambition, and it is basically the same as Kate's, though it proceeds out of a different weakness: 'Having so often concluded on the fact of his weakness, as he called it, for life—his strength merely for thought—life, he logically opined, was what he must somehow arrange to annex and possess' (p. 37). Densher's response to 'life', for all his general vagueness, is more concentrated and compressed than the response of any other character in the book, since it can virtually be summed up as his response to Kate ('Deep, always, was his sense of life with her'). Her 'talent for life', which he admires, combines with all her other personal attributes to turn Densher into one of James's most possessed and driven figures. To Kate's own judgement, Densher represents her greatest lack, intellectual culture: 'all the high, dim things she lumped together as of the mind'. But it is a minor peculiarity of the book (coming perhaps from some change of emphasis in the process of writing) that Densher never strikes the reader as truly intellectual, in an analytical or widely speculative or even aesthetically appreciative way. Certainly, he is contemplative and self-communing, but not profoundly so—rather more at the end, of course, but even then a man whose conscience is at the behest of his one great passion. Kate seems to be at least as intelligent as Densher, and considerably less befogged by feeling; and his grasp of moral scruple is, to say the least, insecure. But of course the real nature of Densher, and of his charm for Kate, is perfectly clear. He is a man 'of the mind' to the extent of not being a man of practical action. He is mentally unattached, unmoulded, a cosmopolite; an ironist in his way, but belonging to no social system. He is capable of thought; but has found little in the world to seize him. There is a pleasantly unaggressive quality about him; yet his temperament is far from placid. He is a *flâneur* without money, and has the grace not to be happy about being a *flâneur*. And as such a man he is singularly liable to be quite overthrown by encountering an experience in the shape of Kate Croy. If it is in his sexual urgency, rather than his strength for thought, that Densher comes to represent Kate's lack—in our eyes, though not in hers—Kate nevertheless always strikes us as a woman whose potentialities certainly include passion. She is alarmingly controlled and lucid, but we feel she has a side of her nature that requires control. And it is the idea of two attractive, sensitive, and intelligent persons uniting through mutual passion that gives such force to the relationship of Kate and Densher, and moves James, typically, with its promise of fruition and harmony:

> if the great possibility had come up for them it had done so, to an exceptional degree, under the protection of the famous law of contraries. Any deep harmony that might eventually govern them would not be the result of their having much in common—having anything, in fact, but their affection; and would really find its explanation in some sense, on the part of each, of being poor where the other was rich. (p. 36)

Aunt Maud, who wishes to stop the growth of their relationship, is in fact an important catalyst in its early stages. Kate comes to appreciate her own potential the more she hears Aunt Maud value it highly in social terms, and is confirmed in her ambition to include Densher in the vision of 'everything' that Aunt Maud dangles before her. She will set her sights on 'personal happiness' as well as social greatness ('to be as rich and overflowing, as smart and shining, as I can be made'). And Densher in turn sees new elements of richness and attraction in Kate as a result of his visits to Aunt Maud, which initiate him into the vision of material and social power, and in particular into an awareness of what society, through Aunt Maud, can see in his lover. Aunt Maud's ambitions for Kate—her 'fond, proud dreams'—are not easily dismissable, and are allowed a certain nobility behind their self-seeking. Densher's sense of helplessness when faced by the Juggernaut of Lancaster Gate and the vulgarity of her power always includes a strong element of reluctant respect. Such power *is* power. It is one aspect of the whole 'real thing' that is to be aimed at and fought for. And his passion for Kate, no matter how resentful in one way of those values that stand in its way, cannot remain untouched by them: Kate's desirability can only be increased by his seeing her, so highly priced, in the social market-place.

From the start this passion is bound to be an affair of conflict—mirroring as it does the whole conflict between private and social life. The tension comes most directly from Densher's perpetual emotional frustration: 'Life might prove difficult—was evidently going to; but meanwhile they had each other, and that was everything. This was her reasoning, but meanwhile, for *him*, each other was what they didn't have, and it was just the point' (p. 44). There is no book by James more sexually *aware* than this one, in the continual ache of specific desire and disturbance that fills Densher's broodings. It is Kate who can postpone the act and live in the idea, and Densher who rages for physical possession of her—so little is he the man of pure reasoning, or she the woman of action. But there are other notes that seem to threaten the 'deep harmony' of Kate and Densher's relation: notes that are difficult to be certain about, but that can be detected more clearly in the light of later developments. It is not a question of an unreality in their love. In some ways it is a flaw that comes from an excess of certain qualities in it, or from certain over-wrought intensities. In the early exchanges between them in Kensington Gardens—which so many critics see as being only positive, rich, and passionate within their very mannered high style—I wonder if there are not, even so early, several touches of falsity and of a tone that seems to quaver just a little. For example, what are we to make of Kate's remark to Densher that during her visit to her father she had offered to give Densher up for ever if her father would take her in? That is, what are we to make of the truth of the remark when we certainly heard her say nothing of the kind during the visit in question (in Chapter 1)? Is Kate led into an exaggeration for the sake of highlighting her own heroic family feeling? And what are we to make of the peculiar taste of saying this, in a scene between committed lovers? If this is to be explained as part of the high style's urbane irony, then is there not a certain sourness in that style? Again, having seen Kate in the milieu of Lancaster Gate, we find it very difficult now to believe in Kate's self-abnegating protestation to Densher that she would still go to live with her sister 'in a moment if she'd have me'. That is, not all of Kate's large gestures are at once acceptable as a part of

G

the sophisticated 'manner' between her and her lover. It is a question of a razor's edge, no doubt—as to where a certain ominousness breaks through the hyperbolic and courtly dalliance of the dialogue. Does it verge on the preposterous because James knows that the high style is not quite enough, and intuitively puts a question-mark into his rendering of it? Or is James simply unsteady and a little too dazzled by glamorous surfaces? The latter possibility must always be raised with James—but only, in this instance, to be denied. He knows the highly complex nature of his subject-matter, and evaluates it in the only possible way, by nuances and shades. He sees the intense and elegant self-consciousness of Kate and Densher as a great asset that can nevertheless betray. And the perilousness of the path they tread, even in their language with one another, is revealed in the various little qualifications and hesitations of such a passage as this:

> They were talking, for the time, with the strangest mixture of deliberation and directness, and nothing could have been more in the tone of it than the way she at last said: 'You're afraid of [Aunt Maud] yourself'.
> He gave a smile a trifle glassy. 'For young persons of a great distinction and a very high spirit, we're a caution!'
> 'Yes', she took it straight up; 'we're hideously intelligent. But there's fun in it too. We must get our fun where we can. I think', she added, and for that matter, not without courage, 'our relation's beautiful. It's not a bit vulgar. I cling to some saving romance in things'.
> It made him break into a laugh which had more freedom than his smile. 'How you must be afraid you'll chuck me!'
> 'No, no, *that* would be vulgar. But, of course, I do see my danger', she admitted, 'of doing something base'.
> 'Then what can be so base as sacrificing me?'
> 'I *shan't* sacrifice you; don't cry out till you're hurt'. (p. 51)

But most unambiguous of all is the way James catches up all these slight doubts about Kate and Densher at the very moment of their deepest pledge to one another, when Kate pronounces 'with extraordinary beauty: "I engage myself to you for ever" '. The moment between the two *is* of 'extraordinary beauty', as they take 'final possession' of 'their prospect', full of faith and clarity, and with a communicated feeling that has the 'fullness of a tide': 'They were in the open air, in an alley of the Gardens; the great space, which seemed to arch just then higher and spread wider for them, threw them back into deep concentration.' But quickly we notice how Kate smilingly passes over Densher's objection that their secret engagement will cease to be honest whenever Aunt Maud finds a particular candidate for Kate's hand—a moment that echoes with the unspoken name of Lord Mark, whom she knows well to be already Aunt Maud's candidate. And then they find themselves trapped, almost by a trick of their own words—a trick of their high style—into a disconcerting avowal of the fact that from here on their love is solidly attached to a lie. They stumble together on 'a possible, a natural reality': the reality that it will have to be Kate who does the lying to Aunt Maud, and that Kate is the one best fitted for lying, by virtue of those 'refinements . . . of consciousness, of sensation, of appreciation' that she now claims to possess, resentfully and defensively. The transition, here at the end of the novel's opening section, from the lovers' refinements to their dishonesty, from their full tide of feeling to their mutual watchfulness, from joy to fear, and then quickly back again, is very subtle, and for the reader even a little frightening. It is frightening because we feel we are at the inmost pulse of a relationship: we can feel its life, and we can feel its life flicker and hesitate. 'So quick bright things come to confusion.'

II

One of the most remarkable features of *The Wings of the Dove*, and essential to its effect of 'life', is the almost tangible quality of its complex structure of personal relations. The structure is virtually an architectural one. Everyone is engaged in supporting everyone else, making up for the various lacks of others, and finding their own individual 'account' in what others offer. The aim is to sustain—to bear someone up, to be 'nice', to be 'kind', to be 'civilized'. And at the same time to accept, with a wise ruefulness, that others inevitably offer themselves up to be used. The principle of annexation is so emmeshed with the principle of sacrifice as to become an essential factor in the kinetics of the whole system. 'Life', the book says, is a community—perhaps a damned community, often a tragic one—of self-aggrandizing charity. And it is a community of 'usage', in both senses of the word.

It is typical of the book, therefore, that we should first approach Milly Theale through her dependent Susan Stringham, and that the 'account' Susie finds for herself in Milly should lead us into the account that Milly hopes to find for herself in the world at large: the world as considered first from her ledge in the Alps and then, at closer quarters, in the dining-room at Lancaster Gate. These two prospects taken by Milly not only grow out of Susie's prospect—they also grow out of Kate Croy's, the one taken from Chirk Street and the other from her private citadel that looks down on a social world and on Densher, waiting in Kensington Gardens. The destinies and patterns—the community of relationships—are already gathering, even before the two girls have met.

Almost the first thing we are told about Susan Stringham is that (rather as we saw with Kate) from the moment she leaves the 'narrow walls' of her private 'little life' and confronts the challenge of something greater, in the shape of her complicated companion, she finds herself necessarily engaged in the dishonesty of a 'manner': 'The woman in the world least formed by nature, as she was quite aware, for duplicities and labyrinths, she found herself dedicated to personal subtlety by a new set of circumstances, above all by a new personal relation' (p. 70). Susie, in her small way, is a woman of imagination and 'freedom'. James calls her, with mild amusement, a 'romantic'; but what he means in this case is that she discovers a thousand 'impressions' and 'aspects' and 'relations' in things. She is an 'adventurer' of consciousness—with 'duplicity' and the subsequent loss of 'freedom' as one of her adventures. A Bostonian by nature but educated in Europe, open to novelty and change, deprived of husband and children, she finds in Milly a 'revelation' of 'the real thing, the romantic life'. And in particular she is held by the pathos of seeing 'the potential heiress of all the ages' reduced by fate and ill health to humility. Her relationship is one of service to another (which includes filling Milly's only lack, that of 'culture'), in which she will also find fulfilment for herself. James gives a wonderfully sympathetic, comic sketch of Susie's stereotyped life which the advent of the New York girl's greater 'reality' has now transformed:

It was for the surrender of everything else that she was, however, quite prepared, and while she went about her usual Boston business with her usual Boston probity she was really all the while holding herself. She wore her 'handsome' felt hat, so Tyrolese, yet somehow, though feathered from the eagle's wing, so truly domestic, with the same straightness and security; she attached her fur boa with the same honest precautions; she preserved her balance on the ice-slopes with the same practised skill; she opened, each evening, her *Transcript* with the same interfusion of suspense and resignation; she attended her almost daily concert with the same expenditure of patience and the same economy of passion; she flitted in and out of the Public Library with the air of conscientiously returning or bravely carrying off in her pocket the key of knowledge itself; and finally—it was what she most did—she watched the thin trickle of a fictive 'love-interest' through that somewhat serpentine channel, in the magazines, which she mainly managed to keep clear for it. But the real thing, all the while, was elsewhere; the real thing had gone back to New York. (p. 73)

Susie makes a 'general surrender' of her own life to Milly's greatness—the first phenomenon ever fully to have satisfied her imagination—in the way that so many figures surrender at least a part of themselves to others to help bear up the system we have looked at. Like the others, Susie receives her *quid pro quo*: a 'mine of something precious', the 'treasure' of Milly's personality. And James proceeds to establish the 'grand scale' of this personality by the same mixture of analysis and dramatic impression that he used to convey the 'presence' of Kate Croy:

the vagueness, the openness, the eagerness without point and the interest without pause—all a part of the charm of her oddity as at first presented—had become more striking in proportion as they triumphed over movement and change. She had arts and idiosyncrasies of which no great account could have been given, but which were a daily grace if you lived with them; such as the art of being almost tragically impatient and yet making it as light as air; of being inexplicably sad and yet making it as clear as noon; of being unmistakably gay, and yet making it as soft as dusk. Mrs. Stringham by this time understood everything, was more than ever confirmed in wonder and admiration, in her view that it was life enough simply to feel her companion's feelings; but there were special keys she had not yet added to her bunch, impressions that, of a sudden, were apt to affect her as new. (p. 78)

James asks us for the moment to approach Milly in the same spirit as her friend, that of 'a consenting bewilderment' to her special kind of charisma: 'When Milly smiled it was a public event—when she didn't it was a chapter of history.' One of the elements that make her charisma so special is her wealth, never more forcefully used by James as one of the qualities that can constitute individual human 'greatness': wealth that empowers, that confers the freedom to exercise the imagination and the feelings; and wealth that creates, for good or bad, new challenges and new complexities of relationship. And at the very centre of James's vision of power, in the person of Milly Theale, lies the perception of her death—perceived by Susan and by Milly herself. Susie, aware from the outset of the quality of doom that hangs over her ailing friend, at once thinks of some 'latent intention' of suicide in Milly's dangerous posture on her Alpine ledge. And the idea of her death, the question of whether she will have much of life, is obviously present within everything else that Milly is considering as she sits there, since it spills out in her immediately subsequent talk with Susie.

The nature of Milly's fatality is of course of the highest importance to the novel: not the actual name of her disease, which James rightly omits as not belonging to the essence of the case or to the way in which Milly and the others choose to react to it, but the question of whether James uses the presence of death as a factor that makes for sentiment or for escapist idealism or for something more balanced and realistic. It is one particular emphasis placed on Milly's fatal disease that has produced the familiar 'angelic' view of her character: a wasting, pre-Raphaelite damozel, for ever leaning out from the bar of Heaven; the divine dove, released by the prospect of death, hovering over the stricken world.[10] But I think the clue to James's prevailing view of Milly in this novel, for all the traces of late-romantic morbidity one might detect in other works, is to be found in his description in the Preface of how Milly's dying is viable to the novelist not by its being 'the record predominantly of a collapse' but by its producing 'the unsurpassable activity of passionate, of inspired resistance'—in this lies 'the soul of drama'. 'The process of life gives way fighting, and often may so shine out on the lost ground as in no other connexion.'[11] This 'lost ground' is peopled by all

---

[10] The 'religious' or 'transcendental' interpretation of Milly's character— usually accompanied by references to the Book of Psalms and the dove image in 'Little Gidding'—has been very influential. At its most extreme it is found in Quentin Anderson's view of Milly as an allegory of Christ (*The American Henry James*, London, 1958, pp. 233–80), but it also determines much of the tenor of other important accounts, such as Dorothea Krook's (*The Ordeal of Consciousness*, pp. 195–231); and in many cases (not Miss Krook's) it results in an exaggeration of Milly's qualities of sickly passivity and withdrawal from the world (e.g. Leo Bersani, 'The Narrator as Center in *The Wings of the Dove*', *Modern Fiction Studies*, vi, 1960, 131–44).

[11] *The Art of the Novel*, pp. 289–91.

the other characters in the novel, whose own lives are illuminated
by the remorseless fact of Milly's dying, and are drawn together
by it into the entanglement that constitutes the book's plot. And
the knowledge of death for Milly herself is emphasized as something that affects her life, rather than as an entry into some higher
realm of values. Death being a catalyst as well as an ending, it
obliges her to consider the basis of her own life—as we shall see
in the great central episode at Matcham and at Sir Luke Strett's—
and therefore to enter more fully into the *conditions*, social and
personal, of that life. This is one of James's most important
perceptions in *The Wings of the Dove*, and one that explains so
much of the book's sombre power: that if its main characters'
lives are lived out in the pursuit of completeness, and if, like
Kate Croy, they are determined that the 'broken sentence' of their
inheritance must 'end with a sort of meaning', then it is only the
encounter with death that can provide the ultimate grammar of
that meaning.

Milly Theale in the Alps, empowered by her active imagination
and by her wealth, surveys 'the kingdoms of the earth' (more in
the spirit of a conquistador than of Christ—to whom the allusion
is usually taken to refer). Like Kate Croy, she decides that what
she wants is simply 'everything', and goes down in order to take
'full in the face the whole assault of life'. That is, although her
awareness of her death comes to her now (like Fleda Vetch's
'sense of desolation') in the very moment of plenitude, its effect is
to confirm her motive for action, not withdrawal. And in the
dinner-party scene at Lancaster Gate which follows, and which
signalizes Milly's immersion in those new 'relationships' between
herself and the world that comprise her 'life', the thought of death
comes back to her only to be accepted and worked into the
completeness of the scene before her: her sense of death into her
sense of London life.[12] Indeed, the vividness of the latter sense,
her discovery of the speed with which she can take up new relations, seems to prove to her the irrevocable truth of the former—

[12] When Milly later tells Susie, 'I want abysses', it is clear that 'abyss' means
'complications' and 'relationships' of an implicating kind. Of course the idea of
death is in the word—it at once reminds Susie of Milly's dangerous perch on a
real precipice, and of her illness—but 'abyss' is primarily Milly's involvement
in life, and not simply a chasm of extinction. (See, on the other hand, Jean
Kimball, 'The Abyss and *The Wings of the Dove*: the Image as a Revelation',
Nineteenth Century Fiction, x, 1956, 281–300.)

it suggests to her, in the midst of the glitter, 'that her doom was to live fast. It was queerly a question of the short run and the consciousness proportionately crowded.' She consciously embraces the full prospect of life-and-death, rather than the 'alternative', which can only be a retreat into the self:

while this process [of the dinner-party] went forward our young lady alighted, came back, taking up her destiny again as if she had been able by a wave or two of her wings to place herself briefly in sight of an alternative to it. Whatever it was it had showed in this brief interval as better than the alternative; and it now presented itself altogether in the image and in the place in which she had left it. The image was that of her being, as Lord Mark had declared, a success. (p. 106)

The scene of the dinner-party is one of the fullest representations in the book of the way Milly's mind tests and judges the new life that is around her, and at the same time submits to it and expands through the new modes of experience it offers. There is a superb and witty re-creation of the rise and fall of conversation; of intimate detail and general sonority and light. Pauses occur while dishes are presented, and the attention wanders away from one neighbour to eavesdrop on the next. Palpable glances are exchanged down the length of a table; the unspoken is detectable everywhere in the spoken; nuances make the air heavy and rich; and consciousness hums lika a dynamo inside the formal system of the occasion. The way James can blend the two, the private and the social sense of such an event, may at first remind one of Mrs. Ramsay's dinner-party in *To the Lighthouse*. But basically I think the resemblance may be rather closer to the group-scenes in Jane Austen: Emma's visits to Randalls or to the Coles', for example. In Virginia Woolf, the private world of those taking part is irremediably far beneath the surface of behaviour— so much of life has to stop while its inmost contours are being traced to the furthest verge of the expressible. Both Jane Austen and James, on the other hand, bring the two levels together more subtly—and for that reason more hopefully. It is not just a difference of technique from Virginia Woolf but different estimations of the worth of the life of surfaces and manners. For both Jane Austen and James reveal by such details of technique alone their respective conceptions of how the personal life—at a great cost and a great hazard, in James's case especially—is nevertheless able to flow outwards into the forms and shapes of a more public existence.

Throughout the dinner-party, James gives us Milly's fully awakened sense of life, all excitement and fear as she swims through a whole sea of 'elements . . . positively rich and strange', rejecting nothing, questioning everything, and grappling with such phenomena as the 'great reality' and distinct 'identity' of Kate and Mrs. Lowder and Lord Mark, who is her neighbour. And part of Milly's growth is that she quickly learns to accept the viability—though not the conclusiveness—of 'types'. She is puzzled why Lord Mark should so affect her as having a great reality when—in the English fashion—he so conceals the movements, if any, of his mind. Her explanation is, 'His type somehow, as by a life, a need, an intention of its own, insisted for him.' Her American mind is discovering that identity is partly constituted by external signs and conventions—by customs, a manner, a taking for granted, an established place in a society. As Kate Croy explains to her, with only partial irony, the completeness with which Lord Mark fills out his place and his type is enough to comprise a kind of genius on his part. And as Milly fumbles with various 'categories' to describe Lord Mark—a member of the world of 'fashion', or 'a potentially insolent noble'—she finds that he, more swiftly, has categorized her. She has been 'placed', and 'popped into a compartment'—that of 'the American girl' and the social 'success'. The subtle point—which distinguishes James's attitude here from his more simply critical view of 'categories' in an early work like *Daisy Miller*—is that Milly finds her 'compartment' comfortable and convenient: a useful mode of social travel. And this takes us at once back to the situation of Kate Croy, who herself has discovered, quite recently, that to accept the roles which others cast you in—'the version that met their convenience'—is 'the way to live'. Milly has entered the 'system' with a vengeance, and will be seen from now on playing various roles, in completely normal and 'innocent' duplicity: that is, in growing sophistication and experience. Her roles, which are the sign of a life of manners, are a compromise, being designed to please others and keep the system—the golden bowl of the system—intact; or, if inevitably cracked, to keep it in one piece. And after all, even Maggie Verver reconstitutes the 'golden bowl' of two threatened marriages on a worldly basis of sophisticated concealment, mutual 'convenience', and elliptical 'decency' (rather than of Grace and Redemption, as is often suggested).[13]

Although Milly's roles are active and organic, and not just defensive or totally foreign to her nature, James always allows the voice of natural freedom, the voice of the untyped individual, to question the merits of a life that requires them. Milly, who has wished to suspend judgement and play her roles, now comes out from behind them and makes a judgement against Lord Mark and the English system: 'You're *blasé*, but you're not enlightened. You're familiar with everything, but conscious, really, of nothing. What I mean is that you've no imagination' (p. 107). The temptation for the critic who takes the 'ethereal' view of Milly, or sees the book as a fable of good and evil, is to single out Milly's condemnation here as the first shattering beam of light cast by the Dove into the gathering shadows of the secular world. In fact, the Dove's judgement is at once shown to be itself lacking in imagination. Lord Mark laughs at it: ' "Oh, I've heard that", the young man replied, "before!" ' Her criticism has fallen into the pattern of a cliché—and a very American cliché, against the English, which the English themselves, especially the travelled English like Lord Mark, can easily stigmatize as being glib and naïve (though the criticism retains a sting). And in recompense we then see Milly quite uningenuously using a very 'English', a very social tactic against Lord Mark. In order to protect herself from the growing possibility of too personal an involvement with him, she consciously changes the conversation to the subject of 'the handsome girl' further down the table: 'She accordingly put in Kate Croy, being ready to that extent—as she was not at all afraid for her— to sacrifice her if necessary.' And Milly, to the end of the dinner scene, proceeds consciously to fill out the impersonal role of the American Girl which allows her such safety and such freedom to manœuvre—her tribute to the civilized ease of manners.[14]

---

[13] Milly Theale's role-playing has more often been seen as simply a loss and a betrayal—for Naomi Lebowitz, for example, she is destroyed by the metaphors and the conventions forced on her by this mannered, manipulative society (*The Imagination of Loving: Henry James's Legacy to the Novel*, Detroit, Mich., 1965, pp. 60, 76–7).

[14] Milly's complicated 'judgement' of society is worth contrasting with the judgement made by another such 'innocent' straying through a web of manners as Mr. Longdon, in *The Awkward Age*. His complete moral disapproval, and the lack of any very convincing richness in the manners of the Buckingham Crescent

Milly's 'sacrifice' of Kate is a piece of humour, of course, and a tiny incident. But in the knowledge of Kate's later plot to sacrifice Milly it seems possible to recognize Milly's little gambit with a faint twinge of irony. At least it helps to confirm the important fact in this book that Kate's particular plot is touched and even indirectly supported by many other plots and sacrifices—and especially by the general plot against 'sincerity' that incriminates anyone in a tight social situation, such as this dinner-party, or an impecunious secret engagement. The note of incrimination, in fact, is caught up in a very faint current of unease that runs beneath the lively social graces of the whole dinner scene—like the strain we felt between Kate and Densher in Kensington Gardens. From the beginning of the scene, Milly is 'oppressed' as well as stimulated. She fears her own weakness when faced by a complicated social reality that has something just a little menacing within it—as when she realizes that Lord Mark is trying to extract information about Aunt Maud from her: 'she had, on the spot, with her first plunge into the obscure depths of a society constituted from far back, encountered the interesting phenomenon of complicated, of possibly sinister motive' (p. 102). And her suspicion is confirmed by Lord Mark's offhand references to the whole system of 'usage' into which she has strayed, and according to which Aunt Maud in 'backing' Milly will 'get back . . . her money': 'Nobody here, you know, does anything for nothing.'[15] If Milly has her slight

---

set, point to the comparative simplicity and even thinness of that book's treatment of the theme.

[15] The fullest description of the 'system' in these particular terms comes later from Kate, as she initiates Milly into the knowledge of it:

'. . . the working and the worked were in London, as one might explain, the parties to every relation.

Kate did explain, for her listening friend: everyone who had anything to give—it was true they were the fewest—made the sharpest possible bargain for it, got at least its value in return. The strangest thing, furthermore, was that this might be, in cases, a happy understanding. The worker in one connexion was the worked in another; it was as broad as it was long—with the wheels of the system, as might be seen, wonderfully oiled. People could quite like each other in the midst of it, as Aunt Maud, by every appearance, quite liked Lord Mark, and as Lord Mark, it was to be hoped, liked Mrs. Lowder. . . . She declined to treat any question of Milly's own "paying" power as discussible; that Milly would pay a hundred per cent—and even to the end, doubtless, through the nose—was just the beautiful basis on which they found themselves' (pp. 118–19).

unease, the reader's is greater. At the very start of the dinner we are told, quite casually and without emphasis (which is how it must appear, through Milly's eyes), that Kate Croy has made a point of bringing Lord Mark to Milly to take her down to dinner. And at once we are reminded that there is a significant disparity between Milly's consciousness and the full facts of this social scene: the fact, for example, known to us, that Lord Mark is Aunt Maud's candidate to marry Kate, and that Kate therefore must be using Milly's presence to take the pressure off herself. It is only a little 'plot' by Kate—very far as yet from *the* plot. But the way James simply shows Kate dropping Lord Mark on to Milly, and leaves us to realize that an unseen motive is at work in her, is the beginning of that powerfully effective process by which the movements of Kate's mind are kept distant from us—revealed by surmise and by indirect account—and are thereby made all the more ominous. Milly, therefore, for all her discoveries and her delight through the dinner scene, lags several steps behind her situation, and is to that degree at its mercy. And it is a disparity that will only end much later when Lord Mark, in Venice, puts her at last in command of the facts.

These threats and discords within the dinner-party at Lancaster Gate are as yet minor ones, and what is emphasized is that Milly is on the brink of becoming a 'success' in London society, and that this kind of 'success' will offer to Milly's quickened sense of life exactly what she envisaged for herself above the Brünig pass. To succeed socially is to be taken up by many people and to have the chance of vivid and differentiated relationships with each of them personally, and also for the mind to experience and to discriminate among the endless relations and aspects of so many burgeoning situations. 'Relationships' and 'aspects', like the intelligent borrowing of 'conventions' and 'types', afford the forms that alone make perception possible, and allow the mind and the heart to expand their commerce with the world. In putting this at once into practice, the *confidante*, who is Susie, echoes and extends the experience of her 'princess'. She is 'carried away' by her 'prospect' and 'revelation' of 'the world', which is accompanied by some 'dread' and 'uneasiness'. And 'the world' takes the form of her childhood friend Mrs. Lowder, whose extraordinary 'quantity' as a person is conveyed by one of James's comically elaborated images:

Mrs. Lowder . . . was spacious because she was full, because she had something in common, even in repose, with a projectile, of great size, loaded and ready for use. That indeed, to Susie's romantic mind, announced itself as half the charm of their renewal—a charm as of sitting in springtime, during a long peace, on the daisied, grassy bank of some great slumbering fortress. (p. 112)

A more important touchstone of this new world of reality, for both Milly and her companion, is the looming figure of Kate. It is characteristic of how the book explores the actual techniques of people's responses to one another that it should show Milly and Susie trying at first to apprehend Kate's identity by the aid of analogy and aesthetic image, including the image provided by the social 'type'. Kate becomes 'a figure in a picture stepping by magic out of its frame'; she is the 'flower-strewing damsel', the 'chosen daughter of the burgesses' deputed to meet the 'princess' at the city gate and to offer the princess the pleasures of 'the real'. She is 'the wondrous London girl in person', out of *Punch*; and she is 'the product of a packed society who should be at the same time the heroine of a strong story'—and all this is 'by a necessity of [Milly's] imagination'. After analogy comes direct confrontation—and James beautifully charts the progress of what is at first a real relationship between Milly and Kate, based on certain similarities, exciting admiration and a sense of 'discovery' in each of them, and yet revealing an equally basic incompatibility. Kate finds confirmation of her own driving motive in the advent of Milly—responds to the girl's 'power', the 'extravagance' of her tragic New York history, and above all to the strength of her money. And Milly finds in Kate a confirmation of her latest insight into the ambiguous value of manners: she is a little repelled by the way Kate can reject Susan Stringham as an uninteresting person, and yet she discovers that there might be 'a wild beauty . . . or even a strange grace' in this rather cold sophistication, this social code of self-defence by which objects of dangerous tedium, like poor Susie, are to be avoided 'by the habit of anticipation'. But much more ominously and pathetically, we see Milly soon come upon the fact that there is an unseen side to her new friend, and that in herself there is a side that will always remain unseen to Kate. And the unseen side of both women begins to wear the features of the absent Merton Densher, who is never named between them even though each suspects the part he has played in the private life of the other. Milly detects 'a great darkness' between herself and Kate, and 'a failure of common terms'—another of James's touching breakdowns of friendship and promised unity. We see the two young women begin to watch one another—so early, so long before the famous 'Maeterlinck' image for their watchful separation in Venice. We see Milly discover and utilize a 'manner' towards Kate. We see her sense of their private divisiveness confirmed in wider, public terms when Kate takes her to see her sister Marian and introduces her to the bewildering English 'geography' of social gaps and intervals. And lastly, in the tell-tale nervousness and inconsequence of Milly's voice when she discusses Densher with Susie we detect yet another current that is drawing Milly deeper into the 'abyss' of personal and social relations—and drawing her towards the great crisis and revelation that marks the fulcrum of the book.

III

The centre of *The Wings of the Dove*—not in terms of length but certainly in terms of structure and meaning—comprises Chapters 10 to 13. The density of the writing, the dramatized interaction of shifting feelings and judgements, the endless modifications, and the thorough interweaving with every other part of the book, all reach a new intensity that makes commentary more than usually inadequate. The two chapters devoted to Milly's visit to Matcham, for example, contain some of James's most exalted celebration of the full 'life' achieved through style, and at the same time some of his most calculated exposures of it. And Milly herself appears now as a dazzled *ingénue*, now as a woman of profound spiritual insight, and now in various positions between the two. The passages involved are difficult, and have to be read with painful scrupulousness. And the ultimate effect, as elsewhere in the book, is that these hairline distinctions and contrary evaluations do not lose their separate validity—which is always an important one—but nevertheless cohere to create something larger and more comprehensive. They create the sense of a complicated continuum—the sense of a life, in fact—big enough and natural enough to contain them all, and more. And in this way James's ambiguity, which at its best proceeds from his almost unbearable lucidity of mind, becomes a truly mimetic instrument.

The garden-party (or weekend visit, perhaps) at Matcham is in itself a peculiar triumph of style, of sophisticated manners at their most glamorous, their most benevolently intoxicating. We saw earlier how Kate in her perfection of style had seemed to Milly to step out of a picture-frame. And now, as part of the sense of climax that marks the episode, we see manners become fully identified with art. The result is a grand harmony that includes the detailed and the human as well as the general and the impersonal. Not least, we see that the harmony is a relationship: a harmony between the inherent beauty of these things and the imagination of Milly, the observer and participant, who always contributes to what she observes. It is one of those scenes of near-ecstatic unity in the tradition of Longmore's walk in the French countryside in *Madame de Mauves*—or, more powerfully, it is as if Fleda Vetch had won her Poynton. For a moment, anyway, as 'a high-water mark of the imagination', it seems to represent the grand summation of experience that has been Milly's goal since she looked down on the earth from her high place in the Alps:

The great historic house had, for Milly, beyond terrace and garden, as the centre of an almost extravagantly grand Watteau-composition, a tone as of old gold kept 'down' by the quality of the air, summer full-flushed, but attuned to the general perfect taste. Much, by her measure, for the previous hour, appeared, in connexion with this revelation of it, to have happened to her—a quantity expressed in introductions of charming new people, in walks through halls of armour, of pictures, of cabinets, of tapestry, of tea-tables, in an assault of reminders that this largeness of style was the sign of *appointed* felicity. The largeness of style was the great containing vessel, while everything else, the pleasant personal affluence, the easy, murmurous welcome, the honoured age of illustrious host and hostess, all at once so distinguished and so plain, so public and so shy, became but this or that element of the infusion. The elements melted together and seasoned the draught, the essence of which might have struck the girl as distilled into the small cup of iced coffee she had vaguely accepted from somebody, while a fuller flood, somehow, kept bearing her up—all the freshness of response of her young life, the freshness of the first and only prime. (p. 136)

But Milly—here is the subtle balancing of the scene—stands outside as well as inside the picture. Her mind, which alternates like any other mind, has its freedoms to offset its surrenders, and in the midst of so much 'rose-colour' and so much 'swimming together in the blue' is capable of 'swift crosslights, odd beguilements'. She can accept the 'serenity' evoked by Aunt Maud's ingratiatory murmurings about her being a great 'success'. But at the same time she sees very clearly that Aunt Maud is trying very hard to talk herself into the same state of serenity and social success. Similarly, for all her bedazzlement and for all the soothing compliments that lap over her at Matcham, Milly still realizes that it is Kate, and not herself, who is 'the handsomest thing there' and who is the true hallmark of the Matcham style. And—in a brilliant flash—she recognizes the *objective* quality about Kate that makes her belong more totally than she ever can to the world of manners and style. There is no more striking instance than this—brief insight though it is—of the profound disparity between the two girls. Kate, despite her intelligence and irony, is in some important ways less free-moving and even more trapped than Milly. She can so belong to the life of style as to lose her own identity in it for long periods:

She became thus, intermittently, a figure conditioned only by the great facts of aspect, a figure to be waited for, named and fitted. This was doubtless but a way of feeling that it was of her essence to be peculiarly what the occasion, whatever it might be, demanded when its demand was highest. There were probably ways enough, on these lines, for such a consciousness; another of them would be, for instance, to say that she was made for great social uses. (pp. 138–9)

Milly also perceives that there is some relation between this social and 'objective' quality in Kate and that 'unseen side' of her, connected with the name of Densher, which has already thrown its shadow across their intimacy. Kate's capacity for living is always, in part, her capacity for being 'a beautiful stranger', and for being so 'other'. 'Distance' is integral to her character (and to James's technique of displaying it): it belongs to her strangely attractive 'brutality' and to her partial coldness. It is a quality that Matcham absolutely requires. There is no one more 'other' in the book, for example, more conditioned 'by the great facts of aspect', than the aloof and manipulative Lord Mark, and he, it seems, is the heir of Matcham itself—certainly, in his combination of a decent, kindly conformity and wordless self-seeking he is the true heir to the Matcham manner. It is the quality that Milly noted before in the propensity of the English to fulfil certain 'types', and the quality that she and Susan detected in

Aunt Maud—'her being . . . English and distinct and positive, with almost no inward, but with the finest outward resonance'. 'Inwardness' is the American quality *par excellence*. And 'otherness', like 'type', belongs to the brave Old World of impersonal forms, inherited masks, and studied evasions.

At the centre of Matcham and all its represents—in the very middle of the great house and the resplendent occasion—the Bronzino painting waits for Milly, like a death's head at the feast. As she is led towards it by Lord Mark, to be shown the portrait's resemblance to herself, of which everyone is talking, she has to move with him through the whole 'mystic circle' of the Matcham company. And her progress, dramatized on the page for us in the fluctuations of her response, is a brief progress through the gamut of complex social living: from its heights to its very low places, and back again. The 'circle' may be a 'mystic' one, but it also seems to be made up of 'fellow-strollers more vaguely afloat than themselves, supernumeraries mostly a little battered, whether as jaunty males or as ostensibly elegant women'. Contact with them is a matter of 'soft concussions' and of hearing their 'inveterate "I say, Mark" '. Milly has 'a sense of pleasant voices, pleasanter that those of actors, of friendly, empty words and kind, lingering eyes'. That the kindliness could come from a superior breed of actors, mouthing inanities, is a strong qualification of it. And at the same time, kindliness, charm, and the fine avoidance of harsh concussions are rich compensation for some emptiness. Milly detects the slight hollowness but continues to value the style, since it also has the virtues of charm, some sensitivity, a historical continuity, an aesthetic complexity: features that together 'might be as good a way as another of feeling life'. And immediately before seeing the Bronzino, Milly's hesitant acceptance of the life of style suddenly swells up confidently into another climax of her imagination and feelings: 'Once more things melted together—the beauty and the history and the facility and the splendid midsummer glow: it was a sort of magnificent maximum, the pink dawn of an apotheosis, coming so curiously soon' (pp. 143–4). Even in this 'apotheosis' there is a scrupulous shade of irony in the phrasing: 'magnificent maximum' and 'pink dawn'. James knows clearly what Milly half-intuits: that there is something of a bubble about all this glory and all this slightly facile, even slightly vulgar 'apotheosis'.

And it is death that defines it: death that enforces insight and discrimination.

The Bronzino portrait, like any mirror, is charged with death. It is the record of a beautiful woman, resembling Milly, who is long dead. And Milly's knowledge of the woman's death is part of her aesthetic perception of the picture. The woman in her day and in her life was a triumph of style; and the Bronzino version of her is also a triumph of style.[16] And within the style of the woman's beauty and the cold style of the artist who has commemorated her—so 'unaccompanied by a joy'—there lies the anti-style of extinction itself. Milly's response is very deep. Her 'pale sister' is the reminder of her own death and the confirmation of her suspicions about this Matcham world of *maniera* she has been led into, and partly shaped by. But the reminder of the deathliness in it does not obliterate that world, either for her or for us. The 'magnificent maximum' shrivels for the instant—especially when its representatives now step forward, while Milly feels tearful and faint, in the shape of the fatuous Lord and Lady Aldershaw. And even more chilling, there is the sight of Kate at her most managerial and 'objective', in whose very compassion for Milly at this moment there is a reminder of the conscious, conventionalized virtues of her 'style' and of her social 'set'.[17] But the point still remains that Milly is presented by James as having been perfectly entitled to over-respond in the way she has to Matcham's 'magnificent maximum'. She is so entitled by the innocent altruism and energy of her imagination, and also by the real qualities of the Matcham life. Her perception of death, through the Bronzino, does not amount to an outright rejection of an immoral world but also

[16] Without wishing to give too much to it, one cannot ignore the fact that James went out of his way to choose Bronzino and not Reynolds, say: that is, to choose one of the highest devotees of style, of sophisticated and tense distortion, of *alta maniera*. Also, as has been remarked, Bronzino's flesh—in his portrait of Lucrezia Panciatichi, for example, which may have been the one in James's mind—is singularly white and deathly. (See Miriam Allott, 'The Bronzino Portrait in *The Wings of the Dove*', *Modern Language Notes*, lxviii, 1953, 23–5; and Viola Hopkins Winner, *Henry James and the Visual Arts*, Charlottesville, Va., 1970, pp. 82–4.)

[17] This is Kate's compassion for her sick friend that Milly had already foreseen, and called in anticipation 'the height of the disinterested'. In perfect contrast to Kate's reserved pity, Milly is now shown making a typically warm and quixotic gesture to Kate: she asks her to come to Sir Luke Strett's as a friend and companion in order to make amends in her own mind for having noticed Kate's 'reserve'.

expresses her horror at the prospective loss of consciousness—consciousness that has its rights to take things as they come and as they appear, even after it has discovered their faults and their impermanence, along with its own.

The effects of Milly's brief communion with the Bronzino painting accompany her into Sir Luke Strett's consulting-rooms soon afterwards, and find there a final clarification and even a resolution. This is why it is so important to treat the Matcham scene and the two linked visits to the great doctor's as an integral episode, and not to allow the famous Bronzino 'moment' to stand out by itself. The parallels between the scenes are so close, indeed, as to be a little delusive. Just as all those at Matcham, with their 'kind eyes', are joined in bearing Milly up within their 'mystic circle', so Sir Luke Strett, with a Matcham-like blandness, seems to adhere to the same system of convenience and sustenance by his aim of 'easing her off beautifully'. Milly 'surrenders' to Sir Luke's professionalism and 'general goodwill', and enters into this new 'relation' as into a rich 'possession'. Sir Luke's consulting room, filled with the soothing hum of medical expertise, is another cell in the great honeycomb of manners—everyone bearing up, and living off, everyone else; everyone devoted to the same principle of 'happiness'; everyone engaged in the one conspiracy, more or less benign. But there is a progression and a difference, in that Milly's intensified sense of death, made all the more acute by the increasing desirability of the world, now comes under an extraordinary form of tutelage from the man who is by her own description more a priest and confessor than a clinician.

Sir Luke is more cryptic than any priest, and there is a penumbra of mystery around him that is only partly of Milly's own creating. But the essential meaning of the scene is perfectly accessible and is absolutely crucial. Milly learns from Sir Luke how she must accept her personal destiny: what she must do with the knowledge that has been growing inside her like death itself, and that flowed over in her tears before the Bronzino. Why Sir Luke avoids the direct medical issues and tells Milly that she can *decide* to live is because the question is no longer one of physical survival for her but of 'defeating' death by consciously seizing every chance of happiness that life still offers her.[18] It

---

[18] His exhortation to Milly to 'take the trouble' to 'live' is an ironic counterpart to Strether's similar exhortation to little Bilham in Gloriani's garden, in

must come from Milly herself. Sir Luke can do no more than suggest this in his elliptical way, and he can only help by giving her confidence in her own powers of consciousness—including her power to love. And this, after all, is profoundly different from being 'borne up' by the 'kindly eyes' of Matcham. It is a process of self-scrutiny and gathering together her own resources that affords Milly 'something firm to stand on', even if the purely medical diagnosis means 'being let down'. That is, she is being helped to discover a meaning for her life that will include, at the centre, the certainty of her early death. Milly's quest, like that of the other characters of the book, has been for some fulfilling experience and knowledge. And just as those others find something of their 'account' in friends and lovers, so in Sir Luke Milly has one of her closest encounters with 'the real'—the encounter being the more productive that it forces her to find the real within herself, within the capacity of her own will and imagination. Sir Luke offers her the necessary stance of seeing her situation temporarily from the outside—which is why he appears as confessor rather than healer. And the 'beautiful, beneficent dishonesty' of his evasive manner is in the end a way of making her interpret the signs and arrive at the facts for herself: a manner so full of affectionate pity can only mean the case is a terminal one. By being tactful to the point of the sphinx-like, Sir Luke is acting like any emissary of destiny, who states the riddle and leaves it to the traveller to make that destiny his own by the way he reads its tokens and uniquely lives it out. Sir Luke is an authority— impersonal, though concerned—and he holds the scales on which Milly can freely choose to place her life. And for all these reasons his figure takes on a paternal grandeur in her eyes, and his consulting-room becomes a whole world in which at last she can find a permanent place: a compendium of those 'kingdoms of the earth' she once looked down on, and a quintessence of innumerable other lives and other disburdened truths:

The very place, at the end of a few minutes, the commodious,

The Ambassadors. She *can* live, *can* experience in consciousness, like Bilham; but her life *in time* is within sight of its end. James, as in his essay, 'Is There a Life After Death?', allows these two senses of 'life' to play against one another: the life that is dependent primarily on the energies of consciousness and the life that is more clearly dependent on time and the body. (The essay appears in F. O. Matthiessen, *The James Family*, New York, 1947, pp. 602–14).

'handsome' room, far back in the fine old house, soundless from position, somewhat sallow with years of celebrity, somewhat sombre even at midsummer—the very place put on for her a look of custom and use, squared itself solidly round her as with promises and certainties. She had come forth to see the world, and this then was to be the world's light, the rich dusk of a London 'back', these the world's walls, those the world's curtains and carpet. She should be intimate with the great bronze clock and mantel-ornaments, conspicuously presented in gratitude and long ago; she should be as one of the circle of eminent contemporaries, photographed, engraved, signatured, and in particular framed and glazed, who made up the rest of the decoration, and made up as well so much of the human comfort; and while she thought of all the clean truths, unfringed, unfingered, that the listening stillness, strained into pauses and waits, would again and again, for years, have kept distinct, she also wondered what *she* would eventually decide upon to present in gratitude. (pp. 154–5)

In this 'brown old temple of truth' Milly can conceal nothing. She exposes herself in order to discover herself and to absorb the fact of her irremediable loneliness and responsibility, which she sees without self-pity or undue pathos: 'one's situation is what it is. It's me it concerns. The rest is delightful and useless. Nobody can really help.' Milly repeats the phrase, 'I like you to see me just as I am.' And these are words we will remember when Kate and Densher, too, in *their* journey towards the truth about themselves, come to their crossroads like Milly's: one marked for Densher by his challenge, 'Will you take me just as I am?'; and for Kate by her valediction, 'We shall never be again as we were.'

Milly bears her new certainty out of the private consulting-room into the surrounding world of London, and discovers in that 'grey immensity' that her personal fate is also the world's fate. It is a perfect stroke on James's part, and one that creates the most general extension of this whole episode's significance. The significance is at first one that brings a strange hope and zest, under the shadow of annihilation—a 'military posture' and a new daunting 'freedom' in exchange for the old 'freedom' of health and safety. Milly has preserved her will and her freedom at the very point where Roderick Hudson lost his: by deciding to join all her intrinsic energies and spiritual creativity to whatever her destiny has in store for her, and by 'taking this personal possession of what surrounded her'. She takes possession of the full remnant of her life through having entered into possession of her death. And she now walks across London (she, too, descending from her 'terrace') to celebrate 'the idea of a great adventure, a big dim experiment or struggle in which she might, more responsibly than ever before, take a hand'. But of course Milly's mood shifts, as it must—we are at the very quick of the girl's inmost life: it comes and goes like a flame—and as she enters Regent's Park and speculates on all she has just learned from Sir Luke the exaltation of the 'adventure' sinks into resignation and even towards despair:

she had come out, she presently saw, at the Regent's Park, round which, on two or three occasions with Kate Croy, her public chariot had solemnly rolled. But she went into it further now; this was the real thing; the real thing was to be quite away from the pompous roads, well within the centre and on the stretches of shabby grass. Here were benches and smutty sheep; here were idle lads at games of ball, with their cries mild in the thick air; here were wanderers, anxious and tired like herself; here doubtless were hundreds of others just in the same box. Their box, their great common anxiety, what was it, in this grim breathing-space, but the practical question of life? They could live if they would; that is, like herself, they had been told so; she saw them all about her, on seats, digesting the information, feeling it altered, assimilated, recognizing it again as something, in a slightly different shape, familiar enough, the blessed old truth that they would live if they could. (p. 163)

It is an intense, spotlighted moment: unusual for James in its plainly symbolical use of a general crowd of people. All of life, the human lot itself, seems to be concentrated into one place and one time—'the dog-days in the Regent's Park'—and is given the shape of idle lads and wanderers, shut in a box. Milly sits motionless on her bench of desolation among all the others, recognizing that she is one of a large company, and divided between a sense of bleak comradeship and of total denudation:

It reduced her to her ultimate state, which was that of a poor girl—with her rent to pay, for example—staring before her in a great city. . . . She looked about her again, on her feet, at her scattered, melancholy comrades—some of them so melancholy as to be down on their stomachs in the grass, turned away, ignoring, burrowing; she saw once more, with them, those two faces of the question between which there was so little to choose for inspiration. It was perhaps superficially more striking that one could live if one would; but it was more appealing, insinuating, irresistible, in short, that one would live if one could. (pp. 165–6)

The image of a despairing humanity burrowing into the grass is equalled for effect only by James's word-play at the end of the passage, where 'one could live if one would' fades away into 'one would live if one could', and Milly and her companions are left together staring into the abyss that lies between all desire ('one would') and all possibility ('if one could').[19]

Milly, by confronting her private destiny in Sir Luke's back room, and her destiny as one of the whole race of human burrowers in Regent's Park, has in fact touched bottom, and has found a strength that will see her through to the end—or almost to the end. Her 'adventure' now is to return to the life that awaits her in the fashionable terraces outside the Park—never forgetting what she learned in her intimate confessional and on her public bench. This is the superbly logical function of the remaining scenes of Book 5. Milly, enlightened, destined, and 'under arms' for the purposes of survival, will take up more avidly than before the roles and some of the weapons of the terrace-world. We at once see her choosing to act out the role of mysterious princess that Susie has placed her in. And when Kate Croy arrives at Milly's hotel that very evening, in all the unconscious insolence of her health and handsomeness, asking for 'news' of her stricken friend's consultation with Sir Luke, Milly sees with new clarity that her only possible relation with Kate must henceforth be one of self-defensive concealment. All through Kate's next visit—that lurid, menacing scene where a rabidly cynical Kate tries to complete Milly's initiation into the jungle nature of English society and warns her, 'You may very well loathe me yet'—we watch Milly learning how to deal with Kate, while Kate to her own belief has been dealing masterfully with Milly. Kate, pacing the room 'like a panther', is on the brink of conceiving her full plot against Milly—we can surmise this from her strange warning and from her being so nervous and so irritated at the sight of her friend's 'residuary innocence of spirit'—and it is because she is looking

---

[19] Barbara Hardy, in a sensitive essay, makes the point (with which I would not completely agree) that it is Milly herself who is creating the symbolism in this scene: 'The very flaunting of the act of interpretation admits, within the novel, that there is a gap between the world outside and the use she makes of it in formulating her plight' (*The Appropriate Form*, 1964, pp. 22–5).

into her own dark spaces that she discovers this image for
Milly: 'You're a dove.' Milly takes up the image as one of the
best of her defensive weapons. Henceforth, she tells herself,
coming out a little breathlessly from this claustrophobic encounter,
she will be a dove, and study the dovelike. And the first act of the
dove is to tell a lie—to protect herself by telling Mrs. Lowder
that she has the impression from Kate's behaviour that Densher
has not yet returned from America, when in fact she believes the
opposite. This will be part of her 'form' and her 'manner'—her
contribution to the great honeycomb of social relationships, from
which, in recompense, she will continue to draw sustenance for
her own imaginative and emotional life, as Sir Luke Strett has
prescribed. It will be Milly's own little conspiracy: she will
manipulate the system, giving and taking, and challenging it
radically only where necessary. And of course the part she is
going to play is partly true. Milly does contain the dovelike,
alongside the Byzantine. And this is the nature of acting among
the complex and the sophisticated, of whom Milly is becoming
one: a consciously adopted role enables one to act out a truth
about oneself, as well as to conceal other truths. And though
Milly, in going to visit the National Gallery, is in retreat from
the strain of such acting, it can only be for a little while. She seeks
refuge in the impersonality of art, and even envies the life of the
lady-copyists there, so earnest and so detached. But in discovering
Kate and Densher surprisingly together in the Gallery, Milly has
at once to leave her peaceful post of observation ('to watch the
copyists and count the Baedekers') and return to the ceaseless
game and struggle of social manners. The meeting is fraught with
deep embarrassments and unaskable questions all round. The
only way for intercourse to proceed is by a courteous arrangement
of responses that marks 'a characteristic triumph of the civilized
state'. And remarkably, disconcertingly, it is Milly the dove,
much more than Kate, who steers them all through and controls
the whole incident. She invites the two others to lunch, acting
out the free American girl, playing 'her own native wood-notes',
with a deliberate masterfulness—'What Milly then gave she
therefore made them take'. For an hour or two Milly in her way
is almost as much a Juggernaut as Mrs. Lowder. And throughout
this lunch we have one of the subtlest analyses in the book of how
four people (Milly, Susie, Kate, and Densher) can conceal private

uncertainties, pains, and affections by throwing themselves with practised skill into the various gambits (places to sit, topics to discuss) laid down for them by the needs of others and by the needs of a complex and specific 'situation'. As in the case of that four-sided situation that animates James's last great novel with its demands for 'equilibrium', here in Milly's room is a precarious 'golden bowl' in the making—alongside a germinal conspiracy. Something of value to a civilization and to a small group of talented people must be preserved, as they all sit after their lunch in the hotel in Brook Street. Everywhere in the air around them is the thought of Sir Luke's recent visit there to Susie, telling her the worst, and the thought of Kate and Densher intimately con-joined in the National Gallery—a thought of death and a thought of deceit, to which their civilization will always succumb in the end. It is Milly in her worldliness who is the inspiration of them all, and who bears up their flawed golden bowl—Milly, burning afresh in her full adventure, advancing after every retreat, with her flaw diagnosed yet her strength redoubled, and with the last desired element in her search for what life offers now seated there beside her, a little abstractedly, in the person of Merton Densher.

7

The Sense of Life in
The Wings of the Dove: II

I

THE study of Merton Densher in the second half of *The Wings
of the Dove* has often been recognized as one of the book's
triumphs.[1] The line it follows seems clear: a man's maturing
involvement in 'relations' with others; an intensifying struggle
between his conscience and his passion; a battle to understand his
contradictory impulses and to discover what he himself really is.
But if the outline is obvious, the details are dense and shifting: as
caught up in the lifelike uncertainties and changes of each specific
moment as those of any other portrait in the novel. Our dominant
sense of him, as at the very beginning, is of a man virtually ill with
desire. If Milly wants fulfilment from the kingdoms of the earth
and Kate from worldly 'success', Densher wants to possess his
woman. Hampering practical details, well observed by James, add
to Densher's desperation: the all-important fact, for example, that
he and his lover have simply nowhere to go to be alone. We see
them meeting in the refreshment rooms at Euston Station and the
National Gallery, parting at the doors of hansom cabs, snatching a
momentary caress in Aunt Maud's drawing-room, unlinking their
arms as they feel observed, from far off, in the middle of St. Mark's
Square. The pressures on them both are enormous—and the
intolerable sense of their social circumscription, including their
lack of wealth, duly adds to the internal pressure of their physical
passion. Each pressure makes for tension between them: what
James calls finely, at one instance of their having to part in
frustration at the door of Densher's lodging, 'one of those strange

---

[1] That is, when it has not been seen as one of the book's failures—'unequal
to his ambitious role', is F. W. Dupee's complaint (*Henry James*, London,
1951, p. 248); while Richard Chase can give no more than 'a slightly baffled
assent' to the character (*The American Novel and its Tradition*, London, 1958,
p. 137). The usual Babel of opinions about anything Jamesian prevails.

instants between man and woman that blow upon the red spark, the spark of conflict, ever latent in the depths of passion'. The game of social concealment they have chosen to play brings about its own peculiar stresses, but it also provokes the most ancient game of all, the sexual power game. Densher's perpetual smothered resentment is a combination of thwarted desire, anger at being so manoeuvred and used by a skilful woman, and humiliation at the degree of helpless infatuation in himself that makes him accept her half-explained orders and suggestions. And all of this runs beneath his sense of absolute delight in his lover. He goes through a series of crises in which he challenges Kate—'Will you take me just as I am?' is the cry that marks one of them—and which always end in an overflow of sexual feeling for her that blinds him to everything but its own forceful reality.[2] It is a brilliant dramatization of a man's emotional and intellectual life being lived out on a knife-edge. Densher knows with a growing abhorrence the little falsities and lies that are beginning to pile up around him and Kate—in particular he is perturbed by the unexplained way they seem to be using Milly for their own convenience—but equally he can appreciate that Kate has a keener practical intelligence than he, and has an exacting passionateness of her own. And she is always able to play on his acute sense of tact and delicacy as effectively as on his sexuality. It is no mystery that Densher should go along with her demand to do what he is told and try to 'console' Milly—he only *just* goes along, time after time. To explain his obedience as due to self-delusion or moral timidity is only an explanation, after all, and not a full response. Unquestionably, he is shown to suffer from these failings—but just as certainly this is a case for painful recognition and understanding rather than for stark disapprobation alone.

Densher's unease about his personal relations with Kate grows at times into something of wider scope, and touches on the largest issues with which the book is concerned. For example, he recognizes, like Milly, that the necessary histrionic element in the life of manners to which he and Kate are now committed can also be an

[2] In an affecting contrast with Milly, Densher's sense of promised fulfilment in Kate becomes one with his 'act of renewed possession' of London, on his return from America. He sits, like Milly, on a bench in Regent's Park, staring at his very different 'prospect'—not for him the melacholy comrades burrowing into the grass but the thought of Kate waiting for him like the great globe itself (Chapter 17).

appalling burden, and even a dehumanizing one. He watches Kate, as actress, making her grand entrance into the drawing-room at Lancaster Gate, under Aunt Maud's gaze, and reacts with a mixture of spellbound excitement and frightened nausea, perceiving the high cost of such high art:

> That was the story—that she was always, for her beneficent dragon, under arms; living up, every hour, but especially at festal hours, to the 'value' Mrs. Lowder had attached to her. High and fixed, this estimate ruled, on each occasion, at Lancaster Gate, the social scene; so that our young man now recognized in it something like the artistic idea, the plastic substance, imposed by tradition, by genius, by criticism, in respect to a given character, on a distinguished actress. As such a person was to dress the part, to walk, to look, to speak, in every way to express, the part, so all this was what Kate was to do for the character she had undertaken, under her aunt's roof, to represent. It was made up, the character, of definite elements and touches—things all perfectly ponderable to criticism; and the way for her to meet criticism was evidently at the start to be sure her make-up was exact and that she looked at least no worse than usual. Aunt Maud's appreciation of that tonight was indeed managerial, and Kate's own contribution fairly that of the faultless soldier on parade. Densher saw himself for the moment as in his purchased stall at the play; the watchful manager was in the depths of a box and the poor actress in the glare of the footlights. But she *passed*, the poor actress—he could see how she always passed; her wig, her paint, her jewels, every mark of her expression impeccable, and her entrance accordingly greeted with the proper round of applause. (p. 217)

Here is Kate's Matcham quality of 'otherness' at its extreme— and a powerful representation to Densher of what she is doing for him, and to him. Further, this 'entrance' of Kate begins a jaded out-of-season dinner-party in which Densher hears his fellow guests relentlessly discuss and 'place' the absent Milly Theale to such a degree that their whole glamorous society, the object of all Kate's violent ambitions for them both, suddenly turns to 'twaddle' and banality—'if *this* was civilization—!' And then, of course, Kate, momentarily alone with him on a small sofa, disperses his qualms in the usual warmth of her personal presence.[3]

[3] It is perhaps a little puzzling why, in this same dinner scene, James makes so much of the strong 'relation' suddenly and intuitively established between Densher and Susan Stringham. Susie's later visit to him in his lodgings at Venice is really the most that comes out of it, and it may be that James had in

Densher's moments of detachment from his 'actress', and from the world through which she moves so much more tolerantly and expertly than he, are as yet only intervals in his steady progress towards conspiracy. It is impossible to say at what precise point in the book Kate conceives her full plot—that Densher must marry the fatally ill Milly in order to inherit her wealth for himself and Kate to marry on. But it grows, almost as an inevitable process, out of her early and much less invidious plot—that Densher should capitalize on Milly's fondness for him in order to lull Aunt Maud's suspicions about himself and Kate and to provide more ways in which the two of them can meet socially (while at the same time allowing Milly the pleasure of feeling affection and sympathy for a supposedly lovelorn Densher, 'rejected' by Kate). The device by which the private operations of Kate's mind at this stage in the book are kept distant from us—after our closeness to her in the opening chapters—is a peculiarly effective one. The sinisterness of her thinking is immensely increased, and yet at the same time the definite evil of her plot remains very human in scope—complicated always by its elements of pity and generosity—and is no more diabolical than Milly's goodness is divine. If we are not taken into Kate's mind, we are helped to know it by analogy: the book is full of its shadows, pronounced or faint. For example, by sharing so closely in the process of Densher's slipping into subterfuge—a gradual process that makes this section of the novel, between Densher's return to London and the general departure to Venice, more inward and more static on the surface than any other section of the book—we are better able to imagine how Kate herself must have slipped gradually from a limited and even mildly compassionate little 'plot' to the more hideous one that neither she nor the half-aware Densher can bear to articulate. And there is, of course, the most general analogy of all: despite Kate's individual responsibility for what is a personal and heinous decision, her conspiracy is also a reflex of the general 'conspiracy' of being civilized.

---

mind a fuller development of the relationship. No doubt it serves the further function of drawing Densher, like Milly, into more and more complicated involvements, and to that degree it is a part of his moral and psychological growth. It also increases the pressures on him later, within this 'circle of petticoats', when Susie can confidently add *her* expectations that he will help her with Milly by maintaining the fiction of being unengaged and therefore accessible to the girl's affections.

For example, as part of this 'conspiracy' of being 'kind' to Milly—
in the London way—Mrs. Lowder now joins those forces that are
all pushing Densher towards Milly ('The pieces fell together for
him as he felt her thus buying him off, and buying him—it would
have been funny if it hadn't been so grave—with Miss Theale's
money'). Even Sir Luke Strett, trying to 'bear up' Milly like the
rest, though with a more complete disinterestedness, wishes his
patient to come to terms with her possible young man. And in a
telling stroke, Susan Stringham becomes a fully fledged con-
spirator when she agrees with Mrs. Lowder to lie to Milly to hide
the all-important fact—fatal to Milly's hopes of love—that Kate
is as much in love with Densher as Densher with her. Even if
Susie feels she cannot lie directly she is prepared to lie by omitting
to tell the truth—which is exactly the same damning position that
Densher has adopted. And so we watch the purest duplicity and
the purest charity grow into one another, as involved as a love-knot.

Densher is by now caught in a 'wondrous silken web'—for
example in the notable scene at the hotel in Brook Street (Chapter
21) where he finds himself for the first time alone with Milly,
having called there at Kate's command. His motives for obeying
Kate here are not purely abject, but those that properly belong to
a social man: 'good sense and good humour', 'imagination',
'understandings and allowances', the avoidance of 'barbarity'—
that is, a code of gentlemanly tact as laid down by any system of
manners. To refuse to visit Milly would be hurtful and impolite,
in view of the fact that they have a friendship of sorts dating from
his stay in America. And it would also, he imagines, be too offensive
a gesture against Kate, whose own motives for sending him to
Brook Street are not all selfish. If he fails to go on seeing Milly in
the natural way that everyone would expect of him then the
results can only be 'gross', bringing pain to various people,
including the woman he loves. 'It was that he liked too much
everyone concerned willingly to show himself merely impracticable.'
And as he later formulates it, in Venice: 'The law was not to be a
brute in return for amiabilities'—the social law, once again, of
quid pro quo. Densher drifts towards Milly almost in the way that the
Prince becomes Charlotte's lover in *The Golden Bowl*: it is the
only thing, in the peculiar circumstances, that a *galantuomo* can
do. And in addition, to be provincial and over-scrupulous would
only 'bore' Kate, and would prevent him cultivating those amoral

qualities of vitality and style which he admires in his lover. To try to keep up to Kate's stringent and slightly mysterious demands of him, which after all do include being 'decent' and 'kindly' to everyone in sight, is even something of a 'romance', Densher can tell himself in his phases of confidence. It provides the adventure of 'living handsomely' and complicatedly, and seems to offer an aesthetic ideal of human behaviour that appeals to his contemplative mentality.

Nevertheless, faced by Milly's 'beautiful delusion' and 'wasted charity', and caught up in a rapid 'relation' with her, Densher finds himself in the grip of 'a case of conscience', realizing that to do the civilized thing is also to connive at a lie. The aesthetic ideal cannot quite overcome this: 'this inward ache was not wholly dispelled by the style, charming as that was, of Kate's poetic versions.' And we soon see that Densher's real 'adventure'—his full discovery of 'life'—is to take the form of a perpetual struggle, a see-sawing of rebelliousness and passivity, rather than the application of a gentlemanly code alone. The 'real thing', for him, is proving to be larger than what Kate on her own had promised. And in the scene where he has called at Milly's hotel there is a powerful effect of his two relationships, the one with Milly and the one with Kate, eating at one another. Beneath the words that are creating a new relation with Milly, the old one with Kate is subtly changing. Kate, always in his mind even as he responds to Milly, can only appear in a new light when compared to the American girl, and with a disturbing reminder to Densher that his knowledge of her is far from comlpete. So that when Kate herself unexpectedly arrives in Milly's room, and finds him waiting, there is a new note of challenge in his voice even as he accepts her usual emotional bribe to carry on with the plan of being 'kind' to Milly—a note of moral irritation as well as his old sexual irritation, and an ominous insistence on the responsibility that Kate is incurring: 'I do nothing for anyone in the world but you. But for you I'll do anything.' No love, we begin more and more to feel, can bear such responsibilities, or such a charge of energies that have turned in on themselves.

Densher's becomes a search to realize himself and his personal will in various terms that directly oppose one another—it is the quintessential search and agony of the Jamesian hero. For example, in gaining Kate he will clearly find satisfaction and fulfilment of a kind. But he wishes also to be whole and fulfilled in terms of his conscience, which speaks against certain of the conditions that Kate has imposed. As for Milly, she seems to offer little of a truly fulfilling nature to Densher at this stage. He is touched by her; he is charmed by her 'disconcerting poetry' and the 'old-fashioned melancholy music' of her personality; and her presence serves to stimulate his moral self. But his imagination does not possess her in the way that it possesses and is filled by Kate. Only nearer the time of her death does Milly come close to filling his life—and even then he does not seem to find his total 'account' in her in the way that characters in this book do find their 'account' in another person or event. He is always a little bored by her, even when he feels her charm, and her 'reality' for him is not ultimate but one that is always affected by the context of his other relationships. The faculty by which Densher best appreciates Milly will be, significantly, the faculty of memory.

The Venetian phase of his search for himself is ushered in by Densher encountering his own past, with the sight of the house where he had once, long before, rented rooms.[4] The house, and the white papers on its shutters that signify it is again available, become an image that brings to a point of concentration his whole crisis of will. The papers, as he stands meditating on them, are an emblem of his youth, of freedom, and, more specifically, of the possibility of finding an independent basis, physical and moral, for his present life in Venice (the importance of the building for Densher gains by its appearing immediately after the picture of Milly in *her* appropriate setting of the Palazzo Leporelli). The private lodging offers Densher a chance to stand outside the 'circle of petticoats' that has surrounded him and sapped his masculine will. It means a chance—which is also a challenge, for such an assertive man—to get something for himself out of the whole affair, and to make Kate pay at last for her domination and for their long sexual constraint:

It was thanks to her direct talent for life, verily, that he was just where he was, and that he was above all just *how* he was. The proof of a decent reaction in him against so much passivity was, with no great richness, that he at least knew—knew, that is, how he was, and how little he liked

---

[4] Unlike the editor in *The Aspern Papers*, Densher is not shown seeking for 'reality' in terms of the Venice that surrounds him, or in art, or poetry, or history, but only within himself and his relations with two women.

it as a thing accepted in mere helplessness. He was, for the moment, wistful—that above all described it; that was so large a part of the force that, as the autumn afternoon closed in, kept him, on his traghetto, positively throbbing with his question. His question connected itself even while he stood, with his special smothered soreness, his sense almost of shame; and the soreness and the shame were less as he let himself, with the help of the conditions about him, regard it as serious. It was born, for that matter, partly of the conditions, those conditions that Kate had so almost insolently braved, had been willing, without a pang, to see him ridiculously—ridiculously so far as just complacently— exposed to. How little it *could* be complacently he was to feel with the last thoroughness before he had moved from his point of vantage. His question, as we have called it, was the interesting question of whether he had really no will left. How could he know—that was the point—without putting the matter to the test? It had been right to be *bon prince*, and the joy, something of the pride, of having lived, in spirit, handsomely was even now compatible with the impulse to look into their account; but he held his breath a little as it came home to him with supreme sharpness that, whereas he had done absolutely everything that Kate had wanted, she had done nothing whatever that he had. So it was, in fine, that his idea of the test by which he must try that possibility kept referring itself, in the warm, early dusk, the approach of the southern night—'conditions' these, such as we just spoke of—to the glimmer, more and more ghostly as the light failed, of the little white papers on his old green shutters. By the time he looked at his watch he had been for a quarter of an hour at this post of observation and reflection; but by the time he walked away again he had found his answer to the idea that had grown so importunate. Since a proof of his will was wanted it was indeed very exactly in wait for him, lurking there on the other side of the Canal. (pp. 310–11)

And yet to prove his will by possessing Kate physically also means that Densher must commit himself more completely to her, to her plan, and therefore to her power: a paradox at the centre of his predicament that only adds to the irritability of his desire. The more he longs for her the more he opposes her supremacy, and begins to look for an 'advantage' over her, singling out any 'failure of perception' and 'weakness of vision' in her. These opening scenes in Venice are filled with a sense of the violence and of the passionate, separate manoeuvring that runs right through their relationship—always threatening that relationship yet always compatible with its reality and its binding power. Their inner turbulence wells up as the two of them walk in apparent 'solitude

H

and security' through St. Mark's Square, where the 'bright, historic air', filled with 'the flutter of doves', speaks only of 'the joy of life'—whereas in their talk there is sharp fear and conflict: a bitter ultimatum from Densher, 'I'll tell any lie you want, any your idea requires, if you'll only come to me'; and the 'cold quietness' of Kate's noncommittal response. Above all, there is the unbearable contrast between such private tumult and the composure of manner which their eternally public situation requires, St. Mark's Square being in this instance, as they stand in the middle of its space, the general arena as much as the drawing-room of Europe. 'They suggested nothing worse—always by Kate's system—than a pair of the children of a super-civilized age making the best of an awkwardness'—while the eyes of their companions appraise them in the distance, from the shadow of the arcades. And the strain imposed by these lovers' roles is brought to a celebrated climax in the even more theatrical publicity of the scene of manners that follows: the great scene of Milly's last party, where she, too, makes her full and final entrance into the drawing-room and the arena of her society.

II

First we must go back a little, to the beginning of Milly's stay in Venice:

Not yet so much as this morning had she felt herself sink into possession; gratefully glad that the warmth of the southern summer was still in the high, florid rooms, palatial chambers where hard, cool pavements took reflections in their lifelong polish, and where the sun on the stirred sea-water, flickering up through open windows, played over the painted 'subjects' in the splendid ceilings—medallions of purple and brown, of brave old melancholy colour, medals as of old reddened gold, embossed and beribboned, all toned with time and all flourished and scolloped and gilded about, set in their great moulded and figured concavity (a nest of white cherubs, friendly creatures of the air), and appreciated by the aid of that second tier of smaller lights, straight openings to the front, which did everything, even with the Baedekers and photographs of Milly's party dreadfully meeting the eye, to make of the place an apartment of state. (p. 282)

That great serpentine sentence embraces everything for Milly: the one mood of possession that momentarily fulfils her Alpine vision and Sir Luke's prescription together, and contains everything from the Tiepolo-like ceilings to the domestic photographs, the historic and the bathetically contemporary, the land and the sea, darkness and light, exterior and interior. Her whole consciousness has itself become an 'apartment of state', crammed with perception and response and with what Lord Mark, walking now into her *palazzo*, recognizes as 'the pride of life'. The possession is more complete than at Matcham, and when it is taken away, the deprivation is greater. As at Matcham, her sense of glory is partly dependent on how she is 'supported' by others—who by now form a whole retinue of the devoted (the comparison is made to Catherine the Great's attended progress across the steppes), and include her courier Eugenio as the latest of those who 'bear up' the Princess with adoring sincerity and also get their own 'account' in real or metaphorical currency. The bearing up of Milly is partly a social process, and is made possible only by the adoption of the false, the donning of roles and masks. Partly, it is a con-spiracy of silence among her friends, the 'common duplicity' at which she fully connives and by which no reference must be made to her ill health. But the whole process is now imaged, in little, in the description of her masked relationship with Kate—a relation-ship of masks within masks. The two girls, when alone together, act out a charade of intimate relief at having dropped the masks they have to wear in the more general charade of public appearance: 'It was when they called each other's attention to their ceasing to pretend, it was then that what they were keeping back was most in the air.' The famous 'Maeterlinck' metaphor which illustrates this seems strangely overwritten at first: Milly as the 'pale princess, ostrich-plumed, black robed' in her defended tower, with Kate as the 'wondering, pitying sister', the 'upright, restless, slow-circling lady of her court', looking wistfully at her from the other side of the moat's black water in the twilight, 'in the likeness of some dim scene in a Maeterlinck play' (pp. 286–7). But its 'atmospheric' quality is perfectly appropriate to the metaphor's range of sugges-tion: in particular to the way it moves rapidly from the thought of 'acting' to the thought of death. Milly is herself shut up in a tower behind her protective masks. But the tower also contains two other treasures, both of which have determined her social roles. There is the treasure of 'her own conception of her validity'—that is, her secret, hoarded knowledge of her own death, which she will reveal to no one. And there is the treasure of her wealth, which they all covet. So that in one image Milly's selfhood and her death and her money all seem compounded together. And the lady of the court's ominous yet wistful exclusion from the tower signifies the loneliness in Kate that accompanies her cupidity for Milly's wealth—for there is something in Kate, in this mood at least, that desires Milly's affection as well as her money. Just for a moment, the moment in which an elaborate metaphor unfolds, the two girls seem to be caught up in a movement beyond their individual volition: as though trapped amid the masks and scenery of an unchanging, mirthless human comedy.

James can now return to the picture of Milly's 'possession' of her *palazzo* with a difference of key: one of those profound yet delicate modulations of mood and meaning that make *The Wings of the Dove* so rich and so difficult a work. It is the presence beside her of Lord Mark, clearly full of his intention to propose marriage, that ushers in the change—less cruelly than the later and final change that will also be his responsibility. It is as if the comparative impersonality of Milly's feelings for him suddenly allows her to relax in her 'adventure', and in the defence of her tower, and to watch the vision of happiness slip from her 'possession':

She couldn't have said what it was, in the conditions, that renewed the whole solemnity, but by the end of twenty minutes a kind of wistful hush had fallen upon them, as if before something poignant in which her visitor also participated. That was nothing, verily, but the perfection of the charm—or nothing, rather, but their excluded, disinherited state in the presence of it. The charm turned on them a face that was cold in its beauty, that was full of a poetry never to be theirs, that spoke, with an ironic smile, of a possible but forbidden life. (p. 292)

The 'heiress of all the ages' is for the time as 'disinherited' as any of her fellow wanderers—Lord Mark among them, since he, too, has just arrived in Venice in pursuit of a 'perfection' (it is not just Milly's money that Lord Mark seeks, clearly: though her fortune would always be an integral part of life's 'poetry' for him, as for all of them). The taunting face of the *palazzo*'s beauty reduces Milly's 'adventure' to a tremulous, passive, and deathly withdrawal. Momentarily, she abandons her vision of the social kingdoms of the earth, with all their complex forms and roles and relations, and turns to 'the adventure of not stirring':

The romance for her, yet once more, would be to sit there for ever, through all her time, as in a fortress; and the idea became an image of never going down, of remaining aloft in the divine, dustless air, where she would hear but the plash of the water against stone. The great floor on which they moved was at an altitude, and this promoted the rueful fancy. 'Ah, not to go down—never, never to go down!' she strangely sighed to her friend. (p. 292)

Here is one of the few moments in the book where Milly adopts something of the 'angelic' state, the 'divine, dustless air'. It is like that period of withdrawal into a 'cold, still chamber' of aesthetic contemplation that came to Fleda Vetch, as she waited in despair at her sister's for an ending to *her* inner strife between commitment to the world as it is and to the mind's pattern for the world—the strife and drama within which all human values are created.[5] And surely the important point of this episode in *The Wings of the Dove* is not that the Dove is retreating in order to spread her wings aloft in the dustless air but that at once she descends, and that the drama of moods and values continues? 'Never to go down', she sighs to Lord Mark; but, drawn by the interest of his situation, she does go down, into yet another 'relation'. James creates a scene between Milly and Lord Mark that shows her in a phase unlike any other in the book—suddenly frank, appreciative, totally self-revealing ('I'm very badly ill')— and in a brief relationship, full of their mutual liking and inevitable divergences, that grows up on the spot. That is, immediately following on a moment of apparent transcendence or retreat we have, through Milly's reawakened alertness to the immediate possibilities of life, one of the most real and even tender encounters in the book. Milly is able to understand and to like Lord Mark more fully than ever before. She sees the ways in which he could be suited to her friend Kate, and tries, a little clumsily, to suggest Kate as a better match than herself. She can see in him the fine gracefulness of the English world's 'intonations' and 'shades', its dispassionate expertness, its kindliness—'it was the pleasant human way, without depths of darkness.' And equally, she can see in him and his world the self-blinding avoidance of the tragic and of 'the offensive real' ('the chill of the losing game'). After all the attractiveness that she now discovers in such a man, she can measure how her own life has begun to embrace much more than his: both Matcham in its glory and the death-pale Bronzino sitting

[5] See above, pp. 155–6.

in the heart of it. In the end, '[Lord Mark] was not good for what she would have called her reality.'

And it is Milly in possession of her full 'reality'—in possession of the Palazzo Leporelli's 'pride of life' and of the knowledge of its loss—who descends the staircase, uniquely dressed in white, to her final reception for her friends (in Chapter 28). The cracks have begun to open up even as Lord Mark left her, in the scene we have just looked at—he has walked off in sudden suspicion and bitterness at being rejected, leaving behind, for Milly, his troubling imputation that there may be more in Kate's relation to Densher than Kate has accounted for. But if the cracks are those that belong to the life of style, to the life of beautiful duplicities, then Milly's descent is directly *into* such style. She descends, not as the redeeming Dove, but as the active mind and personality taking on the necessary style of the human world. The whole evening in the *palazzo* is shaped by 'the pervasive mystery of Style'. It is Susan Stringham, the most loyal of the friends, loyal even in her plotting for Milly's happiness, who establishes the aesthetic analogy for the whole occasion. In conversation with Densher she converts it all into 'a Veronese picture'—and is thereby associated with Lord Mark's social stylishness, since he, too, in his 'proposal' scene, had invoked Veronese. Susie finds it necessary to stylize her own relation with Milly: she sees herself as 'the inevitable dwarf, the small blackamoor, put into a corner of the foreground for effect', or a retainer in 'one of the courts of heaven, the court of an angel'. And she also places Densher in the Veronese picture as the figure of 'the grand young man who surpasses the others and holds up his head and the wine-cup'—though Densher's awareness of his own falsity ('his attitude lacked the highest style') keeps him for a while outside the scene's harmonies and composition.[6] Milly herself, once again playing the role of 'the American girl' for all she is worth, is the source of this harmony. And so far is James from disowning the world of secular style—even while it is in the very process of betraying his heroine—that he shows Milly to be the manager of the whole splendid masque of manners:

[Densher] felt her as diffusing, in wide warm waves, the spell of a general, a kind of beatific mildness. There was a deeper depth of it,

---

[6] See Laurence Holland's elaboration of the Veronese analogy in *The Expense of Vision*, Princeton, N.J., 1964, pp. 306–13.

doubtless, for some than for others; what he, at any rate, in particular knew of it was that he seemed to stand in it up to his neck. He moved about in it, and it made no plash; he floated, he noiselessly swam in it; and they were all together, for that matter, like fishes in a crystal pool. The effect of the place, the beauty of the scene, had probably much to do with it; the golden grace of the high rooms, chambers of art in themselves, took care, as an influence, of the general manner, and made people bland without making them solemn. They were only people, as Mrs. Stringham had said, staying for the week or two at the inns, people who during the day had fingered their Baedekers, gaped at their frescoes and differed, over fractions of francs, with their gondoliers. But Milly, let loose among them in a wonderful white dress, brought them somehow into relation with something that made them more finely genial; so that if the Veronese picture of which he had talked with Mrs. Stringham was not quite constituted, the comparative prose of the previous hours, the traces of insensibility qualified by 'beating down', were at last almost nobly disowned. (p. 334)

But the masque is always a masque, and the picture is never quite constituted. Milly's presence also catalyzes conflict. Everyone is watching everyone else—stares and glances of private interest, envy, exhortation begin to stretch across the scene between the scattered groups and the whispering, appreciating couples. Kate and Densher together watch Milly's rope of pearls. All their quarrelsomeness, their conflicting wills, and their shared desire, come to a point at the far end of their glance, in the pearls. For Densher, more and more watchful of his Kate from the outside, the pearls are Milly's 'embodied poetry': an almost spiritual presence. For Kate, just as cogently and as validly, the pearls are Milly's enviable wealth; and Milly's 'dove-like' flight is simply the soaring 'great power' of her money. Densher now forces Kate towards exposing to him in words for the first time her full plot against Milly. We realize the nature of his pressure on her: to make her say what will humiliate her, to confirm his own angry self-abandon to a shameful process, and to place Kate the more abjectly within the circle of his desire. His desire is fed by his shame—and by the shame of his lover. And it is fed by the extraordinary way in which their intimacy is once again on a general stage: their quiet asides in a corner of a busy public room, filled with light and watchfulness. Kate is moved to tears by the pressure of it all upon her, and counter-attacks by suggesting to Densher the impossible alternative of his abandoning the plot, giving her up, and leaving

Venice. Her aim is now to force him to share her burden with conscious knowledge and guilt, and though he does so, it is at the fullest price he can exact of her: the consummation of their relationship, a consummation which therefore becomes as much one of guilt as of love. And as they approach their final commitment, the eyes of the lovers, filled with their increasingly destructive knowledge of one another, momentarily encounter Milly's:

[Kate] turned her head to where their friend was again in range, and it made him turn his, so that they watched a minute in concert. Milly, from the other side, happened at the moment to notice them, and she sent across towards them in response all the candour of her smile, the lustre of her pearls, the value of her life, the essence of her wealth. It brought them, with faces made fairly grave by the reality she put into their plan, together again; Kate herself grew a little pale for it, and they had for a time only a silence. (p. 345)

It is a brief but dazzling moment of intersection—and it takes place amidst the chatter and the music of the hired orchestra, and amidst all the 'comparative prose' of the occasion that James never forgets. On the pivot of a single look, Milly enters completely into the lives of the other two, and the other two enter into hers: the entry in each case being for loss and gain. In unwitting sacrifice —not in full knowledge as yet, but not passively: with intensity and response—Milly submits to the destructive elements of the 'life' that is represented by her two scheming friends. She will live into them, and find perhaps her greatest 'adventure' in her effect on their lives after her death. And this will be one of the marks of *their* adventure, that they will know their own lives through having preyed on Milly's and been sustained by Milly's. Her glance unites Kate and Densher in the fullest consciousness of what they are doing, and puts the last 'reality' into their plan—'reality', of which any person can face only a little. And Densher, in now mastering Kate—'You'll come?' 'I'll come'—and in taking her conspiracy on himself with the pledge of her body, has also committed himself to intimacy with Milly, and everything that it brings. If there is undoubtedly a sense of fate in this incident, it is hardly to be distinguished from a sense of life. Milly's smile at the two lovers is not really, as R. W. B. Lewis calls it, a 'fragmentary vision of grace', or 'a piercing glimpse of the anagoge', like the smile of Beatrice.[7]

---

[7] *Trials of the Word*, New Haven, Conn., 1965, p. 128.

All three characters are joined together in a fate that has all the lineaments of their essential humanity; and all the poetry, too. Their progress from here to the end is not towards religion or transcendence, but firmly through the natural world—this being the inalienable basis of their tragedy, as of all tragedy.

The place of Milly Theale within the natural world is now her place in the life of Merton Densher. Though she recedes more and more from the foreground of the reader's view, towards seclusion and death, she continues to be apprehended by us in her effects, up to and after her death, on the minds of others. And the adventure of her 'relationships' with the world—the adventure that comprises her life—persists in that prolonged dramatization of a man's inner nature in turmoil that makes the last hundred pages or so of this novel one of the most sustained *tours de force* in English fiction. Densher's entering more fully into his relationship with Milly—after Kate has paid her price by coming to his rooms, and after he has been left alone in Venice to pay *his* price in the form of attentions to Milly—is explicitly set against his experience of consummation, emotional and physical, with Kate. If Milly is to grow in Densher's mind, then she must do it in contest with an event that would seem to allow no replacement. The long description in Chapter 29 of Densher savouring in retrospect his union with Kate is one of the highest evocations in the book of what that particular pair can do for one another: the 'account' and fulfilment they can find. It is effective that James should do it all in terms of a room, just as he created Milly's very different sense of 'possession', then of disinheritance, in terms of the rooms of the *palazzo*. For these seem to have been infinite riches that Densher has won in his little room: they fill it, in memory, as they fill his whole consciousness, till his imagination and the room become identical, each as crammed and achieved as a fruit with its own flesh. This is Densher's equivalent of an Alpine vision: a room and a mind filled with the reality of one woman known, possessing her and possessed by her. And James, as he evokes the experience of fulfilment in his impressionistic, lingering, metaphorical way, turns up a cold seed of fear in the depths of Densher's satisfaction:

What had come to pass within his walls lingered there as an obsession

importunate to all his senses; it lived again, as a cluster of pleasant
memories, at every hour and in every object; it made everything but
itself irrelevant and tasteless. It remained, in a word, a conscious,
watchful presence, active on its own side, forever to be reckoned with,
in face of which the effort at detachment was scarcely less futile than
frivolous. . . .

It played for him—certainly in this prime afterglow—the part of a
treasure kept, at home, in safety and sanctity, something he was sure
of finding in its place when, with each return, he worked his heavy old
key in the lock. The door had but to open for him to be with it again
and for it to be all there; so intensely there that, as we say, no other act
was possible to him than the renewed act, almost the hallucination, of
intimacy. Wherever he looked or sat or stood, to whatever aspect he
gave for the instant the advantage, it was in view as nothing of the
moment, nothing begotten of time or of chance could be, or ever
would; it was in view as, when the curtain has risen, the play on the
stage is in view, night after night, for the fiddlers. He remained thus, in
his own theatre, in his single person, perpetual orchestra to the ordered
drama, the confirmed 'run'; playing low and slow, moreover, in the
regular way, for the situations of most importance. No other visitor
was to come to him; he met, he bumped occasionally, in the Piazza or
in his walks, against claimants to acquaintance, remembered or
forgotten, at present mostly effusive, sometimes even inquisitive; but
he gave no address and encouraged no approach; he couldn't, for his
life, he felt, have opened his door to a third person. . . . Never was a
consciousness more rounded and fastened down over what filled it;
which is precisely what we have spoken of as, in its degree, the
oppression of success, the somewhat chilled state—tending to the
solitary—of supreme recognition. If it was lightly awful to feel so
justified this was by the loss of the warmth of the element of mystery.
The lucid reigned instead of it, and it was into the lucid that he sat and
stared. (pp. 347–9)

And there is another significant item that emerges from the image
of Densher's room. When he makes his regular trip to the *palazzo*
he is helped in his efforts to forget the falsity of his position there
by his knowing that when he shuts the door of his room he leaves
all of Kate locked in there behind him. And this—as he turns with
reluctance yet growing fascination to Milly—is a reminder of one
fatal quality in his passion for Kate: that it is necessarily too
secretive, too enclosed from the world and the world's alleviating
conventions, too much thrown on its purely passional resources.
And this instability is only increased by the paradox that their love

has actually become so enclosed because of Kate's overrriding ambition for expansion.

The growth of Milly's influence on Densher is a much subtler process than that of one woman simply driving another out of a man's mind. There will always be a place in Densher's life that only Kate Croy can fill—a place where Milly has no importance or interest for him. The struggle in his mind between Kate and Milly is as unresolvable and organic as the shifting emphases of his own spirit. For Densher is being enlarged, rather than redeemed, by these three extraordinary weeks he spends, unsupported by Kate, paying his daily visits to the girl who is now too ill to leave her *palazzo*. The detached wanderer through Kensington Gardens, the man with no talent for 'life', the young man, vague, unformed, clever, is up to his eyes in 'life' now: a 'life' bizarrely concentrated into his solitary visits to Milly and into the tense elliptical manner of their conversations, by which each labours to 'spare' the other. For Densher, the weight of so much that is unspoken, the demands made on him by Milly's inscrutable gentleness, the memories of Kate, his agonized self-study, all constitute 'action' and involvement of an unparalleled intensity. And yet—this is what gives it its explosiveness—the situation is on the face of it absolutely static, since the only course Densher can follow is that of very deliberately and tactfully doing nothing. 'Doing nothing' is a very complicated state that vibrates with 'everything'—like 'waiting' in *The Spoils of Poynton*. The stage has long since passed where Densher could end the position by exposing Kate to Milly and retiring from the scene. Even apart from his continuing loyalty to Kate, such brutal candour would be more fatal to Milly than keeping up the present pretence, which, in addition, Milly's own kindliness seems almost to absolve. This idea of absolution has its facile and sophistical side for Densher, but his response to Milly's 'charm' and to the spectacle of her whole nature helplessly, resignedly, and gently in love, is a profound one, and we can almost accept his moments of believing that the wrongs of the conspiracy are less important, morally, than Milly's daily happiness and her bottomless capacity to forgive. At any rate, there is something very different from the mere exposure of a word-juggling swindler taking place in the qualifications, ironies, and sea-changes of such a passage as this:

He then fairly perceived that—even putting their purity of motive at its highest—it was neither Kate nor he who made his strange relation to Milly, who made her own, so far as it might be, innocent; it was neither of them who practically purged it—if practically purged it was. Milly herself did everything—so far at least as he was concerned—Milly herself, and Milly's house, and Milly's hospitality, and Milly's manner, and Milly's character, and, perhaps still more than anything else, Milly's imagination, Mrs. Stringham and Sir Luke indeed a little aiding; whereby he knew the blessing of a fair pretext to ask himself what more he had to do. Something incalculable wrought for them—for him and Kate; something outside, beyond, above themselves, and doubtless ever so much better than they: which wasn't a reason, however—its being so much better—for them not to profit by it. Not to profit by it, so far as profit could be reckoned, would have been to go directly against it; and the spirit of generosity at present engendered in Densher could have felt no greater pang than by his having to go directly against Milly. (pp. 349–50)

The strange dance that takes place in dialogue between Milly and Densher is one of the most artificial instances of manners in the book. The tension of their meetings is almost insupportable: consciously, they both build up a little sustaining bridge of half-truths to cross over the unmentionable fact of Milly's approaching death, and in every conversation it sways dangerously. Civilized half-truths are perhaps justified when it comes to dealing in the open with such ultimate facts.[8] Densher fumbles by asking if it is 'safe' for Milly to leave the *palazzo*; but soon compensates by an extravagant compliment that neither of them believes, calling her 'the freest person probably now in the world. You've got everything.' Then when he says, 'I know you don't complain', with a 'terrible kind gravity' in his voice, this again means a shaking of the bridge. Milly can only look at him hard for the moment, then turn off the awkwardness by a polished, kindly evasion of her own devising. And though the stress they suffer, and control, by such tact is different in origin for each of them, it ends by drawing them even closer together. As the reader saw it in the scene of Milly's party, so Densher himself now recognizes the fateful fact of intersection:

[8] There is another little example of this unmentionability of death in *The Europeans*—so far off in time, style, and tone as to be incongruous here, no doubt—when Mrs. Acton refers to her own coming demise with a New England abruptness that shocks and offends the mannered Eugenia (in Chapter 11). Both are justified from their own point of view, of course—though I think in context Eugenia has the edge.

her pass was now, as by the sharp click of a spring, just completely his own—to the extent, as he felt, of her deep dependence on him. Anything he should do, or he shouldn't, would have reference, directly, to her life, which was thus absolutely in his hands—and ought never to have reference to anything else. . . .

. . . He was mixed up in her fate, or her fate, if that were better, was mixed up in *him*, so that a single false motion might, either way, snap the coil. (p. 358)

A fate is borne up, a humaneness exercised, and two lives lived out, by resorting, as always, to 'a delicate art'. And, in the most affecting touch, the art and the role to which they both consciously resort now, as in the beginning, is the role of 'the American girl'. In an *aperçu* that confirms James's view that roles and manners are expressive and not just defensive, the 'national character' and the 'type' of 'the American girl', which they adopt as an artificial method for communicating with one another, also offers access to a perfectly natural 'reality' of Milly's inmost self:

The type was so elastic that it could be stretched to almost anything; and yet, not stretched, it kept down, remained normal, remained properly within bounds. . . . They really, as it went on, *saw* each other at the game, she knowing he tried to keep her in tune with his notion, and he knowing she thus knew it. Add that he, again, knew she knew, and yet that nothing was spoiled by it, and we get a fair impression of their most completely workable line. The strangest fact of all for us must be that the success he himself thus promoted was precisely what figured, to his gratitude, as the something above and beyond him, above and beyond Kate, that made for daily decency. There would scarce have been felicity—certainly too little of the right lubricant—had not the national character so invoked been, not less inscrutably than completely, in Milly's chords. It made her unity and was the one thing he could unlimitedly take for granted in her. (pp. 359–60)

The game of course breaks down—as it did, momentarily, before the Bronzino's cold mirroring—and the precarious 'peace' is shattered in the weather-change that marks one of the great crises of the novel. Venice is 'profaned and bewildered' by lashing rain and wind, and its sociable people reduced to 'melancholy maskers', as they were when the weather changed for the editor in *The Aspern Papers*. The subtle Eugenio becomes a wordless accuser of fortune-seeking Englishmen, as he denies Densher entrance to the *palazzo*, in the cold and wet. And the disillusioning

Lord Mark, the agent (and also victim) of it all, sitting like the spirit of wicked weather in the heart of Florian's. For a while it seems to be the collapse of a house of cards. Manners and roles, the whole life of style, have been blown away in the autumn storm of Lord Mark's revelation: he has told Milly how Kate and Densher have betrayed her. For Densher, 'shuffling about in the rain', it all appears to have been merely 'a general conscious fools' paradise, from which the specified had been chased like a dangerous animal'. He is thrown into a turmoil of self-blame and self-justification. He condemns Lord Mark for being brutal, and praises himself for being more delicate; then he feels 'no straighter' than Lord Mark, and longs to suffer some punishment that will re-establish his sense of virtue; then he blames the absent Kate for leaving him to face the music; then casts himself totally on Milly's will—and so on: a Densher-like pot pourri. And within the general sense of disaster lies the fact of Milly's pain and the image of Milly with her face turned to the wall.

We see nothing directly of Milly's collapse; but the nature of her discovery, her sense of utter loss, and the approach of her death, are all harrowingly present to our imagination right through the last part of the novel. Yet James presents to us with equal emphasis—mostly through Densher's possession of it—the idea that she is far from extinguished, that she does 'recover', that she has the strength to forgive, to continue to protect, and therefore the strength to remain in 'life' through having entered so completely at the last into her relation with Densher. Few artists were ever more attached than James to the notion of immortality through the memory of others, or to the belief that every act of human relationship has some meaning, influence, and permanence—even an act of loving, like Milly's, built on delusion. And the achievement of spiritual permanence and meaning is made possible, in part, by a restoration of manners. The social house of cards is built up again—which is in accordance with the whole logic of the book. Susan Stringham (in one of the most elliptical scenes in the entire novel[9]) asks Densher to keep up appearances to Milly and to deny Lord Mark's assertions—and she herself shows no shock or disapproval at the extent of Densher's duplicity. Similarly, Sir Luke Strett returns to Venice, accompanied by soothing weather,

[9] See Percy Lubbock's eloquent account of it in *The Craft of Fiction*, 1954, pp. 180–3.

and establishes a magisterial tone of reconciliation around the death-bed. He is as dedicated as Susie to the delicate art of 'letting down' Densher easily so that Milly, too, can be 'let down' easily; and he does it all by civilized silences and by a bland refusal to admit 'the specified':

> it was just by being a man of the world and by knowing life, by feeling the real, that Sir Luke did [Densher] good. . . . He was large and easy—that was the great thing; he knew what mattered and what didn't; he distinguished between the just grounds and the unjust for fussing. One was thus—if one were concerned with him or exposed to him at all—in his hands for whatever he should do, and not much less affected by his mercy than one might have been by his rigour. The beautiful thing—it did come to that—was the way he carried off, as one might fairly call it, the business of making odd things natural. (pp. 392–3)

So that by the time Sir Luke passes on the request for Densher to visit Milly for the last time—the scene of valediction to which we are not admitted—all the strands have been gathered together again. And as always, the ultimate, unseen hand on the loom has been that of the subtle dying girl in the Palazzo Leporelli.[10]

III

The last movement of *The Wings of the Dove*, comprising the whole of Book 10, has something of the quality of an epilogue. It develops and concludes most of the book's major topics, but, equally, it has an effect of independent power and novelty of insight. It is also one of the densest and most complicated episodes in the entire novel, in which the nuances of mental states are played against one another so swiftly that it calls for an immense effort on the reader's part to subtilize his responses to the required degree. Above all, Book 10 is a continuing drama: full of change and life, almost oppressively at one with the critical tensions within Kate and Densher, and offering suspense and fluctuating excitement as the truest conclusion such a novel can reach.

---

[10] The last interview with Densher is apparently run on similar lines to those that took place before Lord Mark's disclosures: avoiding the 'specified' sparingly and humanely, like the ellipses of social manners and roles at their highest. Remarkably, it comes out later that Milly has also 'protected' Densher to Lord Mark, and hence to Mrs. Lowder's whole circle, by telling a 'lie', and persuading Lord Mark, at the very moment of being herself shocked and convinced by his revelation, that the accusations against Densher are untrue (see Chapter 37, p. 441).

Densher's sense of reality has drastically changed in emphasis now that he has returned to London. It is now as much centred on memory as on desire—as much on Milly as on Kate. He seems to be torn equally between these two categories of value: one private and contemplative; the other social, sexual, and active. This is the most important and characteristic feature of the conclusion, that it does not show Densher coming to a state of grace, choosing his good angel and rejecting his temptress. In fact, when Densher broods over the memory of Milly, he is in one way reverting to his earliest condition, as we saw it at the beginning: that of a somewhat dangling and introverted figure. And thus we are shown again how though one character may act critically on another, as Kate and Milly have each done on Densher, there is no magical transmutation, only a change in the balance of elements already in that personality. The conclusion, as is proper, retains the double vision of the whole novel. It suggests that Densher is 'right' to be so influenced by the memory of Milly's supreme charity and forgiveness that Kate and her world, in contrast, seem harsh and suspect. But it also makes clear that to reject Kate and her values represents an irreparable loss and possibly a perpetual unfitness for ordinary living. Kate begins to recover much of our sympathy, our ordinary feelings of kinship, in proportion as Densher recedes from her, and the moral vision of Milly outshines her. And the more clearly we see that Densher has now no alternative but to judge Kate against a higher standard of goodness, the more we can detect the dangers of his moral idealism—which are the dangers of every ideal. James knows and understands these hazards well. We have seen how he indicated them, and accepted them, in *The Spoils of Poynton*—and how, in *The Tragic Muse*, the imagination, like all the highest activities of the human consciousness, reveals a self-destructive element within it. Milly's function in this story, and her fate as a fictional character, has been to bring out these irreconcilable things that lie very deep within life, and we do not expect her, or James, to change or to explain away these ultimate facts of experience. It is not that we deplore as too idealistic Densher's wish to renounce Milly's astonishing bequest to him—the selfless bequest that would enable him to marry Kate after all in the way they had planned. Too much has already gone wrong with their relationship, morally and psychologically, for us to feel that he is wantonly turning down the very best that life can offer. Our fears for Densher are, rather, that his desires and ambitions—his sense of life—are inevitably being forced inwards, into a chamber of memory, from which it is always difficult to escape. It may be significant that he can discuss his last sight of Milly not with Kate but only with the elderly: a somewhat lachrymose Mrs. Lowder, with whom he is thrown into a new intimacy based on a mutual interest in Milly that verges on the religious—and possibly, just a little, the sentimentally religious:

He himself, for that matter, at moments, took in the scene again as from the page of a book. He saw a young man, far off, in a relation inconceivable, saw him hushed, passive, staying his breath, but half understanding, yet dimly conscious of something immense and holding himself, not to lose it, painfully together. The young man, at these moments, so seen, was too distant and too strange for the right identity; and yet outside, afterwards, it was his own face Densher had known. He had known then, at the same time, of what the young man had been conscious, and he was to measure, after that, day by day, how little he had lost. At present there, with Mrs. Lowder, he knew he had gathered all: that passed between them mutely as, in the intervals of their asso-ciated gaze, they exchanged looks of intelligence. This was as far as association could go; but it was far enough when she knew the essence. The essence was that something had happened to him too beautiful and too sacred to describe. He had been, to his recovered sense, for-given, dedicated, blessed; but this he couldn't coherently express. It would have required an explanation—fatal to Mrs. Lowder's faith in him—of the nature of Milly's wrong. So, as to the wonderful scene, they just stood at the door. They had the sense of the presence within— they felt the charged stillness; after which, with their association deepened by it, they turned together away. (p. 416)

Densher's former peril was of surrendering up his moral self to Kate; but now, *as he himself admits*, the risk is of allowing his moral imagination of 'the wonderful scene' of death and beatitude to turn him into 'a haunted man'. So that Densher turns to Kate once again as to a 'reality' and a 'talent for life' that is far removed from the spiritual or the apparitional. He asks her to take him 'just as I am': to tell the truth to Aunt Maud and the others, accept their failure, and rebuild their two lives on—on what? And this is the crux. It is no longer simply a problem of a financial basis for their marriage, but of the fact that too many things have happened to them for 'just as I am' —or just as Kate is—to mean the same as in the old days in Kensington Gardens. Densher tries, to the extent of asking Kate (on the shortest day of the year) to meet him in the Gardens again, where he urges her to marry him as he is and to begin again. But Kate knows with a 'lucidity' that horrifies Densher, yet at the same time matches a new 'cold thought' of his own, that they are both locked in what they freely chose to make of their lives. Mechanically, she adopts her familiar posture of sexual manipulation, and appeals to that desirefulness in him that has become a routine and a treadmill. And so, on 'their old pair of chairs', they lean towards one another, in a deadly parody of their earlier love—and this on midwinter day.

Around the arrival of the two decisive letters—the posthumous one at Christmas from Milly bearing news of her gift to Densher; and the later one from the New York lawyers announcing the bequest that is Densher's to take up or not—is played out a painfully intricate game between Kate and Densher, the prolongation of which is James's testimony to the way such a relationship does die: not in dramatic finality but in slow, reluctant corrosion. Densher takes the first letter unopened to Kate, whom we see once again in her sister's house in Chelsea, set against the background of social squalor and pressure that explains so much of her life. When he offers her the letter—'something I feel as sacred'—it is both an ultimatum and a tribute. It challenges her to choose magnanimity and reject Milly's offer without being requested to do so—Densher prompting her no more than by the cryptic remark, 'It's all I can do as a symbol of my attitude.' But he also offers the letter as a kind of talisman: a 'sacred script' that represents, in Milly's handwriting, something essential of himself, and that might influence Kate for the saving of their love. Kate's comments and her dramatic burning of the sealed letter are therefore doubly disastrous. She has destroyed the proffered symbol and memorial of a supreme moral value, and lost the chance (if chance there ever was) of its moving her in the same direction as Densher—she knows how foreign that direction is to her own 'reality'. And she also burns Milly's letter, she says, because she does not need to read it to know all that truly matters in it, the certain announcement that Densher will get a legacy. And by this forthright evaluation of what 'matters', Kate quite consciously and challengingly defines the limits of Milly's relevance to herself, and to her love for Densher.

As they wait for the final turning-point of the second letter, Kate and Densher begin to recoil in fear from the quality of intimate exposure to one another that has resulted from their passion and their conspiracy. Passion itself is now even to be welcomed as a possible escape from intimacy and lucidity: 'he saw at moments, as to their final impulse or their final remedy, the need to bury in the dark blindness of each other's arms the knowledge of each other that they couldn't undo' (p. 447). But there is a better way for escape—and for parting. In one of the subtlest and most ironic pulsations of their dying affair, they are shown to us finding their refuge from one another in a 'manner'. It is a manner that derives from their old high style, and from the style of their society— but it has a tell-tale hollowness now that comes from its strained self-consciousness and from the shattering of the relationship which it was once used to express and to expand:

They crossed the river; they wandered in neighbourhoods sordid and safe; the winter was mild so that, mounting to the top of trams, they could rumble together to Clapham or to Greenwich. If at the same time their minutes had never been so counted it struck Densher that, by a singular law, their tone—he scarce knew what to call it—had never been so bland. Not to talk of what they *might* have talked of drove them to other ground; it was as if they used a perverse insistence to make up what they ignored. They concealed their pursuit of the irrelevant by the charm of their manner; they took precautions for a courtesy that they had formerly left to come of itself; often, when he had quitted her, he stopped short, walking off, with the aftersense of their change. He would have described their change—had he so far faced it as to describe it—by their being so damned civil. (pp. 448–9)

There is clearly something very perverse about such civility between them now—though after all, as we saw at the time, even in their original courtliness there were faint omens of this present stultification and breakdown. James has preserved his double view of manners throughout the novel, just as he presents a double view of Densher caught between the qualities of Milly and of Kate. The whole duality, on which the book hinges, is expressed at this very point with remarkable clarity and force—and for the last time. Only a few pages from the end, almost juxtaposed within two alternate paragraphs—without conscious arrangement or contrivance—we find two significant descriptions that arise out of Densher and Kate's new manner of civility. The first is an appreciation of 'life' as an affair of senses, formal gestures and conventions, of mannered shapes and surfaces in a social setting, of civilization and culture. The second is of 'life' as a private room and a morally defining pain—an affair of the individual imagination and memory, of the free contemplative spirit, and of the soul. It is possibly the supreme Jamesian antinomy, and it is right that we should see it revealed in this formal way, during a period of waiting and reflection, before his lovers are plunged back into the living drama of that antinomy in action: the drama of their personal separation. Here is the first description: the great 'talent' of Kate Croy, which Densher rediscovers and appreciates even within the hollow courtesy of their latest manner to one another:

It was her talent for life again; which found in her a difference for the differing time. She didn't give their tradition up; she but made of it something new. Frankly, moreover, she had never been more agreeable, nor, in a way—to put it prosaically—better company: he felt almost as if he were knowing her on that defined basis—which he even hesitated whether to measure as reduced or as extended; as if at all events he were admiring her as she was probably admired by people she met 'out'. He hadn't, in fine, reckoned that she would still have something fresh for him; yet this was what she had—that on the top of a tram in the Borough he felt as if he were next to her at dinner. What a person she would be if they *had* been rich—with what a genius for the so-called great life, what a presence for the so-called great house, what a grace for the so-called great positions! He might regret at once, while he was about it, that they weren't princes or billionaires. She had treated him on their Christmas to a softness that had struck him at the time as of the quality of fine velvet, meant to fold thick, but stretched a little thin; at present, however, she gave him the impression of a contact multitudinous as only the superficial can be. (p. 449)

And all the while inside Densher there is something that denies the splendidly multitudinous and superficial. It is 'only a thought', but it is 'of something rare': his mind's retention and active interpretation of the memory of Milly:

The thought was all his own, and his intimate companion was the last person he might have shared it with. He kept it back like a favourite pang; left it behind him, so to say, when he went out, but came home again the sooner for the certainty of finding it there. Then he took it out of its sacred corner and its soft wrappings; he undid them one by one, handling them, handling *it*, as a father, baffled and tender, might handle a maimed child. But so it was before him—in his dread of who else might see it. Then he took to himself at such hours, in other words, that he should never, never know what had been in Milly's letter. The intention announced in it he should but too probably know; but that would have been, but for the depths of his spirit, the least part of it. The part of it missed forever was the turn she would have given her act. That turn had possibilities that, somehow, by wondering about them, his imagination had extraordinarily filled out and refined. It had made of them a revelation the loss of which was like the sight of a priceless pearl cast before his eyes—his pledge given not to save it—into the fathomless sea, or rather even it was like the sacrifice of something sentient and throbbing, something that, for the spiritual ear, might have been audible as a faint, far wail. This was the sound that he cherished, when alone, in the stillness of his rooms. He sought and guarded the stillness, so that it might prevail there till the inevitable sounds of life, once more, comparatively coarse and harsh, should smother and deaden it—doubtless by the same process with which they would officiously heal the ache, in his soul, that was somehow one with it. (pp. 450–1)

This 'room' in Densher's mind that is always filled with the thought of Milly, and with the 'wail' that is virtually the cry of her dying, makes an overpowering contrast with the locked 'room' he once had in his memory for Kate and for the physical passion she had shared with him in Venice. The 'ache' in his soul has its passionate quality, too—it is not all negation or withdrawal into solitary communion with the dead. The 'ache' is the pain of his belated possession and knowledge of the example of Milly's life—a full 'possession' that is now acting against his former 'possession' of Kate, and against his continuing admiration for her 'talent' and her world of manners and 'great positions'. And it is a pain that is always one possible feature of the interplay—or conflict—between our sense of spiritual values and our sense of everyday necessity: that between a Fleda Vetch and a Mrs. Gereth, for example. The interplay shown within Densher's experience at this point is a real one. For there are possibilities of morbidity in the way his imagination possesses the dead Milly[11]—they are con-

---

[11] Just as there are far clearer possibilities of morbidity in James's much-commented-on reaction to the death of his young cousin, Minny Temple, who was the prototype of Milly Theale: 'The more I think of her the more perfectly satisfied I am to have her translated from this changing realm of fact to the steady realm of thought'. (See Leon Edel, *Henry James: the Untried Years*, London, 1953, pp. 328–37.)

tained (and only just controlled) in the emotional language of that last passage, just as they were in the earlier passage where he and Mrs. Lowder together held their breaths in reverence at the thought of his last meeting with Milly. The 'sacred hush' of his meditations contains within itself many positive and some negative possibilities. And as part of this complexity we see that his meditation is in any case resisted by a part of his nature that to the very last turns outwards away from 'the stillness of his rooms' towards the coarser 'sounds of life' and towards Kate's comparatively unspiritual vitality.

It is remarkable how the magnanimity of Milly Theale produces in the end as much disruption as amelioration. There is no sense of redemption or steady wisdom won by Densher, as we see him putting Kate to the test of sending her the second letter unopened. He has an inner light of purpose as he does so—to make Kate choose to join him in actively renouncing the legacy—but it is Kate in some ways who seems to be the clearer-headed and more perceptive of the two. He is still genuinely offering to marry her if she fulfils certain conditions that would seem to be strictly and morally just—even adding , as another and rather cruel turn of the screw, a further 'temptation' for Kate to overcome, in that she will receive his money if she does *not* marry him. She either marries him poor, or she is enriched alone. Kate, who has always had more self-knowledge than he, is able to see the fallacy in his offer, and can enlighten him, even morally: 'she died for you then that you might understand her. From that hour you *did* . . . And I do now. She did it *for* us.' To understand Milly is to love her—as Kate has to remind Densher. And if he has loved Milly, even if only in memory, he can have no room left in his heart for Kate, and no refuge from his knowledge, and her knowledge, of the flaws in their relationship—including those essential differences in their two natures that had once, in the past, seemed hopefully complementary. Densher remains caught in his very human confusions, hesitating between a somewhat harsh and challenging attitude to Kate and moments of his old charmed passivity before her. The harshness is inevitable, of course. Like the bitterness in the dialogue of Nick Dormer and Julia Dallow on their lake in the park, it comes from the inherent falsity of their situation and their bond. And Kate's last 'challenge' to him—that she will accept his 'conditions' if only he can swear to not being in love with Milly's memory—is meant simply to emphasize the impossibility of it all. It is Densher who is left fumbling, blind for the moment to the truth he himself has demonstrated in words and actions. 'I'll marry you, mind you, in an hour', he says—though only 'as we were'. Whereas Kate knows clearly, without delusion, that their old confidence and their old lives cannot be recovered: 'We shall never be again as we were!'

The Dove is not left shining down eternally on such a scene, and the way Kate and Densher will go is far from fixed. There are too many dangers in Densher's life without Kate and without 'Society' for us to feel confident, with F. C. Crews for example, that he has achieved 'salvation' through 'renunciation' of 'the social machine'.[12] And as for Kate, who has regained much of her charm and intelligence in our eyes just when she seemed to be most extinguished, *her* success or failure at 'life', with or without Densher's transferred legacy, is equally an open question. *The Wings of the Dove* forswears the exemplary to the last, and though as a novel it is very formed, it gives no sense of finitude. For like all of James's finest works it remains in the mind as an unexhausted and informing image, only imperfectly grasped as a whole by the memory and by the understanding, but an image nevertheless through which we can go on more clearly apprehending something of the world around us—the world that needs created images if it is ever to be apprehended.

Any great writer makes such images, which take on the quality of touchstones: touchstones of what is 'real', and freshly proved to be real. James, obviously, is no giant of humane realism in literature—his approach to the real is at the furthest extreme from a Tolstoy. His touchstones are not often immediate and absolute, and the manner in which they are expressed, as in *The Wings of the Dove*, is often profoundly and uniquely idiosyncratic. At times we deny the truth of them, and complain quite properly that there are great areas of experience they never include. But when we do find them and accept them it is because they are not the images of the pure dreamer or the voyeur or the detached aesthete, but dramatic images that prove to contain our natural features, even when they are involuted, refined, irradiated with consciousness far beyond the scope of our everyday life. As such images must, they implicate us

---

[12] F. C. Crews, *The Tragedy of Manners: Moral Drama in the Later Novels of Henry James*, New Haven, Conn., 1957, p. 80.

with a new definiteness, through the power of dramatic illusion, in certain imagined scenes of life—exactly as the characters themselves are not (as is so often claimed) all of them irretrievably locked in self-consciousness and isolation but are also torn out of themselves, in delight or pain, by all that lies in other people and things. Consciousness is not often 'pure' in James—certainly not in the books we have examined. Consciousness, instead, is tragically burdened (and therefore redeemed) by feeling and sensation. And very vitally, it is compelled out of singleness into explicitly social forms—the forms of intercourse and relationship—and, equally, into the discovery that experience is not only private but collective and even traditional. Each of these characters—Longmore, Winterbourne, Rowland and Roderick, the editor, Nick, Peter, and Miriam, Fleda, Milly, and Densher—each one of them has seen, in a moment of critical insight, 'the strong current of the world's great life', and has discovered 'the solidarity of all human weakness'. They have all bruised themselves against the world: the facts of infidelity, of stupidity, of death, of all falling-short. But James stresses that there is a firm world there to be bruised against, and that the private sensibility, on which a full life depends, is never quite adequate in itself. Experience may be bitter, and inexplicable, but at least it is not a dream: not self-delusion and somnambulism, as in Conrad, and not the solipsistic word-world of the Joycean artist-hero. The London and the Venice that Milly Theale descends into—down from her Alp, and down from 'the ark of her deluge' high up in the Palazzo Leporelli—is an area of experience that we can recognize, where the paths of individuals cross in their pursuit of a life of fullness, and where the story of a group of people becomes the story of a society and the story of all social living: living through manners, forms, and relations, which give the unfulfilled self access to a great power but also to an appalling trap. It is a quandary and a drama in which all people, as communal beings, have found themselves: giving and taking, in public roles and in privacy, loving, betraying, building up an imperfect little system for human grace and survival. And that drama is one in which we, the actors as well as readers, go on trying to find ourselves in another sense: trying always to grasp what can only ever be found within the fluid terms of drama and process and the intercrossing of paths: a sense of life that will define us to ourselves, and fulfil us.

Index